Israeli and Palestinian Identities in History and Literature

Israeli and Palestinian Identities in History and Literature

Edited by

Kamal Abdel-Malek and David C. Jacobson

St. Martin's Press
New York

ISRAELI AND PALESTINIAN IDENTITIES IN HISTORY AND LITERATURE

 For information, address St. Martin's Press, 175 Fifth Avenue, New York, N.Y. 10010.

ISBN 0-312-21978-4

Library of Congress Cataloging-in-Publication Data

Abdel-Malek, Kamal and David C. Jacobson.
Israeli and Palestinian identities in history and literature / edited by Kamal Abdel-Malek and David C. Jacobson.
p. cm.
Includes bibliographical references and index.
ISBN 0-312-21978-4 (cloth)
1. Palestinian Arabs—Israel—Ethnic Identity. 2. Jews—Israel—Identity. 3. Israeli literature—History and criticism. 4. Arabic literature—Israel—History and criticism. I. Abdel-Malek, Kamal. II. Jacobson, David C., 1947–
DS113.7.I86 1999
305.982'7405694—dc21 99-10907
CIP

Internal design by Binghamton Valley Composition

First edition: September, 1999
10 9 8 7 6 5 4 3 2 1

To my children, Amira and Layla, and to all Palestinian and Israeli children. May theirs be a world of true peace. KA

In memory of my teacher, Rabbi Daniel I. Leifer, who loved peace and pursued justice. DCJ

CONTENTS

Preface and Acknowledgments

For six years, we had the pleasure of working together as colleagues at Brown University, Kamal in the field of Arabic language and literature and David in the field of Hebrew language and literature. We were raised on opposite sides of the Arab-Israeli conflict: Kamal grew up in Egypt during the Nasser and Sadat years; David grew up in America in a Jewish family that staunchly supported Israel, and since the age of eighteen he has spent a considerable amount of time engaged in study, teaching, and research in Israel. Before we met at Brown, each of us had already started to explore the point of view of the "other side" of the conflict: as an undergraduate student Kamal spent a year studying at the Hebrew University in Jerusalem, and after completing his graduate studies in Hebrew literature David developed an interest in a comparative approach to the study of Palestinian and Israeli literature.

Shortly after we both arrived at Brown in 1992, we began to develop a series of collaborative projects based on a comparative study of the Israeli and Palestinian histories, cultures, and societies. Our first project was the creation of a new undergraduate course at Brown, "Arabs and Jews: Their Encounters in Contemporary Israeli and Arabic Literature." In the course we focused on Israeli and Palestinian fiction and poetry published since 1948 in which Arab and Jewish characters discover the limits and possibilities of appreciating their common humanity. As we taught the course, we became convinced that literature can offer important insights into the nature of the conflict between Jews and Arabs over the land the Jews call Israel and the Arabs call Palestine. As an extension of our commitment to provide Brown students with the opportunity to study the Arab-Israeli conflict in a comparative manner, we founded, together with faculty members from Wesleyan University and Trinity College, the Program in Israeli and Palestinian Studies, in which students spend a semester based in Jerusalem studying Israeli and Palestinian culture, politics, religion, and society in courses taught by leading scholars from Israeli and Palestinian universities.

The papers presented in this volume are drawn from a conference we codirected at Brown University in April 1997: Israeli and Palestinian Identities in History, Literature, and the Arts. In addition, we have each prepared papers that complement the contributions of the conference participants. The conference included scholars in the disciplines of literary studies, film studies, history, political science, and sociology, each of whom addressed issues related to the ongoing construction of Israeli and Palestinian identities. The purpose of the conference was to give experts in the areas of Israeli and Palestinian studies the opportunity to engage in exchanges that could prove to be enlightening to those interested in the Arab-Israeli conflict, as well as to a broader audience seeking to understand the development of national identity as a general phenomenon.

The conference had an artistic dimension as well. Two concerts were presented: one a selection of contemporary chamber music by Middle Eastern composers, performed by Brown's resident ensemble, the Charleston String Quartet, the other a concert of Jewish and Arab music by Fusions, a trio of Jewish and Arab musicians from Israel. We also screened Israeli and Palestinian films. Photographs of Arabs and Jews interacting in Israel by David H. Wells were displayed during the conference as well. Unfortunately, the scope of this volume does not include this artistic dimension of the conference, which added much to our deliberations and helped to foster a positive spirit among the participants. The one representation of this dimension is the photograph by David H. Wells that he has graciously permitted us to include on the cover.

We would like to take this opportunity to thank the many colleagues at Brown who gave us so much support as we developed each of these projects. Thanks to a number of Brown University grants from the Dean of the Faculty, the Dean of the College, and the Wayland Collegium, we were able to travel to do research in Israel and the West Bank during the summers of 1995 and 1996. We are indebted to Deans Bryan Shepp, Sheila Blumstein, Kenneth Sacks, and Karen Romer, and to Professor Anani Dzidzienyo for their strong support and encouragement. It has been a pleasure for us to work with Kirstin Moritz, Director of the Office of International Programs at Brown, and Professor Jeremy Zwelling of Wesleyan University as we have developed the Program in Israeli and Palestinian Studies in Jerusalem.

The conference Israeli and Palestinian Identities in History, Literature, and the Arts was primarily supported by a grant from the Thomas

J. Watson, Jr. Institute for International Studies at Brown University. We are most grateful to the Director of the Watson Institute, Thomas Biersteker, for his enthusiastic support for the conference. We also would like to thank the other Brown affiliated sponsors of the conference: the Joukowsky Family Foundation, the Charles K. Colver Lectureship and Publication Fund, and the Department of Music. The conference could not have been as successful as it was without the tireless efforts of its coordinator, Jean Lawlor.

Finally, we thank Routledge, publisher of *Ethnic and Racial Studies* for permission to reprint the article by Gershon Shafir and Yoav Peled, "Citizenship and Stratification in an Ethnic Democracy," [*Ethnic and Racial Studies* 21, no. 3 (1998): 408-427], and we thank Maḥmūd Darwīsh for permission to reprint selections of his poetry.

A Note on Transliteration

The transliteration system for Arabic follows that of the *International Journal of Middle East Studies* (IJMES). The transliteration system for Hebrew follows that of the "general" style of the *Encyclopaedia Judaica* (Jerusalem: Keter, 1972). The consonants *alef* and *ayin* are indicated by the marks ʾ and ʿ respectively only when they occur between vowels within a word. Proper names and other well-known terms are often spelled according to common usage in English.

Introduction

The papers presented here cover a wide range of Israeli and Palestinian identity issues from the point of view of several academic disciplines. Part I includes papers with approaches drawing on the disciplines of history, sociology, political science, and film studies that focus on the ongoing dynamic process of the definition and redefinition of identity that both Israelis and Palestinians have undergone. The papers in part II explore the use of literature as a means to derive insights about Israeli and Palestinian identity issues. In part III, we present an edited transcript of the roundtable discussion we moderated, which took place at the conclusion of our conference, Israeli and Palestinian Identities in History, Literature, and the Arts. During the roundtable discussion each participant was given the opportunity to react to the identity issues that had been raised by the other participants' papers.

In part I, Salim Tamari and Sammy Smooha make clear that the development of Palestinian identity has been fragmented, because Palestinians have undergone a variety of historical experiences in different geographic centers since 1948. In the aftermath of the 1948 war, some stayed on the Israeli side of the cease-fire lines and were granted Israeli citizenship, while others found themselves in exile from their homes either in parts of Palestine occupied by Jordan (the West Bank) and Egypt (the Gaza Strip), or in countries throughout the world. In 1967, those living in the West Bank and the Gaza Strip came under Israeli occupation in the aftermath of the war in June of that year.

Tamari traces the development of Palestinian identity from a more local to a more national identity. In the nineteenth century and much of the twentieth century, he states, the primary identity of Palestinians was not so much national or religious as local, "based on the village, city, or regional unit" or on kinship ties. Over time, national identity came to be more central to Palestinians. After 1948, he notes, the key figures who defined this national Palestinian identity were part of the exile community living outside of the land. Those who remained in Palestine did not play much of a role in the ongoing attempts to define Palestinian identity. This began to change as Palestinian citizens of Israel in the 1970s and Palestinians in the Israeli-occupied territories in the late 1980s began to assert their national rights. As they did so those who had stayed in Palestine in 1948 began to have a greater voice in defining Palestinian identity. This division between Palestinians living outside and inside the land has persisted as leaders from the Diaspora have returned to Palestine to participate in the establishment of the Palestinian National Authority (PNA) in parts of the Gaza Strip and the West Bank. At present, there continue to be political tensions between communal organizations established by the Palestinians who remained in the land in 1948 and the "emergent state power represented by the Palestinian National Authority," led largely by the returnees from the Palestinian Diaspora. Tamari looks to these pre-PNA communal organizations to challenge the PNA as "an oppositional force that would focus on democracy, civic rights, and political pluralism."

Sammy Smooha focuses on that segment of the Palestinian people who stayed or are descendants of those who stayed in Israel after 1948 and accepted Israeli citizenship. As a scholar of Palestinian studies Tamari is interested in the links that these Palestinians have with the Palestinian people as a whole. As a scholar of Israeli studies Smooha is more interested in the question of how connected they feel to Israeli identity. Smooha's study, based on comparable public opinion surveys of Arab citizens of Israel during the period 1976–95, suggests that Arab citizens of Israel have been increasingly drawn to the Israeli side of their identity. Over Israel's first fifty years, he argues, Arab citizens have become bilingual and bicultural, adopted Israeli culture as a subculture, accepted Israel as a state, reconciled themselves to a minority status, and during the 1990s have even shown signs of coming to terms, in a limited manner, with Israel's Jewish-Zionist character. Smooha believes that this process of Israelization can be encouraged even more by public policy that will put into effect reforms aiming at greater equality and integration between Arabs and Jews. In Smooha's opinion, the greatest barrier to the full identity integration of Arabs in Israel, however, is the Zionist ideology of Israel, which assumes some forms of preferential treatment for Jews. Palestinian citizens of Israel, he believes, will not be fully integrated into Israeli society until Zionist ideology is revised in such a way as to create "a dignified, respectful, and useful niche" for Palestinians.

Like Palestinian identity, Israeli identity has also undergone periods of definition and redefinition. Nurith Gertz examines the formative period of the 1940s and 1950s when Israeli Zionist propaganda films reflected the attempt by the Jewish cultural establishment in the land of Israel to transform the Jewish Diaspora identity into a new Israeli Hebrew identity. Holocaust survivors are portrayed in these films as having all the Diaspora Jewish traits that Zionism sought to negate, including being "persecuted, homeless, at the mercy of non-Jews, and haunted by the terror of the Holocaust." These films pay particular attention to the Zionist efforts to transform male survivors into new Israeli Hebrews by negating the qualities of their Diaspora identity, some of which (weakness, passivity, and wildness), are also shared by other elements in the culture, namely women and Arabs. This transformation allows the male survivor to become "a man who demonstrates his virile potency by cultivating the land, . . . by going to war, and by having a 'normal' relationship with a woman." Despite the apparent triumph of the Israeli Hebrew identity in these films, the very presence of alternative identities, particularly those associated with Diaspora Jews, women, and Arabs, suggests their potential for challenging the hegemony of the new identity. Indeed, Gertz notes, in later works of Israeli film and fiction since the 1960s, these elements have emerged as part of a more complex hybrid Israeli identity than that advocated in the Zionist propaganda films of the 1940s and 1950s.

With the passing of time, the Holocaust has continued to play a central role in defining Israeli identity. Neil Caplan examines the ways in which memories of the Holocaust have fostered an ongoing sense of victimhood that has pervaded Israeli identity to this day. This persistent identity as a victim, Caplan asserts, is puzzling given the growing military and economic strength of Israel in the first five decades of its existence. He explores the process in which the Israeli "self-concept as victim" has fostered a problematic obsession with security and a refusal to accept the possibility that Palestinians may too have been victims. There is, he argues, evidence that Israelis are to some extent moving away from this identity as victim, which he believes is part of a necessary process if there is ever to be a true reconciliation between Israelis and Palestinians.

During the conference Yoav Peled presented a paper that drew on the research he has pursued with Gershon Shafir into the changing nature of citizenship and ethnic relations in Israel. Since we held our conference, the results of that research have been presented in an article by Peled and

Shafir that we reprint here, "Citizenship and Stratification in an Ethnic Democracy" [*Ethnic and Racial Studies* 21, no. 3 (1998): 408–427]. In the article they argue that for much of Israel's existence, relations among its main ethnic and religious groups (Jews of European origin, Jews of Middle Eastern and North African origin, Orthodox Jews, citizen and noncitizen Palestinians) were constituted through a hierarchical combination of three citizenship discourses: a collectivist republican discourse, based on the civic virtue of pioneering colonization; an ethno-nationalist discourse based on Jewish descent; and an individualist liberal discourse, based on civic criteria of membership. Over time, they suggest, Israel has undergone a gradual transformation during which the collectivist republican discourse has been replaced by a greater emphasis on liberal discourse, as reflected by changes in the politics and economy of the state. Indeed, they maintain, this shift is a major factor in the greater willingness of Israeli political and economic elites to support territorial compromise with the Palestinians, which these elites see as more compatible with a liberal discourse. The liberal discourse, however, must still struggle in Israel with challenges from a Jewish ethno-nationalist discourse that incorporates themes associated with the collectivist republican discourse. The primary focus of this struggle is the deep divisions between supporters of the Jewish ethno-nationalist discourse and supporters of the liberal discourse over the issue of whether Israel should continue to pursue a peace process based on territorial compromise with the Palestinians.

Part II examines the ways that Israeli and Palestinian identity issues have been explored in Hebrew and Arabic literary works. Each chapter confirms the statement made by the Palestinian poet Fawaz Turki at the conference, "History and history making is everyone's milieu in our part of the world." While Palestinian and Israeli writers write on such nonpolitical issues as the joys and anguish of love, the beauty of nature, and human relations in general, there is a high degree of preoccupation with historical and political issues in this literature. As Turki notes, this preoccupation would most likely seem surprising to most Americans used to their own cultural milieu, in which literature and politics are more typically divorced from each other. The best of Israeli and Palestinian literature often surpasses political rhetoric and even scholarly discourse in expressing sophisticated insights into the identity dilemmas of both peoples by means of such elements of imaginative writing as language style, imagery, narrative structures, and metaphors.

The chapters by David C. Jacobson, Arnold J. Band, and Ami Elad-Bouskila examine a variety of writers of Israeli citizenship who have been forced by historical circumstance to come to terms with issues of Israeli identity. It is clear from the chapters by Jacobson and Band that the questioning of the Zionist narrative and ideals that has emerged in Israeli Jewish cultural discourse over the past several years has been developing virtually since the establishment of the State of Israel in 1948. Jacobson surveys fictional works of the 1948 and 1956 wars in which writers seek to capture the experiences of Israeli soldiers as occupiers of land inhabited primarily by Arabs. He pays particular attention to the ways in which each writer explores the tension between patriotic rhetoric that justifies the occupation, on the one hand, and the moral conscience of the individual soldier, on the other. One can sense in these stories of the 1940s and 1950s that the authors are particularly troubled by the contrast between Zionist ideals and the acts of war in which these soldiers engage.

As Band observes, this sense that the ideals of Zionism no longer play a vital role in Israeli culture is not a unique phenomenon: "it is characteristic of most writers who are sensitive to the inevitable gap between the dreams they had inherited and the realities they must live with." By the 1960s the questioning of Zionist ideals became, Band notes, an "intergenerational conflict between the founding fathers of the nation and the first generation of Israeli writers." Band discusses works of fiction written by Aharon Megged, Amos Oz, and A. B. Yehoshua in the 1960s that express disillusionment with the earlier generation's romantic vision of the Zionist past and lament the malaise and confusion that beset Israel as it faced the challenge of a more "normal" existence as an established state.

Writers who are Arab citizens of Israel have had their own set of identity issues. A central question facing such writers since 1948 has been whether to write in their mother tongue, Arabic, or to adopt the language of the majority, Hebrew. In his discussion of this question, Ami Elad-Bouskila notes that there has been an interesting parallel phenomenon among Jewish writers who emigrated to Israel from Arabic-speaking countries. Like their Arab counterparts, they too had to decide between their mother tongue, Arabic, in which some of them had already begun to write, and the language of most Israeli Jews, Hebrew. The decision of an Arab citizen of Israel to write in Hebrew is fraught with political implications that arise from the fact that Hebrew has been perceived in the Arab world as the language of the enemy. Nevertheless, a number of Arab writers have chosen to do so, thereby exposing themselves to potential condemnation from the Arab world, even while their acceptance as writers in the majority language has the potential of solidifying their position in Israeli society. Elad-Bouskila pays special attention to the Israeli Arab writer Anton Shammas, whose Hebrew novel, *Arabesqot* (1986), he believes, was the single most important work of Hebrew literature by an Arab citizen of Israel to raise "the revolutionary, problematic issue of Arab authors writing in Hebrew and [to] expose it to criticism and serious debate."

Maḥmūd Darwīsh is widely accepted as the leading living Palestinian poet. His biography, outlined for us by Issa J. Boullata, has followed the pattern of exile and longing to return that is shared by an important segment of the Palestinian people, as he has moved from Lebanon to Tunisia, to Paris, and most recently back to Jordan and the West Bank. Darwīsh has also declared his desire to return to his hometown, Haifa, but he has not been granted permission to do so by the Israeli government. Boullata traces the changes in Darwīsh's poetic expression of his identity as a Palestinian as he went through the various stages of his life. The common thread in his poetry is the centrality of the land of Palestine to his identity. His relationship to the land evokes in him anger at Israel, feelings of love for the land, calls for resistance against Israel, and (in his later poetry) elements of existential despair.

It is not surprising that connection to the land is so central to Darwīsh's poetry, for it is often true of national groups engaged in political struggle that the leading writers feel compelled to devote much of their literary output to national concerns. Salma Khadra Jayyusi discusses the centrality of the collective in Palestinian identity and the ways that this is expressed in Palestinian literature. One can discern in Palestinian literature, observes Jayyusi, the ways that Palestinian historical experience has served to give Palestinians a more clearly defined sense of themselves than can be found among other Arabs. As painful as the experience of exile has been for so many Palestinians, Palestinian literature has actually benefited from it, according to Jayyusi. Before 1948, Palestinian writers were not widely exposed to trends in world literature, whereas the writers of the Palestinian Diaspora have been greatly influenced by such trends, with the result that their literary works have reached new heights of sophistication. Indeed, she observes, in the Arabic literary world "Palestinian writers are now major originators and sometimes leaders of new trends."

Kamal Abdel-Malek explores the central role of images of marginality and liminality in literature depicting the experiences of war and exile in the writings of three Palestinian Diaspora writers, Ghassān Kanafānī,

Fawaz Turki, and Maḥmūd Darwīsh. Kanafānī's work of fiction, *Men in the Sun,* portrays the experience of Palestinian refugees who ultimately die seeking to be smuggled over the border of Kuwait, where they hope to find work. In his memoirs *The Disinherited* and *Exile's Return,* Fawaz Turki portrays his personal experience as an exile destined to live in a perpetual state of liminality. In Darwīsh's memoir *Memory for Forgetfulness,* an account of his exile in Beirut during the 1982 Lebanese War, the text is replete with such literary phenomena as intertextuality and metaleptic reversals in which discrete units of text and time blend together, thereby reflecting the dominant experience of Palestinians living on borderlines.

The present condition and future prospects of Palestinian and Israeli identities was a central theme of the roundtable discussion held at the conclusion of the conference. Yoav Peled expressed his concern that as Israel moves toward an accommodation with the Palestinians the earlier group identity that was based on the Arab-Israeli conflict is being replaced with a superficial individualistic identity. He expressed his wish for the development of a more meaningful collective Israeli identity based on an ethos of social cooperation. While Peled assumed the emergence of a new identity in Israel, for better or for worse, Sammy Smooha made clear that he did not believe that Israeli identity had changed significantly over the past fifty years. As far as he has been able to determine as a sociologist, Israeli identity is still solidly Zionist, and the so-called post-Zionist identity crisis affects a minuscule percentage of the Jewish citizens of Israel.

Fawaz Turki presented a scathing condemnation of Arab culture in general and the Arabic language in particular, which, he believes, socializes Arabs to have an excessive fear of authority. He called for nothing less than a cultural "Intifada" that will liberate Arabs from the dehumanizing effect of the Arabic language, which, he claims, prevents Arabs from interacting with other cultures. Issa J. Boullata noted that Turki's critique of Arab culture is not unique: indeed many modern Arab intellectuals have raised serious questions about the degree to which Arab culture encourages such fear of authority.

Given the central role of the Arab-Israeli conflict in the formation of Israeli and Palestinian identities, it is not surprising that a number of participants addressed the question of what each side has actually done or could do to further reconciliation between these two peoples. Salma Khadra Jayyusi stated that while Palestinians are prepared to recognize Israeli national rights, as the aggrieved party they cannot be expected at this time to take the initiative to reach out to their Israeli enemies. Real change can come about, she declared, only when more Israelis raise their voice in protest against Israeli policies toward the Palestinians.

Nurith Gertz, in response to Jayyusi's call for protest in Israel sympathetic to the Palestinians, expressed her surprise at what appeared to be a lack of knowledge on the part of Palestinians of the degree to which Israeli filmmakers and writers have actually anticipated and advanced the peace process. Not only did many Israeli writers publish poetry that protested Israeli policies during the war in Lebanon and the Intifada in the 1980s, she argued, but more importantly, Israeli literature and film has played a central role in uncovering for Israeli Jews the humanity of the Palestinians, thereby transforming the Palestinians from being a faceless enemy to being real people with whom Israeli Jews could consider making peace.

Participants explored the ways in which studying issues of Israeli and Palestinian identity in a larger comparative context could shed light on those issues. Neil Caplan observed that negotiation theory makes clear that it is important to take into account significant differences in terms of the power relations between two negotiating parties. It is also generally true that no two sets of national experience are exactly alike and that in the case of the Israelis and the Palestinians each people's experience of victimization must be seen not as an abstract concept, but as a real and uniquely tragic experience. Ami Elad-Bouskila noted that the question of bilingualism that Arab citizens of Israel face in relationship to Arabic and Hebrew is found in many contexts among modern writers, including North African writers who make use of both Arabic and French. Issa J. Boullata reported on a conversation he had with a member of the audience who declared that based on her experience as a former resident of Eastern Europe, it is language and culture, not land that is central to identity; she therefore could not understand the Palestinian obsession with land as central to identity. Boullata observed that on the level of prophetic ideals, she is right, but that on the level of political reality, there is no escaping the centrality of land for both Israelis and Palestinians.

Two participants strongly disagreed on the relative merits of the humanities and social sciences as academic disciplines that can reveal truths about issues of identity. As a sociologist, Sammy Smooha made an impassioned defense of a quantitative approach as the only sure way of defining identity in a social context. He raised serious methodological questions particularly about the ways in which the literary scholars in the conference asserted that their discipline provides important insights into issues of identity. How, argued Smooha, can a work of literature written by one author, who often takes on the role of social critic, be a source for understanding an entire society's attitudes toward identity issues? Arnold J. Band, in response, defended the humanities as sometimes more in tune with reality than the social sciences. To support his position he cited the classic work by Thucydides, *History of the Peloponnesian War,* which makes an important point most relevant to understanding relations between Israelis and Palestinians, that people on both sides of a conflict are capable of doing both good and evil.

In the introduction to the conference program we wrote that it was "our hope that in the course of the intellectual interchange and artistic experiences of the conference, the participants will arrive at a greater understanding of the common resonances of the fears and aspirations, anxieties and hopes, and defeats and triumphs of Palestinians and Israelis." We also expressed the hope that "all participants will recognize that the destinies of these national groups are intertwined and will consider the ways that genuine peace between Israelis and Palestinians can be achieved by their recognition of their common humanity."

We cannot be certain to what extent the conference had the kind of transformative effect on the minds and hearts of the participants that we hoped for. At the very least, we did succeed in arranging a relatively rare opportunity for scholars in the areas of Israeli and Palestinian studies to meet together and share each other's understanding of what is central to the identity issues of each of these peoples. This mutual endeavor could perhaps be seen as a foretaste of what might be possible if Israelis and Palestinians can figure out a way to overcome so many decades of conflict and begin to cooperate in an atmosphere of true peace.

Part I

Israeli and Palestinian Identity Formation Since 1948

1

The Local and the National in Palestinian Identity

Salim Tamari

This chapter will address the manner in which the issue of identity among the Palestinians in the post-Oslo period has been transformed by the establishment of the Palestinian National Authority (PNA) and by dynamic developments in Palestinian civil society that have redefined the relationship between the Palestinians who had remained in their homeland and the Palestinian Diaspora community. At the risk of oversimplification we can see that before Oslo the images of Palestinian dismemberment and the paradigms of exile dominated the debate over Palestinian identity. After Oslo we notice that juridical aspects of identity (such as citizenship and the Jordanian dimension) and the related issues of residency and access to citizenship under a regime of qualified sovereignty began to dominate this debate. This dichotomy between the politics of exile and the politics of statehood, however, camouflages a more profound and also more interesting aspect of Palestinian identity: the question of localized consciousness, on the one hand, and the tension between the Oslo dimension and the regional dimension in the new Palestinian social formation, on the other.

Localized Consciousness

Throughout the nineteenth and twentieth centuries the local community in greater Syria, whether based on the village, city, or regional unit, played an overriding role in defining Palestinian and other Arab loyalties. These points of reference, together with kinship, took precedence over religious and national identities. Localism was reinforced by a decentralized system of administration and by regional markets, and it was expressed through distinct recognizable dialects. Such communitarian loyalties reached their zenith under the system of *iltizām* (tax farming) through the rule of Ottoman *mashāyikh* and village potentates.

The campaign of Ibrahim Pasha and the Tanzimat following the collapse of the Egyptian occupation, and the later emergence of British colonial rule and of Zionism, contributed to the weakening of Palestinian localism and its contestation by a national identity that often transcended the boundaries of modern Palestine and constituted the core of modern Palestinian regional nationalism. This regional identity, however, was itself riddled with ambivalence. At the turn of the twentieth century this ambivalence resulted from the challenge to regional Palestinian identity made by those who felt that their main allegiance was to greater Syria (*bilād al-shām*) and that Palestine was part of Southern Syria (the Istiqlāl Party), as well as in part by the pan-Arab supporters of King Faisal and the Arab Revolt. Both of these currents were the precursors of the Nasserist, Baathist, and Syrian Nationalist currents that dominated Palestinian political trends in the 1950s and 1960s. Although one can say that they were eclipsed by the rise of the Palestine Liberation Organization (PLO), they nevertheless continue to contribute to its wider frame of reference in the cultural domain today. In cultural periodicals, for example, there is a lot of debate about the need to infuse Palestinian culture with an Arab dimension.

The Politics of Exile and Identity

The decisive marker of contemporary Palestinian identity, however, has been the politics of exile. This is rooted in a social feature of the Palestinian experience, namely the fact that the bulk of the Palestinian leadership, intelligentsia, and professionals—who played a critical role in the formulation of Palestinian national consciousness out of the refugee experience in the 1948 and 1967 wars—were either expelled or exiled, or (as in the case of Maḥmūd Darwīsh) chose exile.

The politics and poetics of exile became so dominant in this formative period that the conditions, aspirations, and outlook of those Palestinians who remained in Palestine (almost half the total number of Palestinians) were virtually forgotten. They were rendered an abstract object of glorification and heroism. In practice they were not only marginalized as a component of Palestinian politics, but were also subsumed as a residue, a remnant of a people whose real place was in the Diaspora. Subliminally there was an element of betrayal in the fact that they were not exiled or chose not to live in exile. This was the height of schizophrenia in Palestinian national identity.

It took two spectacular events to transform this outlook: the assertion of national identity by Palestinians in the Galilee on Land Day (1976) and later by Israeli Bedouins in the Negev, and the Intifada of 1987. The former development established the struggle for equality within Israeli society as a legitimate and recognized current within Palestinian politics. It brought more than ever the perspective and aspirations of Arabs in Israel to the national conscience of the Palestinians as a whole. The Intifada, on the other hand, redressed the imbalance in the hegemony of the PLO over the "forces of the inside."

Inside/Outside

The Intifada itself was the culmination of a protracted process by which the PLO, acting as the torchbearer of Diaspora politics, realized after years of Arab encirclement and Israeli military subjugation that it had to re-anchor itself in the emergent political will of the Palestinian homeland. This shift has been recognized in formal terms as a shift away from a strategy of liberation towards a strategy of independence. Such a shift not only required the adoption of the new pragmatic politics of territorial compromise and dialogue with the enemy, but also constituted a radical rupture with the established ideological heritage.

This heritage revolved around the notion of "redemption through return" as the underpinning of all Palestinian political strategies. Its vision was amplified by a reconstitution of an idealized Palestinian past, which the dismembered Palestinian nation sought to recapture. Its vehicle was a combination of mass mobilization, armed struggle, and the linking of the exiled communities through the leadership of the PLO. The social bases of these politics were essentially the refugee camps in the Arab host countries and the mercantile and professional classes in the Gulf countries and in Jordan. By contrast, the shift in the 1980s towards a territorial strategy was a move in the direction of grounding Palestinian politics in the relatively stable and conservative communities of the West Bank and Gaza. Although they contained a large refugee component, these communities were to a great extent historically continuous with the peasantry of the Palestinian highlands and their regional elites.

These stable communities, however, did not constitute a *national* community. They did exhibit a high degree of nationalist consciousness, and beginning in the 1970s they increasingly began to articulate their political aspirations within the confines of the PLO. But unlike the "external force" in exile, their leadership remained in the hands of the local regional elites, whose power, wealth, and prestige were derived from an extended network of kinship and putative identities rooted distinctively in Nablus, Hebron, Jerusalem, and Bethlehem.

State Formation and Identity

The assumption of power by the PNA after the Cairo agreement (1994) was therefore not only the beginning of the process of state formation, but also of the incorporation of those regional social groupings and political elites within a reconstructed *national* formation. The PLO, through its cadres and relocated diasporan bureaucracy, thus performed a crucial integrating role for the segmented communities in the West Bank and Gaza, which the nationalist movement during twenty-nine years of Israeli rule was unable to do. Because this process is still in a state of flux, we are sometimes unable to see the forest for the trees. In the current debate about the role of the returnees in the allocation of positions and clout, references are made to familial and regional forces being over- or underrepresented. Certainly the PNA and Arafat had to take the weight of these forces into account when allocations were made. Increasingly, however, we see a new *national polity* asserting itself that is gradually transcending its constituent parts. Due to the statist nature of this corporate body its main victim has been not the regional elites but the private business sector.

This trend became more distinct during and after the elections for the Palestinian Legislative Assembly in April 1996. The campaign itself seemed to signal a return to familism and localism, but eventually the dominant forms of mobilization during the campaign reflected a mix of national and local concerns. The result was clearly the triumph of nationalist politics over localism. This was reflected not only in the program adopted by a majority of the candidates, which was mostly rhetorical in content, but also in the preference of the electorate for candidates with a history of national political activism, as well as for candidates of refugee or exile background with little or no local social base.

The New Divide

Despite the current hegemony of the "returnees" in Palestinian politics, I would argue that the hitherto dominant divide in Palestinian politics between outside and inside forces has been transcended by the current consolidation of the PNA. To the extent that the former divide still persists it reflects the contestation over clout and patronage by a minority whose politics, social background, and ideological predisposition is essentially the same as those of the "native" community. Only in matters of cultural socialization can one detect a difference, with the returnees displaying a background rooted in an exile experience that is more urbane, secular, and alienated.

Palestinian pluralism, as a political form, is highly overrated but it is nevertheless real, or at least it has a kernel of reality. It is rooted in the multiplicity of political experiences in exile and in the diversity of forms of resistance to Israeli rule. In the Diaspora it is based on what has amounted to a stalemate in the ideological struggle between nationalist and leftist (or what were leftist) currents of thought. Inside Palestine, as well as within the Arab community in Israel, it is based on the voluntary coexistence between Islamist and nationalist political tendencies. An important contributor to this persistence of pluralism is a style of leadership that so far has preferred the politics of cooptation and patronage over the politics of confrontation and one-party control. Today we witness a significant deviation from this tradition in which the institutions of civil society and the variety of communitarian groups that emerged during decades of occupation are engaged in a new battle for democratic space against an emergent state power.

Conclusion: Civil Society and the end of "Embryonism"

During the 1980s, the strategy that prevailed within Palestinian mass organizations was one of "embryonism." This term refers to the perception on the part of a variety of resistance groups that since Israeli occupation was likely to prevail for an extended period, the task of Palestinian resistance inside the West Bank and Gaza was to establish alternative organs of power at the institutional level (such as municipalities, universities, and schools) and at the level of the provision of public services in the arenas of health, credit, day-care, and so on. Politically these institutions and services would, it was believed, ultimately converge in establishing alternative organs of power to replace the colonial state apparatus.

When the historical moment came, these embryonic institutions would act as the nascent alternative state in the making. Any future Palestinian state would have to establish its power base on the foundations of these nascent organs.

As it happened, this strategy proved to be completely mistaken in anticipating the nature of the power arrangement that actually emerged with the establishment of the PNA. At one level, these institutions of civil society were much more attuned to organizing resistance than to establishing sustainable institutions of governance. Their failure, however, was due basically to a willful choice by the PLO to establish its power base on a combination of alliances with local social elites and the returning cadres of the PLO. The emergent state institutions in Palestine have much more in common with neighboring Arab regimes than with the institutions of civil society established during years of resistance. Whatever future exists for the residual mass organizations that are still active today would seem to be in the search to build an oppositional force that would focus on democracy, civic rights, and political pluralism. The natural arenas for this battle are the legislative assembly, the municipal council, and extra-parliamentary bodies like the press and the media.

2

The Advances and Limits of the Israelization of Israel's Palestinian Citizens*

Sammy Smooha

The 850,000 Palestinian Arab citizens of Israel in 1997 constituted 16 percent of the total population and about the same proportion of the Palestinian people. They have been citizens of Israel since 1948, enjoying human, social, civil, and political rights. They are part of two worlds: Israel and the Arab nation, and being both Israelis and Palestinian Arabs, Israel's Arabs are subject to two processes: Israelization and Palestinization. Are these processes in conflict? Which is stronger? How do they shape the identity of Israel's Palestinian citizens? What are their implications for Arab attitudes toward the Jews and the state? These and other issues will be discussed, drawing on survey data for the 1976–95 period.

The Arab Minority in a Comparative Perspective

The Arabs of Israel are a highly *significant* minority. As an indigenous population, they feel firmly attached to the land and have strong claims to the country. Constituting 11 percent of the electorate in a system that is deeply divided between two political camps, their politics carry considerable weight. They are a *nonassimilating* minority. They differ from the Jewish majority in language, religion, nation, culture, and ethnic descent. They do not wish to assimilate into the Jewish majority, and the

Jews do not want to assimilate them. They have separate schools, communities, and institutions. They keep their own identity and struggle to remain separate but equal. They are, however, an appreciably *disadvantaged* minority. Most of them concentrate in the working and lower strata, while most of the Jews are in the broad middle class. They are excluded from the elites and other higher rungs of society. They are discriminated against in appointments and budgets. The prevailing Jewish norms and practices in Israel make it difficult for an Arab to compete on an equal footing with a Jew.

The Arabs of Israel are a *dissident* minority. They reject Zionism, the state's official ideology, which declares Israel as the homeland of the Jewish people and makes it Jewish in demography, language, symbols, commitment to the Jewish Diaspora, national goals, and policies. They also do not accept the Jewish-Zionist narrative of and approach to the Israeli-Arab conflict, seeing Israel as the aggressor and holding that it should withdraw to the pre-1967 borders, allow the formation of an independent Palestinian state, and acknowledge the right of return of the Arab refugees. Finally, the Arabs of Israel are regarded as a *hostile* minority. As part of the Arab world and the Palestinian people, who have historically been inimical to Jewish settlement and to the Jewish state, they are viewed by the Jews as untrustworthy. They are exempted from compulsory military service and barred from the other security forces. They are placed under control as a preventive measure against possible acts of resistance and subversion.

These features of the Arab minority turn Israel into a *deeply divided society.* To this category belong a small number of societies characterized by a minority of over 10 percent and overlapping differences, disagreements, and disputes between minority and majority. This type of society has a history of violent conflicts and a liability for instability and disorder. To mention just a few of the well-known cases, Northern Ireland, Sri Lanka, Cyprus, Turkey, Iraq, Sudan, Croatia, Rwanda, and Ethiopia are deeply divided societies with a history of violence. Although Israel qualifies as a deeply divided society, it has a record of relative tranquillity in minority-majority relations.

Another way to capture the minority problem in Israel is to depict its special political system. In the literature on comparative politics, a distinction is made between three types of democracy. In liberal democracy, common in most Western states, ethnicity is privatized and people compete and associate freely. The state treats all citizens as equal and promotes their intermingling and assimilation. On the other hand, in countries like Canada and Switzerland, where consociational democracy exists, the state recognizes ethnic differences, grants collective rights, and helps population groups to secure their separation and survival. In both types of democracy, the state is neutral toward all ethnic groups and treats them equally. In contrast, in the so-called Herrenvolk democracy, democratic rights are limited to the "master ethnic nation," as was the case in pre-1994 South Africa. It goes without saying that a Herrenvolk democracy is not a democracy.

Israel fits none of these types of democracy. It is officially and actually both democratic and Jewish. Its system operates according to two conflicting principles: "democracy," which establishes equality of rights and freedoms between all citizens, and "Jewishness," which grants Jews favored status. Israel is neither a liberal nor a consociational democracy, because the state's neutrality and absolute equality between citizens are absent. Neither is Israel a Herrenvolk democracy, because it grants citizenship to the minority.

Israel cannot be classified as belonging to any of the known types of democracy. It is therefore suggested that there is another type, called ethnic democracy, that describes Israel well. This is a system that combines democracy for all with institutionalized dominance of the majority. The state is considered to be the homeland of the majority and caters primarily to its needs, while it casts doubt on the loyalty of the minority and places it under control in order to prevent disorder and instability. In its democratic qualities, ethnic democracy is a system falling somewhere between consociational and Herrenvolk democracy.[1]

Since Israel is prone to intense conflict and instability for being both a deeply divided society and an ethnic democracy, the question is how it maintains law, order, and stability. It is clear that without the enormous strength of the state and the superior power of the Jewish majority, it would not be possible to keep relative quiet in Arab-Jewish relations. Yet asymmetry of power between majority and minority is not sufficient to account for the fact that the Arab minority has avoided unrest and confrontation since Israel's proclamation in 1948. It is likely that change in the Arabs' orientation toward the state and toward Jews also plays an important role in Arab accommodation.

Minorities all over the world are under cross-pressures. They adapt to the dominant groups and norms, on the one hand, and maintain allegiance to an external homeland to preserve their separate heritage and to fight racism, on the other. Globalization reinforces these conflicting influences. Some of the results of these countervailing forces are the formation of hybrid minorities, as in South Africa; hyphenated identities such as those of white ethnics in the United States; bilingualism and biculturalism, which existed throughout the former Soviet Union; and ethnic autonomy granted to national minorities, such as the Hungarians in Romania and Slovakia. The Arab minority is subject to similar cross-pressures, which take the form of "Palestinization versus Israelization."

Palestinization versus Israelization

Most observers, policymakers, Middle East specialists, social scientists, and Jews tend to think that Israeli Arabs have been undergoing a process of Palestinization since the Six-Day War. Before 1967, the Arabs were cut off from the hostile Arab world, saw themselves as Israeli Arabs, and slowly accommodated themselves to Israeli society. After 1967, Israeli Arabs resumed their relations with their Palestinian brethren and together they recovered their lost Palestinian identity. Israeli Arabs' strong solidarity with the Palestinians under occupation and their support for the Palestine Liberation Organization (PLO) demonstrated the advanced stage of their Palestinization.

The pervasive process of Palestinization was further facilitated by modernization, a rise in educational and living standards, better awareness of anti-Arab discrimination, and frustration with the inability to promote Arab status. The Intifada and the resurgence of Islam were additional forces propelling Palestinization during the 1990s.[2]

The common attribution of growing Palestinization to Israeli Arabs can best be illustrated by referring to a new theoretical perspective on Israeli Arab identity set forth by an Israeli Palestinian researcher. Nadim Rouhana wrote in 1993 that Israeli Arabs have "an accentuated Palestinian identity" because they are forcibly denied Israeli identity.[3] The exclusion of the Arabs, he maintained, has left them no choice but to fully identify themselves with the Palestinian people, Palestinian nationalism, Palestinian culture, and Palestinian leadership. They view their Israeli citizenship and identity as a sheer instrument for conducting their daily lives without emotionally identifying themselves with the Jewish state.

Another illustration is a statement by former Prime Minister Binyamin Netanyahu to defend his rejection of an independent Palestinian state. He conveyed a concern, shared by many Jews, that a Palestinian state will lead Israeli Arabs to demands of territorial autonomy and secession from the state.[4] Israel's lingering fears of Arab separatism underpin the grand Galilee Judaization Project, whose aim is to break Arab territorial contiguity and to establish a solid Jewish majority there. The implication is that the Palestinization of Israeli Arabs has already gone very far, posing a danger to Israel's territorial integrity and national security.[5]

Although Palestinization looks natural and obvious in an era of ethnic revival and nationalist resurgence[6] and although the evidence for it seems very compelling, I started to explore this question empirically in the mid-1970s. After completing the first national public opinion survey of the Arabs in 1976, I concluded that Palestinization is indeed potent but not the single and most decisive force in Arab life. I then coined the term "Israelization" in order to capture the parallel trend that the Arabs are undergoing along with Palestinization.[7] For me Israelization also looks natural and obvious. The Arabs cannot live in Israel permanently without adapting to Israeli life and without forming a new identity that combines their Israeli citizenship with their Palestinian national sentiment. My central thesis at the time was that Israeli Arabs were under strong Palestinian and Israeli influence and that Palestinization was effectively restrained by Israelization. After twenty years of research in this area, it is possible to reexamine this tentative thesis.

Israelization means that Israeli Arabs are increasingly absorbed into the Israeli mainstream. They more and more accept Israel's right to exist, appreciate their Israeli citizenship, feel loyalty to the state, adopt the Israeli way of life and thinking, use Hebrew along with Arabic, attend to the Hebrew mass media and culture, compare themselves with Jews, have their main contacts with Jews, define themselves in Israeli terms, and see their fate and future to be tied to Israel. As Israelization advances, the Arabs also develop emotional ties to Israel, cherish the benefits of Israeli life, and view their minority situation in the Jewish state less as an historical injustice and necessity and more as a voluntary choice. Their resistance to Zionism and to Israel's Jewish-Zionist character will diminish, and they will shift away from the standard Palestinian narrative that conceives of Jews as foreign colonizers, usurpers of Palestinian land and sovereignty, Western agents contaminating and destroying Arab traditions, cruel aggressors, untrustworthy expansionists, and people without legitimate rights to the area.

This is not a minimal definition of Israelization but rather a comprehensive and multidimensional conceptualization. Israelization is an ongoing process, an historical trend, not an accomplished fact. It is especially remarkable because it is taking place without Arab assimilation. The Arabs are Israelized while keeping their Arabic language, Arab culture, and separate institutions and communities, and not intermarrying with Jews. They are Israelized while remaining an integral part of the Palestinian people and Arab nation. Furthermore, they are Israelized despite the surge of Islam among them since the mid-1980s.[8]

Part of the evidence bearing on Israelization comes from a large-scale research project on Arab-Jewish relations. Five opinion surveys of the Arab and Jewish populations were conducted, in 1976, 1980, 1985, 1988, and 1995. In each survey 1,200 Arab and 1,200 Jewish Israelis, constituting representative national samples of the entire population, were interviewed face to face about their attitudes toward each other and toward the state. The surveys had a common design and a common core of questions and allowed for the examination of trends over the last twenty years.[9]

The Advances of Israelization

Israelization has made diverse inroads into Israeli Arab life. They include the transformation of Israeli Arabs' social life, language and culture, politics, attitudes toward Zionism and the Jewish-Zionist nature of the State of Israel, identity, and Palestinian orientation.

1. *Social life.* The Arabs have lost their separate economy as subsistence farmers and have become proletarianized.[10] The proportion of wage-earners was 86.9 percent in 1995, which was similar to the Jewish rate of 84.4 percent. They are integrated into the Israeli postindustrial economy unequally. While only one-third of all Israelis are employed in production and agriculture, the gap between Arabs and Jews in 1995 was 58.4 percent to 26.0 percent. Despite the gross Arab-Jewish socioeconomic disparities, the Arabs are an integral part of a consumer and materialist society, enjoying a steady rise in educational and living standards and acquiring the common Israeli petit-bourgeois mentality. The Arab median years of schooling was as low as 1.2 in 1961, far behind the 8.4 Jewish median. In 1994 it went up to 10.0, still less than but much closer to the 12.1 Jewish median.[11]

The Arabs have the same high socioeconomic aspirations as the Jews and take the Jews as a comparative frame of reference. In 1995 over half of them, 2.5 times the proportion a decade earlier, felt that their family socioeconomic status had improved in the past five years (table 1). While in 1976 only 32.9 percent believed that Arab youth could fulfill their occupational aspirations in Israel, by 1995 a majority of 70.6 percent believed they could. Two-thirds reported having Jewish friends, some even with visiting relations.

2. *Language and culture.* Bilingualism and biculturalism are the best

Table 1. Arabs' Social Indicators of Israelization, 1976–1995 (Percent)

	1976	1980	1985	1988	1995
Feel that the socioeconomic status of their family is better today than five years ago	*	*	21.7	24.2	54.4
Compare their socioeconomic achievements with Jews or Westerners	72.3	67.4	68.4	*	63.9
Agree that Arab youth have reasonable chances of fulfilling their occupational aspirations in Israel today	32.9	44.3	40.6	41.9	70.6
Have Jewish friends	61.3	66.4	61.2	65.7	68.4

*Not asked.

indicators of cultural Israelization. Both have increased steadily. By 1995 the great majority of Arabs were able to speak, read, and write Hebrew, in addition to Arabic (table 2). They had also been drawn into the Israeli mass media, which shape the thinking and leisure of all Israelis, except ultra-Orthodox Jews. Two-thirds of the Arabs read Hebrew newspapers and watched Hebrew news on Israeli television. As a result of the ongoing secularization only two-thirds of the Arabs observed religion. The

Table 2. Arabs' Cultural Indicators of Israelization, 1976–1995 (Percent)

	1976	1980	1985	1988	1995
Speak Hebrew	62.3	69.9	68.8	74.2	80.8
Thereof: men, aged 18-25	97.7	97.9	92.3	91.8	94.7
Read and write in Hebrew	48.4	62.9	65.1	71.8	77.2
Thereof: men, aged 18-25	89.4	92.7	91.4	89.9	92.0
Read Hebrew newspapers	27.1	42.4	49.8	53.1	65.4
Watch Hebrew TV news regularly or very often	*	*	*	*	64.2
Think that Arab family should have 1–4 children	48.1	58.9	64.5	58.7	68.0
Nonobservant	53.4	51.8	63.3	66.2	67.1

*Not asked.

rate of Arab observance of religion in 1995 was still twice as high as the Jewish rate, but far lower than what it had been before.

The Arabs have been increasingly drawn to the Jews by acquiring the Israeli Jewish culture as a subculture. They speak Hebrew with the Jews and use Arabic in their homes, schools, and communities. They behave according to Jewish norms in encounters with Jews in Jewish institutions but conduct their internal affairs according to Arab culture with certain Israeli influences. In other words, cultural Israelization takes the form of bilingualism and biculturalism without assimilation.

3. *Politics.* Arab politics is also Israelized in many ways. First and foremost the Arabs accept Israel's right to exist as a state, a necessary condition for taking part in the system. As many as 93.2 percent in 1995, up from 79.5 percent in 1976, accepted Israel as a state, the country that non-Israeli Arabs have for years fought to destroy and the state that has reduced Israeli Arabs to a subjugated minority in their own homeland (table 3). As many as 73.2 percent in 1995, up from 54.5 percent in 1985, were resigned to their fate as a minority in Israel. A majority ranging from 61.4 percent to 85.5 percent felt satisfied with their lives as Israeli citizens, preferred life in Israel to any other country, believed that the Arabs should use voting in Knesset elections as a tool for ameliorating their status in society, and wished to participate fully in the governing of the state.

These Israeli Arab political attitudes are not wishful thinking but rather they fit the new realities of the 1990s. The Labor-Meretz government of 1992–96, the Oslo accords, and the peace process are inconceivable without the Arab vote and without the Arab parties' support. As many as 77 percent of the Arabs voted in the Knesset elections in 1996, only 2 percentage points less than the national average. Two-thirds of them freely voted for predominantly Arab parties, neither for clan or client lists, nor for Jewish parties as in the past. A large portion of the Sons of the Village Movement and the Islamic Movement, the two movements that for years delegitimized and boycotted Knesset elections, participated actively in the 1996 elections. While Israeli Arabs are still not full partners in Israeli politics, (they are excluded from coalition politics, and no Arab has ever served as a cabinet minister), they have moved from the periphery to a position of influence.[12]

4. *Legitimacy of Israel's Jewish-Zionist character.* The legitimacy of Israel as a Jewish-Zionist state and identification with its symbols are the most sensitive indicators of Israelization. It must be emphasized that the state takes for granted the Arabs' rejection of Zionism and does not try to ob-

Table 3. Arabs' Political Indicators of Israelization, 1976–1995 (Percent)

	1976	1980	1985	1988	1995
Accept Israel's right to exist	79.5	89.0	82.4	86.5	93.2
Thereof: men, aged 18-25	85.6	84.5	79.5	81.2	93.1
Are resigned to a minority status	*	*	54.5	67.5	73.2
Thereof: men, aged 18-25	*	*	63.2	68.0	73.0
Are satisfied with life as an Israeli citizen	51.3	44.7	42.1	37.7	73.8
Would prefer to be a citizen of Israel to any other country	*	*	*	*	82.7
Believe that it is possible to change the Arab condition to a great or substantial degree by standard democratic procedures	66.3	55.9	58.0	61.1	77.9
Believe that Arabs should vote in Knesset elections to improve their situation	*	*	*	*	85.5
Favor the inclusion of Arab parties in coalition governments	*	*	*	*	61.4

*Not asked.

tain their consent and legitimacy. The Jewish-Zionist character and mission of the state are actually seen by the Arabs as a constant and serious source of exclusion, discrimination, alienation, and inequality. Even the Israelization thesis does not claim that the Arabs are ready to come to terms with Zionism at this stage, when the Jewish state still practices blatant anti-Arab discrimination and the Jewish majority is still exceedingly ethnocentric.[13]

We find, nevertheless, a declining resistance to Zionism and a significant degree of acceptance of Israel as a Jewish-Zionist state. In 1995 a majority of 64.6 percent of the Arabs accepted with or without reservation Israel's right to exist as a Jewish-Zionist state, up from a minority of 37.9 percent who did so in 1985 (table 4). Half of them no longer considered Zionism to be racism. Most importantly, 85.6 percent would have preferred to live in a Jewish democratic state rather than an Arab nondemocratic state, and 65.9 percent endorsed a solution to their status according to which Israel would continue to be a Jewish-Zionist state but they would enjoy democratic rights, get their proportional share of the budgets, and manage their religious, educational, and cultural institutions. When asked to define their position on Zionism, 47.1 percent

Table 4. Arabs' Legitimacy Indicators of Israelization, 1976–1995 (Percent)

	1976	1980	1985	1988	1995
Accept Israel's right to exist as a Jewish-Zionist state	*	*	37.9	36.8	64.6
Agree that Arabs can be equal in Israel as a Jewish-Zionist state and can identify themselves with the state	30.4	48.4	37.8	33.0	49.9
Disagree that or have reservations about whether Zionism is racism	36.5	39.3	34.7	30.0	49.7
Would prefer to live in a Jewish democratic state rather than an Arab nondemocratic state	*	*	*	*	85.6
Agree that Israel will continue to be a Jewish-Zionist state and that Arabs will enjoy democratic rights, get their proportional share of the budgets, and manage their religious, educational, and cultural institutions	*	*	*	*	65.9
Define themselves as Zionist or non-Zionist (not anti-Zionist)	*	*	*	52.9	75.3
Feel proud of Israel's achievements	*	*	*	*	75.3
Are willing to raise Israel's flag on Independence Day	*	*	*	*	43.0
Regard Israel's flag as representing themselves	*	*	*	*	71.3

*Not asked.

chose the term "anti-Zionist" (rather than "Zionist" or "non-Zionist") in 1985; the figure dropped to 24.7 percent in 1995. As many as 43.0 percent were willing to raise Israel's flag on Independence Day, and as a matter of fact this phenomenon is spreading in the 1990s, although Arabs are neither pressured nor expected to do so.

5. *Identity.* It is remarkable that only 23.0 percent of the Arabs in 1995 chose affiliation with the Palestinian people as their most important identity, as compared with 31.4 percent who selected Israeli citizenship (table 5). Both identities emerged as less popular than religious or communal identity, chosen by 45.6 percent of the Arabs. The decline of national identity allowed ethnic identity to rise. The majority of Israeli Arabs see Israeli identity as fitting them.

Table 5. Arabs' Identity Indicators of Israelization, 1976–1995 (Percent)

	1976	1980	1985	1988	1995
The most important self-identity					
Israeli citizen	*	*	*	*	31.4
Muslim/Christian/Druze	*	*	*	*	45.6
Member of the Palestinian people	*	*	*	*	23.0
When thinking of the term "Israeli," consider both Jews and Arabs	*	*	74.7	*	73.1
Consider the term "Israeli" as an appropriate self-description	52.1	53.0	44.9	45.7	63.2
Consider the term "Israeli Palestinian" as an appropriate self-description	*	*	51.8	*	60.9
Define themselves as					
Israeli, Israeli Arab, Arab	54.7	45.4	32.1	33.2	53.6
Israeli Palestinian, Palestinian in Israel	12.4	28.8	38.7	39.7	36.1
Palestinian, Palestinian Arab	32.9	25.7	29.2	27.1	10.3

*Not asked.

In all surveys, Arabs were asked to choose one of seven identities. The trend over the years is telling. The proportion of Arabs opting for the terms "Palestinian" and "Palestinian Arab" identities, devoid of any mention of Israel, went down from 32.9 percent in 1976 to 10.3 percent in 1995. Over half of the Arabs chose Israeli non-Palestinian identities in both 1976 and 1995, while fewer did so in between. The compound identity "Israeli Palestinian" went up from 12.4 percent in 1976 to 38.7 percent in 1985, stabilizing at this rate. These figures show clearly that Israelization is far superior to Palestinization and that it is inconceivable for 90 percent of the Arabs to think of their identity without Israel.[14] It may be obvious but worth noting that Israeliness carries less import and weight for Israeli Arabs than for Jews. It indicates less identification with the state, less loyalty, no attachment to the Jewish Diaspora, rejection of the Zionist narrative of the Israeli-Arab conflict, indifference to the written and oral heritage of the Jewish people, and much more.

6. *Palestinian orientation.* Israeli Arabs' Palestinian orientation is declining. They increasingly see Israel as their country and feel attached to it. Of those surveyed in 1995, 69.8 percent felt more similar in style of life and daily behavior to Jews than to their brethren in the West Bank and Gaza Strip, 95.8 percent of them would not consider moving to a

Palestinian state if established, and 60.5 percent no longer saw the PLO as representing their interests (table 6).

Israelization has changed the meaning and implication of Palestinian identity for Israeli Arabs as compared to Palestinians on the West Bank and Gaza Strip. While command of the Hebrew language is a vital vehicle for Israeli Palestinian citizens for functioning and integrating into Israeli society, it is just a technical means of communication and survival for the Palestinian noncitizens in their dealings with the authorities and Jews. The Palestinianness of Israeli Arabs is not accompanied by a sense of duty to take part in the legal and extralegal struggle of noncitizen Palestinians for national liberation and independence.

A study of the village of Barta'a, which was divided in 1949 between Israel and Jordan and reunited in 1967, well illustrates these differences in identity of the two segments of the Palestinian people.[15] The inhabitants of this divided village belong to the same extended family, but over the years they have drawn apart. While the residents of the western por-

Table 6. Arabs' Palestinian Orientation Indicators of Israelization, 1976–1995 (Percent)

	1976	1980	1985	1988	1995
Feel more similar in style of life and daily behavior to Jews in Israel than to Palestinians in West Bank and Gaza Strip	*	*	55.5	*	69.8
Feel closer to Jews in Israel than to Palestinians in West Bank and Gaza Strip	*	*	39.6	21.4	49.6
Do not consider moving to a Palestinian state	85.6	91.7	*	92.5	95.8
Agree that the Galilee and Triangle should remain as integral parts of Israel	*	*	54.1	79.8	74.3
Think that if a Palestinian state were established, most Arabs in Israel would be loyal to Israel	*	*	*	*	79.2
Do not consider the PLO as truly representative of the interests of Arabs in Israel	*	51.5	33.8	*	60.5

*Not asked.

tion of Barta'a define themselves as Israeli and Palestinian, the residents of the eastern portion of Barta'a see themselves as Palestinian only. The former are Israeli citizens while the latter are residents of the West Bank. During the Scud missile attack against Israel in the course of the Gulf War in 1991, the Arabs in the western part of the village wore gas masks and felt frightened while their brethren on the eastern side wandered around without masks and felt complacent and joyful at Israel's suffering, like other Palestinians in the West Bank, Gaza Strip, and the Diaspora.

The Limits of Israelization

The advances of Israelization among the Arabs in Israel are impressive, but the limits are considerable as well. Four major factors inhibit Israelization: the Israeli-Arab conflict, the Jewish-Zionist nature of the state, Arab traditionalism, and the nationalist rejection of assimilation.

1. *The Israeli-Arab conflict.* Israelization requires full mutual trust between Arabs and Jews. The transition to the peace era will increase mutual trust but will not remove distrust for years to come. This is because peace is limited to a political-territorial settlement, without a change of hearts, without admission of wrongdoing and guilt, and without forgiveness and compassion. Peacemaking is possible precisely because it is restricted in scope, enabling each side to keep its narrative of the conflict, to make only minimal concessions, and to continue feeling self-righteous, a victim and an accuser of the other side.

Full trust will not be reached also because after the cessation of the Israeli-Arab conflict Israel will continue to live in an insecure and unstable environment. The conflicts in the Middle East will continue to simmer, erupt, and cause damage for the foreseeable future as a result of dictatorships, class polarization, poverty, population explosion, repression of women, Islamic fundamentalism, intolerance of minorities, terrorism, border disputes, and rivalry over hegemony, to mention the most conspicuous ills of the region. Insecurity and instability will encroach on Arab-Jewish trust within Israel and impede further Israelization of the Arabs.

2. *Israel's Jewish-Zionist character.* As long as Israel remains Jewish and Zionist, full Israelization of the Arabs is impossible because complete equality cannot be granted to the Arabs. It is very difficult to accord Arabs first-class citizenship in a state that is officially the state of and for Jews. The fundamental purpose of the Jewish state is the provision of a

favored status for Jews. The Jewish state is bound to make Arabs less equal and less able to identify fully with the state. Moreover, most Jews expect the state to grant them a favorable treatment, although its concrete expressions are not unequivocal. This ambiguity drives many Jews to what can be called "Zionist excesses," namely, demands that would certainly be considered ethnocentric or racist in Western democracies.

Some findings from the 1995 survey can highlight the gravity of the situation (table 7). As many as 30.9 percent of the Jews were in favor of denying Israeli Arabs the right to vote in Knesset elections, 59.9 percent thought that in decisions involving territorial withdrawals there should be a Jewish majority and Arab votes should not be considered, 36.7 percent maintained that the state should use any opportunity to encourage Israeli Arabs to leave the country, 43.8 percent totally refused to have an Arab as a superior in a job, 59.2 percent thought that Jews should be given preference in employment in the civil service or that only Jews should be admitted into the civil service, and as many as 85.9 percent said that according to their religious convictions it is forbidden to appoint an Arab as Israel's state president.

These beliefs are not the standard prejudicial views of majorities toward minorities, common in liberal democracies. They are rather Israeli Jews' bona fide understandings of their rightful entitlements in the Jewish state. Clear excesses of Zionism were also manifested in the surveyed Jews' choice between two undesirable possibilities in the 1995 survey. A minority of 41.9 percent opted for a non-Jewish democratic state, while a majority of 58.1 percent chose a Jewish nondemocratic state.

3. *Arab traditionalism.* An additional impediment to full Israelization of Arabs is Arab traditionalism, common especially among Muslims and Druze, but not so much among Christians. The pace of change is slow and far from being pervasive, as reflected in the superficial nature of secularization, strong communalism, tenacity of the extended kinship system (the continued important role of the *ḥamūla* in marriage and local politics), and tight restrictions over women. This is true of Muslims not only in Israel but also in the West, but change among the Arabs in Israel is inhibited by further conditions. Israeli Arabs continue to live in a huge region characterized by a vital Arab culture and by a resurgent Islam. As an indigenous minority, Israeli Arabs find it more difficult than do uprooted immigrants to detach themselves from centuries-old traditions. Due to a mixture of choice and coercion, they also undergo in situ urbanization, namely, urbanization without migration to urban centers. These

Table 7. Jews' Selected Intransigent Attitudes, 1980–1995 (Percent)

	1980	1985	1988	1995
Deny Arabs' right to vote in Knesset elections	*	24.1	42.8	30.9
Favor the outlawing of Rakah	51.7	44.8	44.8	45.6
Agree that in decisions regarding the future of the Golan Heights and Judea and Samaria, there should be a Jewish majority and Arab citizens' votes should not be considered	*	*	*	59.9
Feel that it is impossible to trust most Arabs in Israel	65.9	59.8	60.0	54.3
Favor a policy of increased surveillance over most Arabs in Israel	42.7	36.9	34.5	32.5
Think that Israel should use any opportunity to encourage Israeli Arabs to leave the country	50.3	42.4	39.9	36.7
Would accept only a Jew as a superior in a job	45.5	47.4	55.1	43.8
Wish to have only Jews as friends	39.1	37.4	40.5	32.2
Think that in a state of unemployment, Arab citizens should be laid off first	*	44.6	*	37.5
Think that Jews should be given preference in employment in the civil service or that only Jews should be admitted	*	*	*	59.2
Feel that, according to their religious outlook, it is forbidden to appoint an Arab as Israel's state president	*	*	*	85.9

* Not asked.

are features known to perpetuate old-time practices and to arrest social change everywhere.

4. *Nationalist rejection of assimilation.* Zionism and Palestinian nationalism concur in objecting to Arab-Jewish assimilation. Bound by their mutually exclusionary ethno-nationalism, the Jews are as nonassimilating a majority as the Arabs are a nonassimilated minority. Israelization cannot proceed too far without meaningful assimilation. For instance, acquisition of the Hebrew language makes the Arabs at most bilingual be-

cause they retain Arabic as their first language. As long as they continue to do so, their Israelization will remain limited. This is in contrast to white ethnics in the United States whose Americanization is advanced by the loss of their original languages and the adoption of English as their only or main language.

Explaining the Primacy of Israelization

How can the primacy of Israelization over Palestinization be explained? Why has Israelization accelerated during the 1990s? Why are Israeli and non-Israeli Palestinians increasingly growing apart? Some of the factors underlying these developments are the following.

1. *Embourgeoisement of Israeli society.* The continuing globalization, economic growth, and rise in the standard of living are making Israeli society more and more materialistic, hedonistic, and individualistic, and less and less ideological, nationalistic, and mobilized. This transformation of Israeli lifestyles and thinking engenders commonalties among Israelis of a similar class position and even across classes, irrespective of ethnic and national origin.[16] The more secular, cosmopolitan, and bourgeois Israeliness is, the more accessible, more attractive, less Jewish, and less offensive it is to the Arabs.

2. *Continued democratization.* Israel continues to democratize, thereby offering Arabs better protection of individual rights and more influence in Israeli society. This liberalization was particularly evident during the 1992–96 term of the Labor-Meretz government, which Israeli Arabs favorably considered to be a government bringing both peace and greater equality.[17] Arabs' conditions have improved and their confidence in democracy has increased during the last decade. Israeli Arabs' Israelization is a response to a more democratic and considerate state.

3. *Withering away of the Israeli-Arab conflict.* Peacemaking appreciably moderates Israeli Arabs' resistance to what they regard as Israel's anti-Arab stands on the conflict. Israel's new policy of the recognition of Palestinian rights, territorial withdrawals, and acquiescence to some kind of Palestinian rule are perceived by Israeli Arabs as the soft and better side of Zionism and of Israeli Jews. Hence, many Arabs no longer see Zionism as uniformly evil, intransigent, expansionist, and rejectionist. Peacemaking forces Israeli Arabs to further differentiate between the various streams of Zionism and between different types of Jews, making Israelization less resistible and more palatable.

Israeli Arabs support the Oslo accords and the Palestinian Authority.

They are, however, highly disappointed with the Palestinian Authority because of its weak democracy, frequent violations of human rights, and slow economic development. Before 1994, Israeli Arabs did not like the idea of moving to a Palestinian state, but since 1994 they have become more convinced of their reluctance, as this possibility is turning into a concrete and unattractive option.

The permanent settlement of the Palestinian question will paradoxically legitimate Israelization and push it a step further. Israeli Arabs will be relieved of the burden to fight for the independence of their people and will be free to devote their attention to bettering their own status in Israel. Their Israelization will not be regarded as a surrender to the Jews and as a desertion of their Palestinian people and Arab nation but rather as a normal adjustment to their life as a minority in Israel.

Furthermore, once Israeli Arabs have the right to move to a Palestinian state, the failure to do so will instill in their stay in Israel a meaning of choice and preference, instead of coercion and misfortune. Israeli Arabs will find themselves in a new situation, reminiscent of the position of American Jews after the proclamation of Israel in 1948. They will identify themselves with the Palestinian state and support it, but also embrace Israel as their country, owe allegiance to it, and fully accept the fact that their life conditions will be determined by developments in Israel and not in Palestine or elsewhere. It is the growing realization of this slowly unfolding reality that has prompted the Israelization of the Arabs in the 1990s.[18]

4. *Israel's anti-Palestinization policy.* All Israeli governments, including those headed by the Likud, have practiced a consistent and firm policy of separating Israeli Arabs from other Palestinians, discouraging contacts between them, and treating them differently. Israeli governments support Israelization of the Palestinian citizens and shy away from Israelization of Palestinian noncitizens. This differential policy has succeeded in dividing these two parts of the Palestinian people because it has been accompanied by tangible and sharp inequality in rights, entitlements, and opportunities. For instance, Israeli citizenship entitles Arabs to employment and social security benefits denied to Palestinians in the Palestinian Authority.

5. *The PLO's pro-Israelization policy.* The PLO not only accepts Israel's anti-Palestinization policy toward Israeli Arabs but also implicitly reinforces it with a pro-Israelization policy of its own. It sees Israeli Arabs as a permanent part of Israel rather than as potential returnees to the new state of Palestine. Its considerations are clear. As long as Israeli Arabs live

in Israel, their problem is considered settled and the PLO is exempted from taking care of them. They are the lowest priority on the PLO agenda, well below Palestinians in the West Bank and Gaza Strip and Palestinians in the Diaspora. In fact, the PLO has an interest in keeping Israeli Arabs in Israel as a lobby on behalf of the Palestinian cause. It uses its clout to channel their votes to help install the Labor Party in power. The PLO also well understands that any Israeli Arab unrest will reinforce Israeli Jews' fears and make them less conciliatory in the negotiations with the Palestinians.[19] For these reasons neither the Israeli government nor the PLO intend to place the Israeli Arab grievances on the negotiation agenda for permanent settlement of the Palestinian question, and both sides welcome Israelization as an accommodating and stabilizing force.

6. *Minority status in Israel as a lesser evil.* Objectively speaking, Israeli Arabs have no better alternative to a minority life in Israel. Immigration to the West is the option of a few, mostly Christian Arabs, who take advantage of it. Immigration to an Arab state or to the Palestinian territories means a multiple loss of opportunities: a welfare state, a modern environment, and a stable democracy. A radical, violent struggle for doing away with the Jewish-Zionist nature of the state and for complete equality will bring about a showdown with the state. The most likely result will be the infliction of great suffering on the Arabs due to the enormous asymmetry in power between the two sides. These are good reasons for pragmatism, realism, and accommodation, conditions conducive to accelerated Israelization.

Alternative Perspectives on Israelization

Is Israelization of the Palestinian citizens of Israel good or bad? What are its broader implications? Four perspectives can be spelled out on this issue.

1. *Israelization as vindication of the status quo.* Israeli Arabs' advanced Israelization can be interpreted as a victory of Zionism and their full resignation with a minority status in the Jewish state. It may be taken as the Israeli Arab disengagement from Palestinian nationalism and identity and incorporation into Israeli politics and society. This logic leads to the conclusion that Arab-Jewish coexistence is sound and that it is, therefore, sufficient to continue the current efforts for greater equality and integration in order to improve it.[20]

This perspective, however, misinterprets Arab Israelization as a passive acceptance of the status quo. Precisely because the Arabs are becoming increasingly Israelized and do not have any other alternative, they will strive for a new, more egalitarian and fair deal with the Jews. After all, a cardinal component in Israelization is equality and active struggle for equality. This approach also errs in treating the Palestinian attachments of Israel's Palestinian citizens as too superficial and unbinding.

2. *Israelization as a mere veneer.* Scholars and observers who conceive of Arab orientation in terms of growing radicalization interpret Arab Israelization as a mere veneer, a superficial and transient adjustment to Israeli realities. Deep inside, Israeli Arabs reject the Jewish state and the Jewish majority, identify themselves fully with the Palestinian people and causes, and wait for the appropriate time to undermine Arab-Jewish coexistence. According to this view, Israelization is a necessity of Arab life in Israel, a concession to the superior Jewish power, a temporary accommodation unaccompanied by acceptance of the legitimacy of Israel, and a lack of real change in the basic hostile position.[21]

This widespread perspective ignores the dynamics of Arab life and orientation. It glosses over the various transformations the Arabs have undergone in their attitude toward the state and toward the Palestinian people. It carelessly dismisses the fact that the Arabs have already come to terms with minority life in Israel and have been fighting to amend it, but not to revolutionize Arab-Jewish coexistence.

3. *Israelization as distortion of Arab life.* According to a contrasting perspective, advanced Israelization is a distortion, a distress, and even an abnormality in Arab life in the Jewish state. This is because Israelization brings about erosion in the Israeli Arabs' Palestinian identity, disengagement from the affairs of the Palestinian people, weakening of their struggle, submission to the gross inequality and exclusion inherent in the Jewish-Zionist character of the state, and coming to terms with the illegitimate and disastrous Zionism. Accommodation with the exclusionary and discriminatory Jewish nature of the state is a sign of confusion, disorientation, predicament, loss of sense of dignity, and a twist of the mind.[22]

Advanced Israelization is the result of the embourgeoisement of the Arabs, the abdication of collective goals, and the celebration of personal interests. Arab leadership is responsible for this deterioration. It is too pragmatic and compromising, lacking vision and courage, failing to tell Arabs the truth that it is impossible to acquire equality as long as the state remains Jewish, and refraining from mobilizing them for intense struggle. This interpretation leads to the conclusion that Israelization has gone too far in deforming Arab life, that it must be stopped, and that a new Arab leadership and a new Arab ideology are needed to fight for the radical change of Israeli society for the benefit of all.[23]

There is no evidence, however, to support this highly critical perspective on Israelization. The Arabs do not appear to be deeply distressed or heading toward a crisis in their relations with the Jews. This approach is also oblivious to the fact that Israelization is a normal reaction to cross-pressures to which minorities are subject all over the world.

4. *Israelization as a normal process.* This perspective views advanced Israelization as a reflection of the complex forces influencing Israeli Arabs. While they are coming to grips with their lives as a minority in the Jewish state, significant segments among them will continue to oppose the status quo and fight for improvement. It is rather normal for the Palestinian citizens of Israel to become Israeli Palestinians, a distinct and new minority that differs in many respects from both Israeli Jews and non-Israeli Palestinians.[24] The implication of this interpretation is that Israel must introduce various reforms in order to increase equality and integration between Arabs and Jews. Such reforms will enable Arabs to proceed with the process of Israelization without assimilating into the Jewish population, without ceasing their struggle for improving their lot in Israeli society, and without giving up their ties and commitments to the Palestinian people.

Conclusion

The Arab minority in Israel is subject to the cross-pressures of Israelization and Palestinization. Israelization means the adjustment of the Arabs to their minority status, the respecting of Israel's right to exist and its territorial integrity, the adoption of Hebrew as a second language and Israeli culture as a subculture, the conduct of struggle according to democratic procedures, and the viewing of their lot and future as firmly tied to Israel. On the other hand, Palestinization means that the Arabs are increasingly drawn to Palestinian nationalism and to feeling more similar and loyal to the Palestinian people than to Jewish fellow citizens. The evidence from comparable public opinion interview surveys conducted between the years 1976 and 1995 and from other sources clearly shows that Israelization among Israeli Arabs is not only a strong force but also stronger than Palestinization. It is paradoxical but true that Palestinization has been on the decline among Palestinian Israelis during the 1990s, precisely at the peak of Palestinian nationalism, with the launching of the Intifada as a liberation movement from Israeli occupation and with the formation of the Palestinian Authority as a significant step on the road to an independent Palestinian state.

The primacy of Israelization is explained by various factors. The embourgeoisement of all Israelis has forged similar lifestyles and ways of thinking among Arabs and Jews. The continued democratization of Israel has provided Arabs with better protection of rights, influence, and a shift from the periphery toward the center, making Israelization more rewarding. Israel's transition to peace since the conclusion of the Israel-Egypt peace pact in 1979 has made Israel more acceptable to the Arab world, pushing Israeli Arabs in this direction. The consistent policies of all Israeli governments of treating Israeli Arabs more favorably than the Palestinians in the West Bank and Gaza Strip and of separating between the two kinds of Palestinians has consolidated and supported the citizenship of Israeli Arabs. These policies have been reinforced by the PLO's policy to recognize the minority status and Israeli future of the Arab citizens, calling on them to act as a lobby in Israel on behalf of the Palestinian people. Israelization is also strengthened by the widespread recognition that Israeli Arabs have no better choice than a minority life in Israel. They benefit by being able to live in their historical land, as well as in a stable democracy, a welfare state, and a modern society.

The advances of Israelization and the macro forces underpinning it constitute a major factor in the relative quiet in Arab-Jewish relations in Israel. Beyond their relative lack of power and their fear of Jewish repression, Israeli Arabs refrain from disobedience, resistance, and revolt thanks to Israelization, which draws them closer to the Jews and reconciles them with a minority status in the Jewish state. They keep law and order because they see positive elements and advantages in life in Israel, gains they wish to retain.

With all its accomplishments, Israelization has its limits. Basic mutual mistrust, resulting from the Israeli-Arab conflict and lingering on for the foreseeable future, mars the relations between Arabs and Jews, deterring Arabs from becoming full members of Israeli society. An even more formidable obstacle is Israel's Jewish-Zionist character, which has turned Arab citizens into unequal outsiders. The semitraditional and nonsecular nature of the Arab community marks off Arabs from the more modern and secular Jews. Israelization is also clearly confined by the rejection of assimilation by both Zionism and Palestinian nationalism. As long as assimilation is lacking, Israelization will have a much more diluted meaning for Arabs than for the Jews.

Israelization, like many historical trends and social developments, is not clear-cut. Public opinion polls, community studies, analyses of political activities, publications of Arab organizations, census data, voting returns, and other material are subject to conflicting interpretations. It is no wonder, therefore, that four rival explanations for Israelization have been suggested: Arab submission and the vindication of the status quo, a mere veneer for basic Arab hostility to Jews and to the state, a distortion of Arab life and an indicator of deep distress, and a normal process of accommodation with life in Israel as a new minority.

The perspective that views the Israelization of the Arabs as a normal process maintains that in order to run its course, Israelization requires certain reforms that will reinforce equality and integration between Jews and Arabs. According to this point of view, the conferral of educational, cultural, and religious autonomy on the Arabs would give Arabs a better control over their affairs, making them more willing to accept Israeli incorporation of the Arabs in the national power structure, and their admission into coalition politics would also encourage their Israelization. In addition, the reduction of personal and institutional discrimination would also make their Israeliness more acceptable.

The transition to the peace era is a proper historical opportunity to inaugurate these reforms and to search for additional, agreed-upon, and satisfactory arrangements. These changes require the reexamination of classical Zionism. This outdated nationalist ideology still conceives of Israel as the exclusive homeland of the Jewish people, leaves no room for the Arabs, and denigrates Jewish life in the Diaspora as incorrigibly abnormal and in need of normalization by return to Israel. These tenets of classical Zionism must be adapted to the realities of the end of the millennium, creating a dignified, respectful, and useful niche for the Palestinian citizens in the Jewish state.

Notes

* This article was written during the author's tenure as a Visiting Skirball Fellow at the Oxford Centre for Hebrew and Jewish Studies (winter 1997). It draws heavily on a public opinion survey of Arabs and Jews in Israel, conducted in 1995 with the collaboration of Dr. As'ad Ghanem. The survey was funded by a grant from the Ford Foundation received through Israel Foundations Trustees and a grant from the Israeli Ministry of Science. All of this support is gratefully acknowledged.

1. For the presentation of the model of ethnic democracy and its application to Israel, see Sammy Smooha, "Ethnic Democracy: Israel as an Archetype," *Israel Studies* 2, no. 2 (1997): 198–241.
2. Eli Rekhess, "Israeli Arabs and the Arabs of the West Bank and Gaza: Political Affinity and National Solidarity," *Asian and African Studies* 23, no. 2–3 (November 1989): 119–54.
3. Nadim Rouhana, "Accentuated Identities in Protracted Conflicts: The Collective Identity of the Palestinian Citizens of Israel," *Asian and African Studies* 27, no. 1–2 (July 1993): 149–70.
4. Interview with Ari Shavit, "A New Middle East? What A Funny Idea" [Hebrew], *Musaf Haʾarets,* November 22, 1996.
5. Arnon Soffer, "The Arabs of Israel toward Autonomy: The Case of the Regional Sub-System of the Galilee" [Hebrew], *Meḥqarim bageʾografyah shel Erets-Yisraʾel* 13 (1993): 198–209.
6. Anthony D. Smith, *Nations and Nationalism in a Global Era* (Cambridge: Polity Press, 1995).
7. Sammy Smooha, *The Orientation and Politicization of the Arab Minority in Israel* (Haifa: The Jewish-Arab Center, University of Haifa,1984).
8. Eli Rekhess, "Resurgent Islam in Israel," *Asian and African Studies* 27, no. 1–2 (March-July 1993): 189–206; Elie Rekhess, "Political Islam in Israel and Its Ties to the Islamic Movement in the Territories" [Hebrew], in *The Arabs in Israeli Politics: Dilemmas of Identity,* ed. Elie Rekhess (Tel Aviv: Dayan Center, Tel Aviv University, 1998), 73–82; Sammy Smooha and As'ad Ghanem, *Ethnic, Religious and Political Islam Among the Arabs in Israel* (Haifa: The Jewish-Arab Center, University of Haifa, 1998).
9. The surveys are reported in the following publications (all by Sammy Smooha): *The Orientation and Politicization of the Arab Minority in Israel; Arabs and Jews in Israel,* vol. 1 (Boulder, CO: Westview Press, 1989); *Arabs and Jews in Israel,* vol. 2 (Boulder, CO: Westview Press, 1992); *Coexistence Between Arabs and Jews in Israel: Attitude Change during the Transition to Peace: Research Report* (Haifa: Department of Sociology, University of Haifa, 1997, mimeographed). The quoted findings are taken from the 1997 research report of the 1995 survey.
10. Aziz Haider, *On the Margins: The Arab Population in the Israeli Economy* (New York: St. Martin's Press, 1995).
11. Central Bureau of Statistics, *Statistical Abstract of Israel 1996,* No. 47 (Jerusalem: Central Bureau of Statistics, 1997).
12. Benyamin Neuberger, "The Arab Minority in Israeli Politics 1948–1992: From Marginality to Influence," *Asian and African Studies* 27, no. 1–2 (March-July 1993): 149–70; Benyamin Neuberger, "The Arab Vote: Between Integration and Delegitimation" [Hebrew] in *The Arabs in Israeli Politics,* ed. Elie Rekhess, 31–39.

13. For a review of the various forms of discrimination against the Israeli Arab citizens, see David Kretzmer, *The Legal Status of the Arabs in Israel* (Boulder, CO: Westview Press, 1990). On the question of ethnocentrism, see Sammy Smooha, "Jewish and Arab Ethnocentrism in Israel," *Ethnic and Racial Studies* 10, no. 1 (January 1987): 1–26. In 1997, the Arab legal association Adalah was established. In 1998, it submitted a report to the United Nations Human Rights Committee in which it enumerated Israel's violations of Israeli Arab rights, presenting a much bleaker picture than Israel's official report to the United Nations Human Rights Committee of that same year. For details, see Richard D. Bardenstein, *Combined Initial and First Periodic Report Concerning the Implementation of the International Covenant on Civil and Political Rights (ICCPR)* (Jerusalem: Israeli Ministry of Justice and Ministry of Foreign Affairs, 1998) and *Legal Violations of Arab Minority Rights in Israel: A Report on Israel's Implementation of the International Convention on the Elimination of All Forms of Racial Discrimination* (Shfaram: Adalah-The Legal Center for Arab Minority Rights in Israel, 1998).
14. For a view that belittles the Israeli component in the identity of Israeli Arabs, see Nadim Rouhana, *Identities in Conflict: Palestinian Citizens in an Ethnic Jewish State* (New Haven: Yale University Press, 1997).
15. Muhammad Amara and Sufian Kabha, *A Split Identity: Political Division and Its Social Reflections in a Divided Village* [Hebrew] (Givat Haviva: Jewish-Arab Center for Peace, 1996).
16. For the liberalization process in Israeli society and its positive impact on Jews' readiness for peace, see Yoav Peled and Gershon Shafir, "The Roots of Peacemaking: The Dynamics of Citizenship in Israel, 1948–93," *International Journal of Middle East Studies* 28 (1996): 391–413; and the chapter by Gershon Shafir and Yoav Peled in this volume, "Citizenship and Stratification in an Ethnic Democracy," which was originally published in *Ethnic and Racial Studies* 21, no. 3 (1998): 408–27.
17. Alouph Hareven and As'ad Ghanem, eds., *Looking Ahead and Looking Back: Progress Made by Government Ministries in the Years 1992–1996 in the Implementation of Basic Government Guidelines Regarding the Arab Citizens of Israel and Major Targets for the Year 2000* [Hebrew] (Jerusalem: Sikkuy, 1996).
18. For a fuller discussion of the implications of peace for Israeli Arabs, see Sammy Smooha, "Arab-Jewish Relations in Israel in the Peace Era" *Israeli Affairs* 2, no. 1 (1994): 51–66. For a pessimistic view, see As'ad Ghanem, "The Palestinians in Israel as Part of the Problem Not of the Solution: The Question of Their Status in the Peace Era" [Hebrew], *Medinah mimshal veyaḥasim benle'umiyyim* 41/42 (Summer 1997): 123–54.
19. For a review of the position of the PLO on Israeli Arabs, see Michal Sela, *The PLO and the Arabs in Israel* [Hebrew] (Givat Haviva: Jewish-Arab Center for Peace, 1996).

20. This view is compelling but not common. It appears in the writings of Ginat on Israeli Arab identity and voting. Ginat attributes little Palestinization to Israeli Arabs. See Joseph Ginat, "The Arab Vote: Protest or Palestinization?" in *The Elections in Israel 1984,* eds. Asher Arian and Michal Shamir (Tel Aviv: Ramot Publishing, 1986), 151–67.
21. This approach is best represented by Soffer and Israeli. See Arnon Soffer, "Full Equality for the Arabs in Israel—Is It Possible?" [Hebrew] *Nativ* 6, no. 2 (March 1993): 50–53; Raphael Israeli, "Arabs in Israel—Are They a Fifth Column?" [Hebrew] *Nativ* 42 (January 1995): 25–31. A similar view is implied by the conceptualization of the Arab response to life in Israel in terms of resistance. For such interpretation and a critique of other perspectives, see Ahmad Sa'di, "Culture as a Dimension of Political Behavior of the Palestinian Citizens of Israel," [Hebrew] *Te'oryah uviqqoret* 10 (Summer 1997): 193–202.
22. Nadim Rouhana and As'ad Ghanem, "The Crisis of Minorities in Ethnic States: The Case of the Palestinian Citizens in Israel" *International Journal of Middle East Studies* 30 (1998): 321–46; As'ad Ghanem, "State and Minority in Israel: The Case of Ethnic State and the Predicament of Its Minority," *Ethnic and Racial Studies* 29, no. 1 (1998): 428–48.
23. Azmi Bishara, "The Israeli Arab: Reflections on a Split Political Discourse," in *Zionism: A Contemporary Controversy* [Hebrew], eds. Pinhas Ginossar and Avi Bareli (Sde Boker: The Ben-Gurion Research Center, 1996), 312–49.
24. Sammy Smooha, *Arabs and Jews in Israel,* vol. 2.

3

The Others in Israeli Cinema of the 1940s and 1950s: Holocaust Survivors, Women, and Arabs

Nurith Gertz

The Zionism that forged the Israeli Hebrew identity out of rejection of the Jewish Diaspora has always needed the Diaspora Jew's identity to define itself by negation. This dichotomy of Diaspora Jew versus Israeli Hebrew was fashioned in many texts of the 1940s and 1950s, including Israeli films that dealt with Holocaust survivors. In such films the survivor was the ultimate manifestation of the culture and history of the Diaspora in view of which, from an ambivalent posture of attraction and repulsion, the Hebrew identity and culture were constructed. Here as in other cases, the one central dichotomy was linked to other dichotomies that defined and were meant to construct a homogeneous national identity out of difference and hybridity.

Holocaust survivors were not the only "other" through whom the Israeli identity defined itself in these films. They were connected in a complex interrelationship with all other outsiders. Israeli society during those years was composed of immigrants and nonimmigrants and of members of different ethnic groups and nationalities. The new Hebrew was a Jew from the Diaspora who attempted to adopt a new identity amid dialogue with the local cultures. The discourse used by the cinema of the time attempts to nullify the dynamism of these differences, to organize them in such a way as to liken the "others" to each other, and to create a hierarchy meant to support the homogeneous appearance of the new Hebrew identity. "Identities are the names we give to different ways we are positioned by and position ourselves within the narrative of the past," writes Stuart Hall.[1] Israeli cinema, like other texts of the time, used various techniques and manipulations to defy this assumption.

In Israeli films dealing with Holocaust survivors, the survivors reach the country bearing the label of the persecuted Jew and represent sterility and desolation. At this stage they are identified with all of the aspects considered most threatening by the Zionist Israeli as alien and "other": the barren land and the Arab who blends into it. Like the land, the Arab has two facets: he is passive and desolate and he is wild. Finally, the survivors are identified with irrational women, who, like the desert, are barren but also wild, seductive, and alluring—a combination of Eve and Mary. My contention is that within this hierarchy of "others" one can distinguish between the different roles that "others" play in the formation of the collective identity and between different degrees of abstraction by which they are described. The Arabs in these films are always more abstract than the Jews, while women are presented more metaphorically than men and serve as tools in defining and sustaining the transformation of the Jewish boy into an Israeli-Hebrew man. These films also make a distinction between "others" who can be transformed and become "the same" (like the survivors) and those who will always remain outside and will sustain the national identity either by negation or by affirmation (like the Arabs).[2] Thus, "others" who are eligible for transformation are contrasted with "others" who are ineligible, and the former are able to benefit from their privileged status in contrast with the latter. It seems as if these films require and sometimes invent an "underdog other" who is ineligible in order to strengthen the will and the motivation for transformation in those who are eligible.[3]

The films to be discussed in this chapter describe the integration of refugees and Holocaust survivors in the country. Their purpose is to tell the Zionist story to the world. As Zionist propaganda films they express, directly and explicitly, the Zionist narrative[4] that prevailed, in various forms, in many popular texts of the time, including theatrical productions, children's stories, journalistic reportage, and commemorative writings. This narrative also appears, if only as a motif, in more complex literary texts, such as *Each Had Six Wings* (1954), by Hanoch Bartov.[5] Bartov's novel describes an outlying neighborhood near the frontier where recent immigrants and Holocaust survivors were settled in the early 1950s. It was the first novel to portray the hardships and immersion of Holocaust survivors in Israel in detail and in a very emphatic way.

Other novels on this theme are *He Walked in the Fields* (1947), by Moshe Shamir, and *Face to Face* (1953), by Abba Kovner.

The films of the time can be described as a cinematic effort to persuade Israelis as well as others of the justness of the Zionist enterprise. They will be reviewed here as a case study in the translation of ideology into the language of cinema and as parallel to similar efforts in other media and genres in Israel. The Jewish Holocaust survivor in these films embodies all the traits with which Israeli identity is meant to contrast. He is persecuted, homeless, at the mercy of non-Jews, and haunted by the terror of the Holocaust. He threatens to dredge up the repressed Jewish past, to turn the equation inside out, to turn the Israeli back into a Jew. He is the "other" whom Israelis see when they look in the mirror and expect to see themselves.

The films cope with the "otherness" of the Holocaust survivor through two opposing, well-known strategies. The first strategy is to emphasize his difference, his "otherness," his being "not one of us." This strategy builds a clear partition between him and Israeli society. The second strategy has the opposite aim: to make him "the same"—a mirror of the typical image of the Israeli. In both cases, the survivor is eliminated as an independent, distinct, and different being with his own past, identity, and experience. In the first strategy, he is a parable and a metaphor for the identity rejected by the Israelis; in the second strategy, he becomes a parable that illuminates the identity adopted by the Israelis. In both strategies, only one identity remains: the homogeneous Hebrew identity.[6]

In the first strategy the national heroic cinema is populated by Holocaust survivors who play the role of secondary heroes.[7] In the second strategy, the survivor's "Jewishness" represents the entire Diaspora. When he is turned into an Israeli his Israeliness" exemplifies "Israeli Hebrewness" in general, and his transformation of identities is structured along the lines of the Zionist narrative. This narrative leads him, in the footsteps of the Hebrew pioneers, down the familiar trail of Jew to Israeli, which is represented metaphorically as the path from death to resurrection, from desert to flowering garden. Israeli films of the 1940s and 1950s, more than any other art form, dramatize this narrative, which starts with a transformation from Jew to Hebrew and ends with growth and prosperity. The Israeli Hebrew, resurrected from the ashes of Diaspora Jewry, from desolation, and from death, expands his territory; builds more settlements, buildings, and factories; and conquers the land with his muscles and his legs. The survivors in the films make it possible to recount this narrative to new audiences through new protagonists who personify it in the most dramatic way—from Holocaust to revival—thereby reaffirming it against the threat from within of a return to exile and the threat from without of Holocaust and annihilation.[8] Thus, the Israeli Hebrew identity is constructed by rejecting, obliterating, and suppressing the Jewish identity of the Diaspora.[9] As the plots of the films progress, the survivors experience a symbolic death and are reborn as Israelis.[10] Additional "others," positioned outside Israeli society or on its fringes, integrate into this process and support it either as real characters or as traits in the Jewish survivor's identity.

The male survivor's rebirth leads to a process of psychological and sexual maturation: the survivor comes to the country as a child (the protagonists of most of these films are children)[11] who has passive, female traits and resembles the indigenous Arabs. When he becomes an Israeli, he becomes a man who demonstrates his virile potency by cultivating the land in what is portrayed as an erotic act, by going to war, and by having a "normal" relationship with a woman. At this stage he sheds the traits that had identified him with the Arabs. The Zionist identity overtakes and dominates him. All that surrounds him appears attractive rather than threatening, dominated by the Zionist entity and united with it: the desert becomes a fertile settlement, and the barren or seductive woman becomes a pure mother. Although the Arab remains the outside "other" and thus has no place in this metamorphosis, he serves it indirectly either in a positive way, by helping the male survivor reach his land and home, or in a negative way, by helping him discover his masculine courageous identity in war. In this fashion, the accounts of the desert that has blossomed, of the Jew who has become an Israeli, and of the transition from death to life, merge into parallel strands in the plot of the survivor's life and are intermingled with the lives of women and Arabs surrounding him.

In these films the male survivor looks to the Zionist future. His erstwhile identity, his memories, and the world he has left behind are mainly elements that inhibit the plot from the start and slow its progression to the happy ending of the substitution of Israeli identity for Jewish identity. This discarded Jewish identity, along with other identities such as those of the Arabs and the women, however, cannot be hidden and erased: they are depicted in other texts, and a subversive reading will even reveal them as integral parts of the same films that try to negate them. Furthermore, under the influence of historical changes that occurred in Israeli society in subsequent decades, these rejected alternative identities that impede the plot and breach its coherence in films of the 1940s and 1950s became major factors in literary and cinematic plots of the 1970s and 1980s. In these later works the repressed past of the Diaspora Jews, like other repressed identities, surfaced and made it necessary to create a new version of the Zionist narrative based on a hybrid, nonhomogeneous identity.

From the Feminine, Arab-Like Jew to the Hebrew Male

The films of the 1940s and 1950s transform first and foremost their Holocaust survivor protagonists' assessment of space. The group of children from Europe constitutes the main protagonist of *Faithful City.* The point of view in this film, however, following the convention of the genre, is that of the objective lens. The children become "filters" of the point of view in two cases only: when this is necessary to underscore their negative Jewish traits, and after they have adopted the Zionist ideological slant. As the film begins, the camera rides the bus that is bringing the children to the Zionist youth village in Jerusalem. The British soldier who boards the bus to search it is observed from the point of view of the children, as is the Arab gang that bombards the bus with stones. Thus, the first people the youngsters encounter as they explore the country are threatening aliens: the British and the Arabs. Not only are they shown from the children's physical point of view; they are witnessed through and personify the children's terror and fear.

After the stoning incident, the children remain in the bus, quarantined with their fears as in the ghetto. In contrast, the camera sets out to explore the Jerusalem landscape of towers, ramparts, and surrounding hills on its own. The camera discovers something to which the children are still oblivious: the existence of a large, spacious country. This country is Jewish, not Arab. Only at the end of the film, in the war of 1948, after Max, the main protagonist, has escaped from the village, met with Israeli soldiers, and helped bring water to the besieged children, is he able to venture into the countryside and observe it. While fighting the Arabs he acquires the right to belong to the country—to be an Israeli.

The correct masculine identity is also revealed at the end of the films with regard to women. At the beginning of the films, neither the male survivor-child nor the male survivor-teenager manages to relate to women properly. All of these male characters display some traits that the films regard as feminine: passivity on the one hand and wildness on the other hand. Only after he displays dynamism, bravery, strength in labor and in combat does the male survivor eliminate his feminine characteristics. Only then can he relate to a woman and experience emotion or love toward her. He always applies his virility, however, to the soil or against the Arabs, never toward women. The asexual morality of these films serves to strengthen the power of the Zionist narrative and to prevent anything from eluding its collective control.[12]

Femininity is not the only obstacle that the male survivors need to surmount; they must shed an assortment of other traits that Israeli culture identifies as the baggage of the Diaspora Jew. The main group in *Faithful City,* headed by the protagonist Max, evades field labor, demands payment for every effort, and cunningly measures every gain and loss. These actions taint the members of this group with several Jewish stereotypes: guile, deceit, preoccupation with trade and commerce, passivity, and idleness. They acquire additional traits on top of these "Jewish" ones: they are violent, uncontrolled, and sometimes akin to wild animals. They reject the order and regimen of the youth village and threaten to replace it with chaos. The Arabs in these films, like some of the survivor women,[13] are portrayed similarly. Thus, the Arabs and the women exist not only as outsiders who underscore the change that the male hero undergoes but also as signifiers of wild, passive, and feminine traits that must be shed in order to build the correct identity.[14] The films lump all these Diaspora Jewish traits into a cluster that will turn inside out when the heroes are reborn—when they stop being feminine, untamed, Arab-like Jews and become civilized workers and warriors.

The Arabs who inhabit Palestine play two roles in these films. In one role, they metaphorically represent desolation and death and, in this sense, correspond to the Jewish Holocaust survivor before his conversion. In the other role, they are expected to support the conversion process and lead the survivor to the new Hebrew identity. In both cases the Arabs help to emphasize the transformation of the Jew into an Israeli.

Films such as *The Great Promise* and *End of Evil* show the Arabs in the exposition. *End of Evil* opens with shots of a desert and Arab convoys with camels, and the narrator introduces the Arabs as part of the old Palestinian landscape that the settlers have come to remake. They are "the thieves and the desert," he says. They hold the country by force. They are part of "these dead hills," which the settlers have come to revive. In *The Great Promise* the Arabs along the Jordan River live the savage lives of uncivilized natives who have not accepted the yoke of culture. They are analogous to the Holocaust survivors, who are depicted as untamed, uncivilized native children, and above all to Tamara, who is described as a savage beast. They resemble the children in *Faithful City* and Binyamin in *Tomorrow is a Wonderful Day.* The Jordan River is childish and innocent, the narrator explains, like the simple folk who inhabit its banks. As he speaks, the camera pans the Arabs, the sheep, and the buffalo. The Jew who has come to settle this locality is defined as a "man," and this definition, by negation, relegates the Arab to the category of pre-man. "Then came the man," the soundtrack states, "with a plan on how to use the land." This definition is also invoked to describe the change that the survivor has undergone: with the help of the soil, he has been transformed from a pre-man to a man.

End of Evil underscores the relationship between the threatening and alluring Arab as a real character and as the representative of an internal Jewish trait. It is the Arab, corresponding to the untamed natural space that lies beyond the fence of the settlement, who warns the group of settlers against inner urges that will destroy them. The Jews Ya'akov and Hava show how telling his warning is. By preferring love over devotion to the collective, they join forces with the Arab, as it were. Thus, the Arab, who represents the untamed world, attacks the settlement from without, and the couple harms it from within.

By creating a parallelism between the Holocaust survivor and the Arab the films suggest that by changing his identity the survivor has also changed his affiliation: from the Arab side to the Hebrew one. As Max circulates in the Old City in search of someone to buy the watch that he has stolen, the radio broadcasts a report on an Arab threat to invade Palestine. After he has "repented," he joins his instructors, Sam and Tamar, in celebrating the proclamation of Israeli statehood. It therefore seems that on the day of his rebirth as an Israeli, which corresponds to the birth of the state, his identification with the Arab side also vanishes.

When depicted as part of a savage, desolate, and infertile world, the Holocaust survivor is given the attributes of the Arab. In contrast, when the Arab is depicted as part of the old bourgeois world that preceded the socialist settlement enterprise, he acquires several classical features of the Jew. "How could I tell the Arab," says the shepherd in *End of Evil,* "that by changing ourselves we lost our path? He would never understand it. He would be rather pleased to live in the old world, not in the new world that we should have built somehow." The two of them, the survivor and the Arab, have to "take a course" in the new Zionist civilization in order to understand it, to be controlled by the Hebrew knowledge, to use Foucault's terms. "Let me show you something that's never been seen in this world," says the Jewish settler to the Arab who has come to visit the settlement in *End of Evil.* "If we Jews want to be more than a memory in this country," he then explains," we have to try a new path." The Arab, like the survivor, is an addressee to whom the Zionist story can be retold. Unlike the survivor, however, he is not expected to participate in this story; he merely supports the process by which the Jews are made into "new men." It is his fate to admire the Hebrew settler's "mastery over the land," but he cannot become a master by himself.

In some of the films, such as *End of Evil* and *Faithful City,* the Arab supports the Jew-to-Israeli transformation by enabling the frightened survivor to become a warrior. In several films his participation in this transformation, like that of other foreign protagonists, is positive. After he arrives at a kibbutz, David, the main protagonist in *My Father's House,* befriends a Palestinian and persuades him to flee with him by donkey in order to look for his father. In a second escape, a Palestinian shepherd helps David by leading him across the mountains to Caesarea. There he encounters a British officer and a man wearing a Turkish tarboosh, who lead him to Tel Aviv. David makes his way from Tel Aviv to the Dead Sea by bus, but he is led from the Dead Sea to Jerusalem by a Bedouin and his camel. Thus, he crosses the paths of members of all the country's peoples. However, instead of unfolding a multinational heterogeneity for him to observe, his escorts guide him toward his one and only identity, that of the Israeli. The Israeli music that is played against the background of the visual depictions attempts to underscore this by imposing Israeli culture even in places where the picture shows other cultures and other possible identities. This Hebrew culture and identity form the core around which the lives of the Arab protagonists are arrayed. The Arab protagonists, like the desert, precede the Zionist man, metaphorically personify his pre-Zionist traits, or lead him in the direction of his Zionist identity.[15] The Arab is thereby a part of the pre-Zionist identity and an instrument for its transformation.

The Arab supports Israeli culture not only by what he does but also by his gaze, which, like the gaze of the transformed Jew, is a bearer of the Israeli Zionist ideological point of view. In *End of Evil,* this look encapsulates his very essence. The soundtrack opens with an account of the Arab convoys that had traversed the country's sand dunes undisturbed until the Jewish settlers came. The convoys are not shown, and a full view of the camel and its rider is not provided. The camera focuses exclusively on the camel's face, its legs, and parts of its hump.[16] Then the convoy encounters the fence of a settlement. The camera abandons its objective point of view and switches to that of the convoy, from which it observes in dazzling sunlight the watchtower and the rifle-clutching Jewish settler who moves toward the gate. The Arab and the camel are utterly nonexistent in the picture, both now and before. Therefore, their entire existence boils down to the way they look at the settlement and the conclusion they draw from it: admiration at the courage of the Jewish settlers, who place themselves amid the desolate dunes and shatter a desert tradition that has prevailed for millennia. In either case, the Arab supports the Jewish presence, either straightforwardly or in the manner of the biblical figure of Balaam, who watched his curse turn into a blessing.

Thus, the Arabs, like the women, serve in these films as "the other of the other": like women, they represent some of the male survivors' non-Hebrew, non-Israeli traits. Like them, they help the survivors to acquire their new identity. Unlike the women, however, the Arabs do not participate, even metaphorically, in the transformation process itself. Their role is thus to stress, by contrast, the survivors' transformation. This point is made very clearly in *Faithful City.* In this film, after the protagonist Max goes through the well-known transformation, he runs away from the children's village, becomes a fighter in the 1948 war, and encounters a frightened Arab boy who has lost his mother and is prostrate and crying. Now Max is a newborn Hebrew. Courageous and strong, he can console the Arab boy who plays his previous role, that of the frightened Jew. The film always makes sure to leave somebody outside in order to strengthen the transformation of those allowed inside.

From Diaspora Time to Zionist Time

The survivor's past in these films is one of exile, suffering, and wandering, all of which are synthesized in the final drama, the Holocaust. The exchange of the Diaspora past for the Israeli past includes an exchange of the survivor's personal, individual past and identity for collective Zionist ones. It is this account that drives the main plot of *My Father's House.* As David hunts for his father, of whom he knows nothing, he is offered various collective substitutes. At first, his Arab friend's father serves him as a father figure by helping the children midwife the donkey on which they rode. Later, David comes to Tel Aviv and visits the philharmonic orchestra, having heard that a violinist named Halevi, who he thinks may be his father, performs there. The musician refers him to a laborer in Sodom named Yehuda Halevi and remarks, with a smile, that he remembered the man's name because of his namesake, the famous medieval Hebrew poet. Thus, in lieu of a personal father who plays a violin, David is offered a national father, the poet Yehuda Halevi who likened his yearnings for the land of Israel to the song of a violin. In Sodom, Yehuda Halevi asks the child about his father's name and mentions the possibility that it was Yisrael. The child confirms this, thus anticipating his Zionist transformation by connecting him with the name of Israel, the collective father of the nation. However, the end is still far off; David will still migrate among many other names before he comes to the name of his true father. In the Old City of Jerusalem he stops two priests and asks them where he might find "the names of the fathers," which refers to a list of parents who vanished in the Holocaust. The priests tell him about the Christian son who ascended to his father in heaven in this city, but they understand that he is looking for a different sort of father and send him to the Jewish quarter. There, a rabbi attempts to find out which father he has in mind: Abraham, Isaac, or Jacob. Like the priests, however, the rabbi realizes his error and sends the boy to the New City, where he discovers that his father has perished in the Holocaust.

Only after he has exhausted all possibilities and potential fathers, from the Arab father through the Christian fathers to the Orthodox Jewish father, and after he forgoes his personal father and acknowledges his death, can David acquire a real father. This father's name is Avraham, thereby symbolically connecting him to Abraham, the patriarch of the nation. As a member of the new Zionist community of the kibbutz Avraham also can be seen as a collective national father. Now that David has adopted a Hebrew father and a Hebrew present, both of whom are strongly connected with the Hebrew past in the land of Israel, he confirms his attachment to them at the founding ceremony for a new settlement. When Avraham shows him a potsherd inscribed with the name Halevi that he has found in the soil, the transformation is complete: David's new Israeli Hebrew identity is now based on past memories that allow him to discover his own roots in the land of Israel at the moment that the land is being settled.

From the Ghetto to the Expanses of Palestine

David takes his journey from the personal past to the national past over a special road: the geography of the country. The films posit an "optimistic geography" from the very outset: a country that one can cross, become part of, and control by walking, labor, and observation. Many elements in Zionist ideology are associated with space: the transition from Diaspora to the land of Israel, from ghetto to open space, from ethereal existence to a life rooted in the soil. This ideology was the infrastructure on which one of the most basic components of the sabra (native-born Israeli) persona was mounted: that of a person who "walks in the fields," is familiar with them, and controls them.[17] With this in mind, one may understand how the films use space to remake the Holocaust survivor into a Hebrew.

In all the films that deal with Holocaust survivors, the children are taken to a flourishing settlement, a kibbutz, or a youth village. True, the place is small and encircled with fences, but it represents a large, spacious, and open world—the entire country or perhaps the entire globe. *Tomorrow is a Wonderful Day,* for example, begins with footage shot from the interior of a room. The camera moves toward the window, the shutter is opened, and the camera steps out, into the youth village; it then heads into the countryside and scans it, first horizontally and then vertically, from heaven to earth. Thus, it emerges from the sealed room in the children's residence to focus on the country's great open spaces. As the film continues, the camera crosses repeatedly from interior to exterior and back again, and the village children move together with it amid the perpetual motion of wagons, processions, and groups.

The strong interaction of interior and exterior corresponds to the close relationship between details and the whole. In all of his films, the photographer and director Helmar Larsky merges close-up and distance shots in order to express the significance of every detail in the "big picture,"—the country and its history. The close-ups in these films are montages of objects and bodily parts linked to each other in detail after detail, in correspondence with the Zionist settler strategy of settling the land "dunam by dunam." The distance shots illuminate the setting to which the details belong and position the details in an inclusive geographical and historical context. Pieces of machinery, the shoulders of a man at work, and two people plowing a field all merge into a single progression of building and planting roots in the soil. As the films approach their end, the series of montages become longer and wider, thus portraying a process of development and growth in which the entire space is filled with settlements, homes, factories, and fields. The account, which begins with a transition from death to resurrection and from withering to efflorescence, ends with a process of growth, prosperity, and expansion.[18]

In most cases, the survivor becomes a "filter" of the camera's point of view as soon as he is born into his new Hebrew identity. After having observed the Israeli landscapes objectively thus far, the camera now contemplates it through the survivor's eyes. When he comes to the country, the survivor is the object of the sympathetic, compassionate, caring gazes of Israelis that are also disparaging, judgmental, and accusative. They have the power of the look, which, according to Foucault, is the power of knowledge, the power of control. Only after his rebirth, after he has acquired the knowledge and the ideological point of view of the Israelis, can the survivor look back at both the landscape and the people.[19]

In the course of the plot, the survivors acquire more than the right to look about: they also gain the right to move around the country freely and to enter its public and private places. These two matters, movement and gaze, are interrelated and attest not only to the protagonist's ability to dominate the space but also to the transformation he experiences after changing from a passive Jew into an active Hebrew. At first, the survivors identify their new home with the ghetto and the concentration camp; they feel imprisoned there and attempt to escape. After effecting this escape, they acclimate themselves to the new country and acquire their new identity as people who inhabit a large, spacious country and not a ghetto and who can circulate in their landscape fearlessly and dominate it with their legs and eyes. At first glance, the escape from the closed institution may challenge its frontiers and represent a criticism of its existing order.[20] In fact, the escape does not rupture the existing order but solidifies it. Its purpose is meant to expand the limits of this order and impose it on the entire space.

In *My Father's House,* the change is embedded in the geography itself. The boy, David, who has fled the Shefeyya children's village, reaches the Dead Sea and is adopted there by Yehuda Halevi, who introduces himself to David as his uncle. As they frolic on the beach, the children and the adults start up a conversation, and David proposes to revive the Dead Sea and use its water to generate electricity. "If you have plans for the Dead Sea, it's a sign that you are already Palestinian," a friend of the family tells him. The next conversation takes place among the children only after the adults have placed themselves at a distance. David mentions the possibility of being reborn to a new father and a new family. The children try to imagine the father they would choose if they were given this opportunity. Thus, a geographical act, a trip, takes the boy to the lowest place on earth, the Dead Sea. There, in the midst of death, the idea of revival surfaces in connection with both the Dead Sea and the Holocaust survivor.[21]

After David realizes that Yehuda Halevi is not his uncle, he flees from the Dead Sea area and begins to ascend through the desert to the Old

City of Jerusalem and afterward to the New City. It is a journey from low to high elevation, from old to new, from death to life, and from the Arab, who leads him from the Dead Sea to Jerusalem, to the Israeli. The film, however, does not content itself with such delicate symbolism. When the boy discovers in Jerusalem that his father is dead, he collapses, prostrates himself on the floor, and sucks his thumb like an infant. Only after he recovers can he effect his rebirth. The gap between the Jewish and Israeli Hebrew identity is so wide in these films that only death and rebirth can bridge it.[22]

It is precisely at the driest and most desolate place on earth that David chooses to begin his journey to rebirth. Other films, too, prefer to stress resurrection and efflorescence in the same place. In *The Great Promise* the survivor remains at the fence of his camp throughout the film, but the Zionist soldier, the brigade fighter, tells him a tale concerning the death and rebirth of the Jordan River in the Dead Sea as a parable of his own resurrection: "The river taught me that there's no end. There's an ascent out of the ashes," he says. The Jordan River is initially described as an unruly child and is likened to the Arab natives who inhabit its banks. Afterwards, it "matures" and accepts the yoke of the Zionist civilization that uses its water for agriculture. Finally, it reaches the Dead Sea and dies. However, the settlers do not yield. They excavate the parched soil, search for water, and find it. The story ends with footage of the water that irrigates their fields and delivers a promise: "One day the water of the Jordan will come here, to the desert, and life will again come forth from the wilderness and erupt from the ashes."

The story of the Jordan River corresponds to David's biography in *My Father's House* and the biographies of immigrants and nonimmigrants in other films. They reach the country as children, and as natives resembling the untamed and uncivilized Arabs they accept the yoke of Zionist culture and undergo a process of death and resurrection. The water bursting forth in the wilderness is one of the most salient symbols of this process, engraved in the country's geography and the history of each of its inhabitants. The survivor merely reconstructs the process. As the eruption of water in the desert serves as a symbol of his resurrection, so does his resurrection symbolize the Israeli resurrection as a whole. Both are emblematic of the same object, the new Israeli identity.[23] The survivor serves this object as a symbol of the highest rank; the country's landscapes, wilderness, and water, like the Arabs who inhabit them, serve it as symbols of secondary rank.

From Desolation to Efflorescence, from Barrenness to Fertility

The path from desert and wilderness to efflorescence, from what is considered an Arab landscape to an Israeli one, is the road traveled by most Holocaust survivors in these films. Where the heroes are heroines, the transition from desolation to fertility symbolizes a changeover from infertility and licentiousness to motherhood. In *My Father's House* the changeover is effected in a sub-plot, the story of Miriam, David's adoptive mother. Miriam was known as Maria in her previous life, but there, in the Diaspora during the Holocaust, she was not allowed to be a holy mother.[24] She was deprived of her children and became a whore of the SS. When she comes to Israel, she refuses to assume the duty of caring for the kibbutz children. She even finds it difficult to promise to care for David, to whom she has become closely attached. In other words, the Holocaust has left her with the negative, threatening images of a woman: those of the childless wife and the prostitute. Here on the kibbutz, she is asked to resume the function of the holy mother, the unsullied mother, a collective person who cares for collective children, either those of the kibbutz or a Holocaust survivor who is not really her son. The film goes out of its way to maintain her pure appearance even to the extent of her not developing an intimate relationship with Avraham, the child's intended father. The fact that they are about to become the child's parents allows one to assume the existence of intimacy between them, but such a relationship is neither consummated nor alluded to in any form in the course of the film. Miriam remains throughout the whole film a mother only, not a lover. Becoming a lover would shift her from her one and only role, which is to support the national existence metaphorically as a sign of fertility.

The transformation from whore to mother that occurs in Anna, the heroine of *Faithful City,* is even more acute and emphatic. At the beginning of the plot, Anna is untamed and disruptive, like her friends, the boys. However, she is a girl and her wildness takes on a sexual connotation. She threatens, attracts, and tempts the men around her, especially her counselor, Sam. She displays individualistic tendencies that others perceive as sexual deviations. By the end of the film, she changes into a modest and disciplined woman, like the other Hebrew women and like the other women survivors who have changed their identity, including Tamara in *The Great Promise,* who changes from a wildcat into a disciplined child, and Miriam in *My Father's House,* who, despite herself, is transformed from a barren whore into a mother.

Miriam, the heroine of *Tomorrow is a Wonderful Day,* does not undergo this kind of process. She is introduced to us as a mother from the outset. Binyamin first observes her tending small chicks and surrounded by children. He is attracted not necessarily by her femininity but by the noble maternity that she radiates. When they reach the location of the new settlement and one of the girls complains, "There's not even a tree here," it is Miriam who replies, "Soon there'll be a whole forest." Thus, she speaks in the name of growth and efflorescence. Indeed, when Binyamin finally approaches her and starts up a relationship, he recalls, "I knew you would gather the first fruit with me." Miriam, like all the survivors, says nothing about her past. The film tells us nothing about her life, identity, and personality. She is but a pure symbol of motherhood and fertility. The male hero communes with her, just as he communes with the land, to give birth and to be born.

In *My Father's House,* it is the camera that connects Miriam's infertility with the desolate landscape that surrounds her. One of her fateful conversations with Avraham begins with a lengthy, slow panning motion of the camera over the Judean Desert and Arab villages. Then the camera focuses on the couple as they stand on Mount Scopus and contemplate the landscape. Avraham is talking. He loves this wasteland, he says, because one can begin everything anew here. He attempts to persuade Miriam to forget her past, to dedicate herself to David's upbringing, and to begin a new life. She refuses, because she explains after what the Nazis did to her she really should have died. She has no strength to embark on a new life. The camera responds to both Avraham's and Miriam's attitudes by echoing them. It observes Avraham against a background of blossoming trees and captures Miriam against the wasteland. When Avraham tells her, "You want to destroy everything that is feminine in you," a barren-branched tree is shown in the background, and when he tells her, "What was done to you there does not exist. I believe in you," a blossoming tree is shown. When he moves away from her and leaves the decision in her hands, she is again filmed against a desert backdrop. In the end, her decision to bring David home and be his mother represents her choice of efflorescence and fertility, and this is confirmed when she joins the circles of dancers at the settlement founding ceremony.

David's first mother in Palestine had been mother earth. After he dies and is reborn in the depths of the Dead Sea, he acquires an additional mother, Miriam, who, like his first mother and like himself, has evolved from a wasteland into a blossoming garden. Miriam's role in the film is the same role assigned to the Arab. Like the Arab, she represents several markers in David's identity. Like the Arab, she helps David change this identity. Unlike the Arab, however, she will take part in David's change in identity, both literally and metaphorically. The Arab, unlike the woman, is condemned to remain the "other" outside, like the desert and the wilderness, and thus has no place in the main metamorphosis of the films.

From Text to Subtext

By analyzing films from the 1940s and 1950s that placed Holocaust survivors in central roles one may probe the Zionist narrative that the films attempt to affirm and thereby distinguish elements of Israeli identity that they wish to preserve from those that they wish to expunge. The films attempt to preserve a coherent history of progress[25] that follows a homogenized, progressive path from one origin only, the biblical past in the land of Israel, to one future only, a flourishing Zionist community in the land of Israel. Death, desolation, and destruction play a mythical role in this account, one of descent into hell preceding an ascent to paradise.

It is a cohesive account that overlooks nothing. Women, Arabs, Holocaust survivors, Christian priests, and British army officers all have one function: to integrate into the story or drive it forward. It does not offer alternative pasts, identities, and possible futures. It has one tradition, one past, one people, and one future. Every individual integrates into its causal progression from the reversal (from curse to blessing, from Holocaust to redemption, from desolation to efflorescence) to accrual and growth. The plot reflects this process, and the camera dramatizes it.

Neither the Holocaust survivor nor the veteran settler is given any leeway in this process. The details of the survivors' lives in and before the camps are incorporated into the films only insofar as they can merge into the Zionist narrative, be redeemed by it, and acquire meaning by its merit. The biographies of immigrants who preceded the survivors are treated similarly. The Holocaust survivor in *The Great Promise* pleads that he lacks the strength to begin anew, and a soldier in the Palestinian brigade replies, "When I came to Palestine, I was a broken man just like you." In this respect, there is no difference between them. All of them are fated to follow the same path. The Holocaust survivor accepts the Israeli redemption account so easily because the details of his life, his past, his suffering, and his every experience, are presented as being devoid of a story that would organize them and invest them with meaning. The films correct this flaw by organizing the details into the Zionist narrative.[26]

The Zionist narrative shown in the films, however, is not the only one that existed in the culture of the time. Other narratives existed and eventually became more prominent. Initially, they occurred in marginal cultural systems or were integrated, as marginal components, into texts dominated by the Zionist narrative. They were also buried in the "subtext" of the films discussed here. Thus, if one stops searching for the engine that drives the plots toward their happy endings and attempts to consider what had to be overcome in order to attain these endings one discovers that the retarding factors are not arbitrary and random: they attest to ideological contradictions that the plots have silenced. In the films at issue, these factors are shown only in the first stages of the plot and for the sole purpose of being obliterated. They are also disseminated in the subtext throughout the work and overshadow the harmony that the plot has created. They are composed of the Holocaust survivor's memories, hardships, consciousness, and identity, all of which have been repressed, banished from memory, and replaced by the Hebrew identity. In later works of Israeli literature and cinema, however, they advanced to the forefront and acquired full significance.

Homi Bhabha describes the national discourse as an ambivalent one that contains its own negation. The minority, he says, exists as "a referent of the dominant discourse; it is therefore an addition that diminishes the ability of this discourse to generalize and generate social stability." The minority shatters the coherence of the dominant narrative and pollutes it with inexpressible contradictions and irrationalities, day-to-day details that do not fit in, and repetitions that inhibit its general progression.[27] The ambivalence of which Bhabha speaks can be translated into terms of plot structure and interaction between elements that advance and retard the plot. From this point of view, arguably, there is no plot that does not undermine its basic assumption, since no plot can reach its end and achieve its goals without overcoming some obstacles. The elements that the plot overcomes are those that express the ideology that the plot strives to suppress, those that the text negates.[28] In most cases these obstacles also merge in the course of the plot in the form of contradictions that break its continuity and coherence, in repetitions that inhibit it, and in day-to-day details that do not coincide with the overall message and that deviate from what Bhabha terms the teleological, pedagogical structure of the national discourse.[29]

Later Israeli works dismantle the narrative that guided the earlier films, expand the contents shown in the initial stages of their plots, and modify their judgment toward these elements. In most instances, however, they dredge up contents that the earlier films repressed throughout their entire plots. Whereas in the initial phases of the films of the 1940s and 1950s the survivors' past obstructs the progress of the plot and is fated to give way to a Hebrew past, the survivors' past begins to dominate the plots of Israeli literary works and films in the 1960s.[30] In works that portray Holocaust survivors the protagonists begin to inquire about their past (*Tel Aviv Berlin*). That past erupts time and again in these later works, dictates the present lives of all the protagonists, including their children, and obstructs their integration into the Israeli reality (*Avia's Summer, Searing Light).* In all of these cases, the survivors' past is judged as superior to the Israeli present, which the plot blurs either through total obfuscation (*Tel Aviv Berlin)* or by presentation, along with recollections of the past, as part of a chaotic, brutal, and incomprehensible reality (*Searing Light*).

Along with the past, the new works are overtaken by scenes from the survivors' settings culled from the earlier films. Through the survivors' subjective eyes, the country seems dark and closed (*Avia's Summer, The Wooden Gun*), akin to a reincarnation of a concentration camp (*New Land, Searing Light).* Arabs or lunatics circulate in its open spaces (*Hide and Seek, The Wooden Gun),* and the heroes form real friendships with them. In any case, the heroes do not integrate into the country. Their fate is the opposite: they become lost in its broad, desolate brightness (*Avia's Summer),* try to flee to a new land (*New Land*), or continue to inhabit Diaspora landscapes (*Tel Aviv Berlin*). In all of these cases, it is the heroes' subjective point of view that dominates and is accepted by the work as a whole. Throughout these works, the survivors remain unredeemed, at the same initial stage that they occupied in the films of the 1940s and the 1950s.

As with time and space, the new works also draw the outlines of the survivors' image in the films of the 1940s and 1950s, but they change the judgment of this image. The trait formerly considered egoism is portrayed as individualism, idle Jewish lassitude is portrayed as spiritual wealth, seeming cowardice is shown as sensitivity, and feminine traits and affiliation with Arabs are much more appreciated than masculine traits or affiliation with Israelis (*Searing Light, Our Tree on the Hill, Hide and Seek,* and *Avia's Summer).* These works do not turn Jews into Hebrews in the course of their plots; they do the opposite. Many of the plots induce the Hebrew to admit that he is in fact a Jew, an orphan (*Hide and Seek*), and the son of Holocaust survivors (*The Wooden Gun*) who inhabits a Holocaust-survivor society, still enclosed within the ghetto walls and immersed in the Jewish past (*The Wooden Gun, Avia's Summer, Searing Light*).

On the one hand, the expositions earmarked for change in the old plots become the main engines of the plots in the new works. On the other hand, the narrative of the old plots, the resurrection of the Jew in the form of the Hebrew, disintegrates into unconnected episodes in the new plots. It is presented as a collection of clichés that the protagonists do not understand (*Searing Light*), is couched in irony (as for example in a laughable attempt to change one's clothing in *New Land*), and leads not to the beginning of a new Zionist life in Israel but to a life of orphanhood, bereft of parents and educators (*Searing Light*).

In the early films, the resurrection process ends with the survivors' adoption of Hebrew parents. In the new plots, the Hebrew fathers are unable to function as sources of authority and strength. They are false (*Searing Light, Avia's Summer*), they are absent (*Hide and Seek*), they communicate false values (*The Wooden Gun*), or they are depicted as parodies of paternal authority (*New Land*). Neither do the mothers fulfill the role given them in the early films. The mothers in *Avia's Summer* and *The Wooden Gun* are insane, the farm manager in *Searing Light* is an unsavory unmarried woman, and the mother in *Hide and Seek* is the mother of an entire children's village, not just her own son. Consequently, these new works dismantle the narrative that guided the early films, expand the contents shown in the initial stages of their plots, and modify the early films' judgment of these contents. In most instances, however, they dredge up contents that the earlier films repressed throughout their whole plots.

At first glance, the later works reverse the older films' hierarchy of judgment by preferring Jewish survivors over Israeli Hebrews. In fact, such preferences are also embedded in the early films. In the very first part of *Tomorrow is a Wonderful Day*, the camera, the editing, and the sound track express the subjective feelings of the protagonist, the young survivor, with great intensity and dynamism, whereas in its second part, after he has become a Hebrew, his persona melts into the collective experience and vanishes there. In fact, he has ceased to live since he was swept along by the great change. His entire life has become one large symbolic celebration. First he celebrates a concert, then the founding of a settlement, and then the Sabbath, the harvest festival, and the festival of first fruit. Then the film skips over the lengthy summer, in which he presumably experiences difficulties in adjusting to work and to communal life, and moves on to a Hanukkah celebration. In other films, the celebration is merely a final chord; here it dominates the plot. Thus, the film seems to identify most strongly with the fearful teenage survivor, whereas the "new Hebrew" is portrayed more as an ideological peg than a flesh-and-blood human being.

The later works transferred the point of view of the early films from the nonimmigrant Hebrews to the survivors. In fact, however, the early films had already surrendered the point of view to the survivors at the most meaningful moments of the plot. The point of view in *The Great Promise* is that of kibbutz children who observe the survivor girl, Tamara, and attempt to define, analyze, and understand her. Nevertheless, at a certain moment in the film she manages to elude her comrades' gaze and let her own point of view slip in. The film anticipates this moment by providing horizontal footage of the kibbutz in the dark as well as melancholy music that attest to the change of consciousness that filters the account from that of the kibbutz children to that of Tamara, the survivor. The horizontal footage is followed by a close-up of Tamara's face in the dark. She removes a necklace from a hiding place and contemplates a photograph of her mother. The girls sleeping next to her climb out of their beds and observe her, and one of them narrates: "We don't know what she's going through." At the critical stage in the account, the spectator sees what the children can neither see nor comprehend: the girl's inner world and past, of which they are allowed to know nothing. The themes of the later works focus on this world and this past.

In the early films, the survivor heroes ostensibly conquer the country's landscapes and find a new identity in them. A focused look at the more disguised components of these films reveals that in them too, as in the later works, the heroes often remain estranged from the landscapes and the surroundings. In *My Father's House,* the boy David does not actually acclimate himself to the Israeli countryside until the end of the plot, and the angle at which this landscape is filmed attests to this. It is true that he crosses the desert, the sea, and the mountains, and the camera provides splendid footage of all of them. However, they are invisible to him. To the very end, the camera does not physically, ideologically, or psychologically adopt his point of view. The boy, stubbornly and obsessively preoccupied with the search for his father, is uninterested in Israeli scenery. In most of the early films, the hero is given the "privilege" of looking around after he has forfeited his Jewish identity. This never occurs, however, in *My Father's House.* Even at the end, when David runs to his new father, Avraham, and falls into his arms, the camera wanders around the new settlement and observes the builders and tree planters. David is not the observer. In the plot, the boy eventually stops looking for his father and integrates into the Zionist narrative, but in fact his deepest identity, the one illuminated by his look, remains that of a stranger in the society he has joined and an alien in the landscapes of the country, which he does not see. Thus, he does not integrate into the attempt to impose the stable order of the National Home on the expanses of the country. The contradiction created by this film between the plot and its resolution fits into the contradiction between plot and gaze that we described here and allows us to depict David, the hero of the film, as a person who largely remains alien to the Zionist time into which he is supposed to integrate. In this sense, too, he prefigures the heroes of the later works.

The successive episodes introduce David to the Zionist narrative in its various details: working the land, the history of the country, and the cemetery where the early pioneers are buried (an attestation to the possibility of resurrection after death). He responds to each of the episodes shown him in one way: he searches for his father. His persistence and his allegiance to his father's memory threaten the Zionist progression of the plot by leading it firmly and coherently in a different direction: to the Diaspora and the past. David's fixation with the past actually guides the major events in the film: his escape from the boarding school, the trek to the desert, the trip to Jerusalem, and so on. The climax of the plot, David's discovery that his father is dead, does lead David to the "correct" solution: he abandons his parents' memory and exchanges his past for a new past, that of Israel. Until the end, however, the plot leads him down a different path: the quest for his real father. The conclusion of the plot in *My Father's House* gives the child survivor a Hebrew homeland, past, mother, and father. The point of view, the footage of the countryside, and the progression of the plot to its resolution, however, all leave him in his real past, with his real father, an alien to the country and its landscapes.

In other cases, it is the circular structure of time that impedes the progress of the early films' plots toward the attainment of the Zionist goals. In *The Great Promise,* the resurrection account is torn apart by a structure of repetitions. In one episode, the film follows the Jordan River in its journey to the Dead Sea and then proceeds to show the revitalization of the wilderness. However, it does not content itself with this; it repeats the resurrection story again and again, five times in all. Thus, whenever we think the process has been completed and the desert has indeed been revitalized, we are taken back to the beginning. The reiterations retard the process and return the plot to death whenever death seems to have been overcome. In so doing, they threaten the dynamic optimistic advancement of the Zionist account and, thereby, anticipate not only the later films that parody it openly but also the literary works of the 1960s and 1970s, which depict the country's history in cycles of death and destruction. ("Facing the Forests," by A. B. Yehoshua, is the most salient example.)[31]

These Israeli films of the 1940s and 1950s attempt to portray the multinational Palestinian space as a large and tranquil one, in which Hebrew pioneers, Orthodox Jews, Arabs, and Christians coexist, and all communities support the Israeli Hebrew one. Unwittingly, however, the footage of the Arab landscape, filmed from its Arab inhabitants' point of view, sometimes clashes with the Jewish patriotic jingles that are heard on the sound track: "Our Tiny Land," "My Motherland Canaan," and so on. The songs attempt to "Judaize" the landscape, but the picture refuses to go along. Similarly, the gaze of the Arab in *End of Evil* is meant to express admiration of the Israeli, but subliminally it also confirms that the Jew needs the gaze of the "other" in order to define himself. The practical strength of the Arabs and other aliens is manifested by the boy David in *My Father's House* when he forms friendships with them. If we observe his interaction with members of other nationalities (the Palestinian boy, the Bedouin, the British soldier, and in a certain sense the religious Jewish children) we may regard these relationships not as part of the plot that leads David to his Israeli identity, but rather as the kernel of a totally different plot, that of a boy who considers himself a stranger in his own society and finds a bond with those who live outside it. This is the story of the survivors in literature and cinema from the 1980s on: strangers in a strange land, "others" within who join the "others" without in order to deconstruct the national narrative and identity.

Contradictions between the plot and the montage shots also undermine the function of the war with the Arabs in strengthening the masculine Zionist identity. At the conclusion of *End of Evil,* Yosef returns to the kibbutz that his parents had left and is given a festive, emotional welcome. The War of Independence erupts in the middle of the revelry, and the text explains, "Yosef has come home. Yosef has a home to defend." Although the war allows Yosef to be reborn as a hero and an Israeli, the picture does not exactly confirm this opportunity. The camera shows lengthy close-up montages of terrified faces and shifts from them to close-ups of a tank, rifle muzzles creeping along, and Arabs astride galloping horses. These scenes recall the footage of the Arab riots at the beginning of the film. There, too, we are told that the pioneers have come to Palestine to defend it, but the footage belies this message by showing scenes more reminiscent of a Diaspora pogrom than a war: shredded parchments, shattered eyeglasses, strewn belongings, a prostrate corpse. The film describes the success of the settlement enterprise in Palestine and the rebirth of Yosef, the Holocaust survivor, in the War of Independence, but recurrent scenes of terror and dread contradict both accounts.

The earlier films also threaten the depiction of the woman as a collective mother by revealing the woman-figure that they repress and stifle. In *Faithful City,* for example, the hero Sam is attracted by the unrestrained, impulsive Anna, of all people, and not by Tamar, who adheres to the right ideology but comes across as an anemic, sexless character. Unlike the other survivors, Anna retains the ability to contemplate and control her surroundings by means of her gaze. In an outing with her comrades in town, they stop at a movie theater and notice a sign with an actress's burning eyes over the caption: "My Way." In the next shot, these eyes—are they the actress's or are they Anna's?—are drawn on a sheet of paper and posted in Sam's room. Sam seems to be perturbed by them, and when Anna enters his room he evidently submits to her allure by giving her a blue ribbon as a gift. However, the film immediately rules out the possible direction of Sam's forming an attachment to the impulsive, threatening, lawbreaking girl. Sam crumples the page on which the eyes are drawn, throws it away, and asks Anna to gather her hair with a ribbon, to comb it like all the other girls, and to behave like them. The film discloses its overt ideological preference for the maternal girl, Tamar. Sam's relationship with Tamar, however, is solely platonic. They share the starring role in the film. They work, live, and pursue the same goal together. It is but natural that an affair would blossom between them. Nevertheless, in this film as in *My Father's House* and other films of the time, Sam and Tamar relate to each other only in the context of their shared parenthood, as the adoptive parents of the survivor children. The survivor girl as temptress is the true focus of the hero's attraction. She is the shadowy side of matters that, like the Jewish survivor and the Arab alien, lies beyond the overt fashioning of time, space, and heroes in the film. The hero of *Tomorrow is a Wonderful Day* builds a fence around the new settlement and explains to himself and to others that "A wall sets a limit for man and place. What lies beyond is sometimes a grave." This wall is the boundary with which the films attempt to circumscribe a stable homogeneous culture. Anything that threatens its unity is hurled past it.

The protagonists in the opening stage of the plots of the films of the 1940s and 1950s indeed congregate on the other side of this wall. In the subsequent works of literature and film, they display the personal human sensitivities that were silenced in the previous films. They yearn for the distant Diaspora past that the earlier plots took pains to obliterate, and they seek a different history and space, for which the previous plots had had no room. They expose the possibilities and the repressed terrors and impulses that the early plots obfuscated. Wasteland and desert, a strange countryside, the Arabs, the non-Jews all around, and also seductive, tempting women, all of which had been tamed and silenced by the plots in the earlier films, evoke terror and attraction in the later works. However, as I have tried to show, these later works did not invent anything; they merely brought to the fore what had been hidden in the plots of the earlier films.

Notes

1. Stuart Hall, "Cultural Identity and Diaspora," in *Identity,* ed. Jonathan Rutherford (London: Lawrence and Wishart, 1990), 225.
2. See Toril Moi, ed., *Sexual/Textual Politics: Feminist Literary Theory* (London and New York: Methuen, 1985), 104, 195. On this subject see also Daniel Boyarin, *Unheroic Conduct: The Rise of Heterosexuality and the Invention of the Jewish Man* (Berkeley: University of California Press, 1997); Yosefa Lushitzki, "From Orientalist Discourse to Woman's Melodrama: Oz and Wolman's *My Michael,*" *Edebiat* 5 (1994): 99–123; and Yael S. Feldman, "Otherness and Difference as Strategies of Subjectivity: The Perspective of Gender Studies" in *The Other as Threat: Demonization and Antisemitism* [a paper presented for discussion at the International Conference, The Vidal Sasson International Center for the Study of Antisemitism] (Jerusalem: Hebrew University, 1995), 67–98.
3. One may compare this phenomenon with parallel narratives in other cultures, such as that of immigrants to America (eligible others) versus American Indians (ineligibles).
4. For the term and its uses see Ella Shohat, *Israeli Cinema* (Austin: University of Texas Press, 1989).
5. These films are described in Natan and Ya'akov Gross, *The Hebrew Film* [Hebrew] (Jerusalem: the authors, 1991) and Meir Shnitzer, *The Israeli Cinema* [Hebrew] (Tel Aviv: Kinneret, 1994). They include *My Father's House* (1946), directed by Herbert Klein and scripted by Meyer Levin; *The Great Promise* (1948), directed by Joseph Leits; *End of Evil* (1946–1949), directed by Helmar Larsky and Joseph Krungold; *It Is No Dream* (1948–1949), directed by Joseph Krungold; *House on the Hill* (1949), directed by George Lloyd George; *Tomorrow is a Wonderful Day* (1946), directed by Helmar Larsky; and *Faithful City* (1952), directed by Joseph Leits. Although most of these films were

scripted in English and addressed to American audiences, some were created by people who had come to the country for the purpose of settling there (examples are Joseph Leits, Meyer Levin, George Lloyd George, and Helmar Larsky). Israeli artists and actors participated in some of them, and local institutions such as the Jewish National Fund and Keren Hayesod funded all of them. An analysis of commemorative booklets can be found in Emmanuel Sivan, *The Generation of 1948: Myth, Image, and Memory* [Hebrew] (Tel Aviv: Am Oved, 1991). For a discussion of literary works, see Gershon Shaked, *A New Wave in Hebrew Literature* [Hebrew] (Merhavia: Sifriat Poalim, 1971) and Gershon Shaked, *Hebrew Narrative Fiction, 1880–1980* [Hebrew], vol. 4 (Tel Aviv: Hakibbutz Hameuchad and Keter, 1993). For a discussion of the attitude of the Israeli cinema toward the Holocaust see Judd Ne'eman, "The Empty Tomb in the Post-Modern Pyramid: Israeli Cinema in the 1980s and 1990s" in *Documenting Israel,* ed. Charles Berlin (Cambridge, MA: Harvard College Library, 1995).

6. Bhabha would term it as a mere sign, whose signified is the Israeli. See Homi K. Bhabha, "The Other Question: Difference, Discrimination and the Discourse of Colonialism," in *Out There,* eds. Ferguson, Russell et al. (New York: The New Museum of Contemporary Art, 1990), 316. Clifford calls this kind of structure a pedagogical allegory. See *Writing Culture,* eds. James Clifford and George Marcus (Berkeley: University of California Press, 1986), 100.
7. For example, in the film *He Walked in the Fields,* Semyon fought the Nazis in World War II but is subjected to his comrades' contempt and scorn in the film. He attempts to emulate them and their behavior, but his efforts are perceived as somewhat ridiculous. The only possible heroism in this film is that of the Israeli-born kibbutz member; the only story in the film is his.
8. On the pretensions of the Western narrative to express the entire nation, see Clifford, *Writing Culture* and Stuart Hall, "New Ethnicity," in *Stuart Hall: Critical Dialogues in Cultural Studies,* eds. David Morley and Kuan-Hsing Chen (London and New York: Routledge, 1996), 441–59. Bhabha defines this plot as one that tells a progressive story of growth and prosperity. See Homi K. Bhabha, *The Location of Culture* (London and New York: Routledge, 1994), 40–65. On this subject, see also Ne'eman, "The Empty Tomb" and Shaked, *Hebrew Narrative Fiction,* vol. 4.
9. These methods of rejection and suppression are described by many. See inter alia Pnina Werbner, "Essentializing Essentialism, Essentializing Silences: Ambivalence and Multiplicity in the Constructions of Racism and Ethnicity," in *Debating Cultural Hybridity,* eds. Pnina Werbner and Tariq Modood (London and New Jersey: Zed Books, 1997.)
10. See Ne'eman, "The Empty Tomb."
11. See Moshe Zimmerman, "Hebrew Cinema for the Wallet and the Emotion" [Hebrew], *Cinemateque* (1989): 48 and Gross, *The Hebrew Film,* 167–71.

12. Boyarin refers to the effeminate, homosexual traits of the Jews. See Daniel Boyarin, *Unheroic Conduct.* Much of my discussion is based on the attempt to show the way the Israeli text tried to convert the process: to turn the homosexual effeminate Jew into a masculine, heterosexual man.
13. As the wild and rebellious Anna, or as Miriam in *My Father's House.*
14. On the fashioning of the Arab character in Hebrew culture, see Ehud Ben-Ezer, ed., *Sleepwalkers and Other Stories: The Arab in Hebrew Fiction* (Boulder, CO: Lynne Rienner, 1998); Robert Alter, "Images of the Arab in Israeli Fiction," *Hebrew Studies* 18 (1977): 60–69; and Dan Urian, *The Arab in Israeli Theatre* [Hebrew] (Tel Aviv: Or Am, 1996).
15. Ella Shohat describes the Orient in the Israeli cinema as lacking any active historical narrative function, as a passive object to be studied and observed. See Shohat, *Israeli Cinema,* 43. In fact, the Orient is not passive in most of these films. The Arabs gallop across the countryside, crisscross it, threaten the Jewish settlers, or move them from place to place. Nevertheless, their passivity is evident in the plot: everything they do merely sets the stage for the Israeli identity and the Zionist overarching narrative.
16. As we will recall, shots of segments of a picture are an element in the poetics of the film. However, while the Arab remains segmented, shots of Jews come together to form a complete picture.
17. The Israeli landscape plays a blatantly propagandistic role in films meant to "sell" the country to American audiences. However, the films also give the landscapes ideological functions.
18. See Jean Cristophe Horak, "The Penetrating Power of Light" in *Fictitious Views of the Israeli Cinema* [Hebrew], eds. Nurith Gertz, Orly Lubin, and Judd Ne'eman (Tel Aviv: The Open University, in press).
19. Such a reversal occurs in Tamara in *The Great Promise.*
20. See the discussion of nomadism in M. Jane Jacobs, *Edge of Empire: Postcolonialism and the City* (London and New York: Routledge, 1996).
21. His journey corresponds to that of the epic heroes from the grave to rebirth, as described in Jurij Lotman, "The Origin of Plot in the Light of Typology," *Poetics Today* 1, no. 1–2 (1977): 161–85.
22. The same reversal of identity occurs in *Faithful City* after the hero flees to Jerusalem. He celebrates the reversal with his instructors on the day that Israel declares its independence. The birth of the state, like the founding of the new settlement in *My Father's House* and the first-fruit celebrations in *The Great Promise,* is a ceremonial event that characterizes the survivor's change as a rebirth and emphasizes the metaphoric aspect of this change.
23. Shohat and Ne'eman describe the role of water in these films. See Shohat, *Israeli Cinema,* 44 and Ne'eman, *The Empty Tomb.* Shohat picks out saliently colonialist elements in Zionist culture and Israeli cinema. In films such as *The Sabra* and *Oded the Nomad,* she identifies the point of view of a Westerner who comes to a new location, crosses its expanses, and strips it of its mystery. The

Arabs who live here, in Shohat's view, are treated as extensions of the landscape and are likened to the desert and the marsh, which await the revitalizing advent of Western man. The present chapter bases itself on several insights in Edward Said, *Orientalism* (New York: Vintage Books, 1977) on the ways colonialist cultures manufacture the concept of "Orient," but does not accept the Zionism-equals-colonialism equation that constitutes a central fixture in Ella Shohat's book. The Zionist settlers did not come to a country alien to them, did not intend to disseminate their culture there, and did not exploit the country to enrich their country of origin (see Boyarin, *Unheroic Conduct*). Therefore, Zionism does not meet several basic criteria of colonialism.

24. In the matter of the woman pioneer as a great mother, see Shohat, *Israeli Cinema,* 44.
25. A teleological history, to use Bhabha's term. See Bhabha, "Interrogating Identity," *ICA Documents* 6 (1990): 5-11.
26. According to Aharon Appelfeld, the survivors indeed accepted this account with little resistance because the beliefs that had informed their lives had collapsed. "The Jew considered himself immersed in the great march of progress," a march "in which nationality and sectorialism are nullified and the world is remade in a new human unity of some kind. This belief, of which he was a leading exponent, blinded him. He did not see, and could not see, that forces of darkness and evil, which for years had been lurking for him, were about to spring from the thicket and dismember him alive." Aharon Appelfeld, "Subtotal" [Hebrew], *Yediot Aḥaronot,* May 9, 1994.
27. See Bhabha, "Interrogating Identity," 295, 296, 306, 313. See also Homi K. Bhabha, *The Location of Culture*, 49 and Elisabeth Bronfen, *Over her Dead Body* (New York: Routledge, 1992), 105.
28. In all these cases, the texts are not really subversive, because the progress of the Zionist narrative is not so much halted as it is postponed when the difficulties that impede the fulfillment of the plot's driving ideology are only insinuated. However, it is the reader, not the text itself, who reveals these difficulties. See Shaked, *Hebrew Narrative Fiction,* vol. 4, 16, in which he speaks of postponing the advancement of the Zionist "superplot," and Orly Lubin, "The Woman in Israeli Cinema" in *Fictitious Views of the Israeli Cinema* [Hebrew], eds. Gertz, Lubin, and Ne'eman (in press), in which she analyzes the role of the reader in fulfilling the subversive dimension of the film.
29. See also Frederic Jameson, *The Political Unconscious* (London: Methuen, 1981). The prevailing argument is that the narrative articulates the hegemonic ideology and the expressive devices subvert it. See also Jean-Louis Camolli and Jean Narboni, "Cinema/Ideology/Criticism (1)" in *Screen Reader* 1 (1977): 2–11. The assumption in this article is that the coherent, processed, and unifying level is the one that expresses the overt ideology of the work, whereas the less coherent, less processed levels may contain ideological lacunae and contradictions.

30. This subject is not fully analyzed in the present chapter. It is discussed in my books *Ḥirbet Ḥizaʿah and the Morning After* [Hebrew] (Tel Aviv: Porter Institute and Hakibbutz Hameuchad, 1983) and *Motion Fiction* [Hebrew] (Tel Aviv: The Open University, 1994). The present discussion of later works on Holocaust survivor themes, too, is sketched in outline form only. It is based on my two articles "From Jew to Hebrew: The Zionist Narrative in *Searing Light*" [Hebrew] in *Between Frost and Smoke: Studies in the Writings of Aharon Appelfeld,* ed. Itzchak Ben-Mordecai and Iris Parush (Beersheva: Ben-Gurion University, 1997), 125–44 and "A New Look at Holocaust Survivors: The Israeli Cinema in the 1980s and 1990s" [Hebrew] (unpublished).
31. In this matter, Bhaba speaks of various repetition strategies that inhibit the development and accumulation of time in the national-progress story. See Bhabha, "Interrogating Identity," 1, 297.

4

Victimhood and Identity: Psychological Obstacles to Israeli Reconciliation with the Palestinians*

Neil Caplan

At a time when Israelis and Palestinians are struggling, not always peacefully, through the implementation of the middle and later stages envisaged in the Declaration of Principles signed at Oslo in 1993, it is important to look beyond the well-known, concrete issues dividing the two peoples to examine the underlying attitudes, stereotypes, myths, images, and self-images that will continue to act as obstacles to full reconciliation between them. We must not be misled into presuming that we will see a definitive end to the Israeli-Palestinian conflict once the remaining "final-status" issues are resolved. Even if one can imagine the onset of some imperfect but workable solutions to the concrete issues of land (territory, settlements), refugees, and Jerusalem, Israelis and Palestinians will still be a long way from true reconciliation. Much creative post-conflict work will be required to guide the longstanding enemies through important psychological transformations in hopes of healing generations of serious emotional wounds.

Victims versus Victims

This chapter focuses on one of the psychological obstacles that must be overcome before we can realistically expect ordinary Palestinians and Israelis to benefit fully from the fruits of what has come to be known as the "peace process." This obstacle is the set of competing, ingrained, and mutually exclusive self-images many Israelis and Palestinians have of themselves as the victim of the other party's aggressiveness and hostility.

Two well-known writers have already put their creative fingers on this theme. The first is the renowned historian and self-described "non-Jewish Jew" Isaac Deutscher, who developed a much-quoted allegory in the wake of the June 1967 Arab-Israeli war:

> A man once jumped from the top floor of a burning house in which many members of his family had already perished. He managed to save his life; but as he was falling he hit a person standing down below and broke that person's legs and arms. The jumping man had no choice; yet to the man with the broken limbs he was the cause of his misfortune. If both behaved rationally, they would not become enemies. The man who escaped from the blazing house, having recovered, would have tried to help and console the other sufferer; and the latter might have realized that he was the victim of circumstances over which neither of them had control.
>
> But look what happens when these people behave irrationally. The injured man blames the other for his misery and swears to make him pay for it. The other, afraid of the crippled man's revenge, insults him, kicks him, and beats him up whenever they meet. The kicked man again swears revenge and is again punched and punished. The bitter enmity, so fortuitous at first, hardens and comes to overshadow the whole existence of both men and to poison their minds.[1]

More recently, the well-known Israeli novelist and peace activist Amos Oz wrote that

> [b]oth parties, in two different ways, are victims of Christian Europe: the Arabs through colonialism, imperialism, oppression and exploitation, while the Jews have been the victims of discrimination, pogroms, expulsions and, ultimately, mass murder. According to the mythology of Bertold Brecht, victims always develop a sense of mutual solidarity, marching together to the barricades as they chant Brecht's verses. In real life [however] some of the worst conflicts develop between victims of the same oppressors: two children of the same cruel parent do not necessarily love each other. They often see in each other the image of their past oppressor. So it is, to some extent, between Israelis and Arabs: the Arabs fail to see us as a bunch of survivors. They see in us a nightmarish extension of the oppressing colonizing Europeans. We Israelis often look at Arabs not as fellow victims but as an incarnation of our past oppressors: Cossacks, pogrom-makers, Nazis who have grown mustaches and

wrapped themselves in kaffiyehs, but who are still in the usual business of cutting Jewish throats.[2]

This mutual sense of victimhood has become one of the most serious psychological complications bedeviling Arab-Zionist and Palestinian-Israeli relations. Like Deutscher and Oz, I am presuming a certain degree of symmetry on both the Palestinian and Israeli sides of this psychological entanglement of self-identified victims struggling against another group of self-identified victims. This chapter outlines only Israeli perceptions and self-images of victimhood, and I must leave it to specialists on Palestinian nationalism and national identity to assemble the evidence that may make a similar case regarding the Palestinian sense of victimhood.[3]

In the following pages I will begin by illustrating how pervasively Jewish, Zionist, and Israeli history and identity are overwhelmed by a morose sense of victimization. I will then indicate how this self-concept as victim has become both politicized and militarized in the Arab-Israeli conflict, most visibly in the well-known Israeli security obsession. In particular, I will examine how the enduring Israeli sense of victimhood became a serious obstacle to reconciliation by excluding the logical possibility that the Palestinians may also legitimately feel victimized. Finally, I will examine recent trends and raise questions about the prospect for change in this unhelpful self-identification as victim.

"Jew-as-Victim" in Zionist and Israeli Identity

Every year roughly in the month of March, Jews around the world celebrate the holiday of Purim. As recounted in the book of Esther, Purim is one of the best-known stories of the Bible. To summarize it briefly, the Jew Mordecai, through the intervention of his niece Esther who had become queen, cleverly (and luckily) succeeds at the eleventh hour in canceling an order by King Ahasuerus, instigated by his wicked chief minister Haman, that would have executed all the Jews of the kingdom. Virtually every child with a minimum of Jewish education knows the story and enjoys the holiday, especially because almost every synagogue or community center has some sort of Purim observance focused on children, usually involving elaborate costumes.

In many respects, Michael Goldberg writes, "the Purim story rings true to Jews' historical experience. Implicit within the holiday's very name—Purim, meaning 'lots'—is the notion that the Jewish People's existence is a dicey thing."[4] Most scholars agree that the Purim story is probably not historically true. Nevertheless, it has become one of the master stories, master narratives, or defining myths and legends for Jewish identity. Most of the history of the Jews in relation to their non-Jewish environment can be understood as variations on the single theme of unrelenting anti-Semitism, expressed in terms of gentile attempts at the conversion, expulsion, or annihilation of the Jews.

In the past fifty years, the Purim master story has been replaced by an even more compelling modern legend, the Holocaust, as the touchstone and rationale for Jewish identity and survival. In the communal life of Jews around the world, and also in the academic world of Jewish studies, most mainstream presentations of Jewish history have accepted and advanced what some scholars have termed the "lachrymose" school of thinking, in which the Jews have always been victims on the receiving end of other nations' power, an endangered species valiantly struggling for survival in a recurrently hostile environment.

There are many anecdotal illustrations of this mentality—critics would call it a form of culturally transmitted paranoia. Let me offer only two contemporary examples. The March 1997 *Jewish Book News* advertised the revised edition of Rabbi Mattis Kantor's successful *Jewish Time Line Encyclopedia: A Year-by-Year History from Creation to the Present* with a sample page taken from chapter 12, "The Rishonim—Early Scholars." Seven of the eight dates listed refer to massacres of or attacks on Jews. The single positive or neutral item on this list is that in 1363, a descendant of the medieval commentator Rashi was appointed chief rabbi by the King of France.[5]

A second area in which this sentiment is widespread is popular culture. In his introduction to *How to Talk Jewish,* veteran comedian Jackie Mason reflects a longstanding view about the connection between Jewish suffering and humor when he writes that

> Jews have always been very free in terms of expressiveness. That's why Jews were always among the best comedians, and still are. Jews always felt alienated from the rest of the world and they had no other way of fighting back against that feeling of alienation except through their humor. They were always a defenseless, helpless minority and they had to hide their true feelings in society at large because they were so suppressed. . . . Humor has been one avenue of escape for Jews throughout history. They managed to find humor in the most tragic circumstances. That's why the Jews, until Israel came about, were never

> known as fighters. Jews knew that things were so stacked against them by the countries in which they were living that . . . they had to find ways of winning the fight by avoiding it, outsmarting their opponent, outmaneuvering him, coddling him, lying to him, hiding from him. Anything except fighting, because he was so outnumbered, so outmanned, so outarmed. . . .[6]

Despite the existence of other intellectually cogent, less lachrymose readings of Jewish history, in the real world of the late twentieth century, we are forced to recognize and deal with the overwhelming staying power of the Jewish self-image as victim. "Jew-as-victim" is a recurring theme espoused and felt, in different ways and to different degrees perhaps, by the majority of Jews around the world, even when their objective successful situation may contradict negative self-perceptions. Diaspora community figures, no less than Zionist and Israeli political leaders, with rare exceptions, play effectively on this theme, exploiting it with varying degrees of cynicism in their efforts to outbid rivals in mobilizing group solidarity, seeking financial support, or pursuing electoral backing in the Jewish public arena.

"Jew-as-Victim" in the Politics and Polemics of the Conflict with the Palestinians

We would be wrong to dismiss this Jewish hypervigilance and suspiciousness as mere fantasy. As one psychoanalyst has remarked, these characteristics are "a response to a cruel reality." Furthermore, writes Jay Gonen, even Israelis cannot rid themselves of these traits

> as long as they are cast as a lonely nation among hostile neighbors. The Holocaust . . . fortified the haunted outlook and suspicious alertness of the Jewish people for generations to come. Mistrust of non-Jews was inevitable. . . . If Jews sound paranoid at times, then it is because all too frequently in their past their worst suspicions turned out to be realities rather than dreams.[7]

This historical *victimization* of the Jews has become transformed into Jewish *victimhood,* and in recent years victimhood has often been used for successful politics. As Michael Goldberg has noted, "claimed victimhood carrie[s] with it significant moral and political leverage over those cast in the role of victimizers."[8] Indeed, Israeli author Shulamith Hareven, in a 1986 article tellingly entitled "Identity: Victim," provides examples, going back to the Sholom Aleichem story, "Lucky Me, I'm An Orphan," of how the identity of victim usually pays off in the short term.[9]

The recent increase in public attention devoted to the phenomenon of victimhood has led some to ridicule the explosion of "the number of squatters staking claims to victimhood on the contemporary American moral and political landscape."[10] If there is today a long queue of those claiming moral and other redress by virtue of their victimhood, many Jews would say that their people was long ago at the head of that queue. Let us review some of the relevant modern history.

1. *Pre-1948 Zionism as an Antidote to Jewish Suffering and Victimization*

At the turn of this century, millennia of suffering, wandering, and lack of a homeland underlay early Zionist appeals for the creation of a Jewish national home addressed both to Jewish coreligionists and to European consciences. The Beiliss trial and early-twentieth-century pogroms in Eastern Europe highlighted the continued persecution and vulnerability of the Jews in their dispersion. The formation and early growth of the World Zionist Organization and the international lobbying efforts of Nahum Sokolow and Chaim Weizmann drew on this theme, which contributed its share to winning British imperial backing for Zionism as enunciated in the Balfour Declaration of 1917.

A wave of anti-Semitism in Poland in the mid-1920s became the main catalyst for a wave of Jewish immigration to Palestine known as the Fourth Aliyah. This was shortly followed by the ascension to power of Adolf Hitler in 1933, which marked the start of the definitive extreme proof of Jewish vulnerability. In the late 1930s and early 1940s, Zionist leaders and spokesmen argued the need for a sovereign Jewish state to serve as a refuge for those seeking to flee the horrors of Nazi Europe. In May 1942, an emergency Zionist conference held at the Biltmore Hotel in New York passed resolutions calling for immediate mass immigration to rescue European Jews and the postwar creation of a "Jewish commonwealth" in an undivided Palestine.[11] When at last the United Nations General Assembly adopted its historic November 1947 resolution endorsing the partition of British Mandatory Palestine into an Arab state and a Jewish state, many observers saw the decision as being motivated, at least in part, by Christian Europe's tacit recognition of guilt or negligence with regard to the victimization of the Jewish people.[12]

2. *1948 and After: Survival or Reprisal?*

Most Jews around the world interpreted the UN partition resolution as a vindication for years of struggle, hardship, and tragedy. Some even went so far as to interpret the events of 1947–49 as a mystical or supernatural recovery (*tequmah*) for the calamity (*shoah*) of 1939–45. Israel's battlefield victories against Arab armies and militias in 1948 and 1949 confirmed the hard-won independence of a state that, according to Zionist ideology, was supposed to mark the end of the "Jewish problem" by ensuring a safe haven for all Jews who wished to be "ingathered" there.

The successful rebirth of Israel was without doubt a cause for celebration among Jews and brought with it a new pride and self-confidence. But the battlefield victory was not translated into a secure peace, and the young country was forced to grow up in a state of siege. Yet, in spite of its rejection by the surrounding Arab states and the permanent threat of renewed warfare, Israel survived and struggled during the 1950s and 1960s and went on to prosper during the 1970s, 1980s, and 1990s. The new state continued to be seen by its supporters and its citizens as a success story, which was all the more heroic when portrayed as tiny David victorious over a mighty Arab Goliath.

Following its striking military performances in October 1956 and especially in the June 1967 war, successful, little Israel also became powerful, larger Israel. But, while post-1967 Israel has been viewed by most nations of the world as a regional superpower, many Israelis have retained the perception of it as a small and besieged state, ever on the brink of extinction at the hands of its unforgiving Arab neighbors. Despite the battlefield victories of its armies and the diplomatic successes of its politicians and spokespeople, the hard-won sovereignty of the young State of Israel did not provide sufficient reason to transform the Jewish self-image of victim into that of victor. While Israel's Arab enemies and her Palestinian sibling rivals experienced firsthand the power of a triumphant Israel in 1948, 1956, 1967, 1973, and 1982, many Israelis continued to develop their identity based not on such victory and power, but on enduring self-perceptions of victimhood and powerlessness.

Why did five decades of Israeli sovereignty not produce, as some might have hoped, a major transformation in Jewish identity and self-image from loser to winner? It seems to matter little that half of Israel's military and intelligence commentators pointed out, for example, that, during the mid- to late-1980s, Israel was much more secure than at any other time in her history; or that in retrospect, the outcome of the 1967 and 1973 wars proved that, from a purely military point of view, there was little real danger of the Arabs overrunning the country; or that Israel did not face imminent annihilation.[13]

To understand this puzzling phenomenon we must probe below the surface of Israel's apparent political and military successes to grapple with the persistent, deep-rooted fears of imminent destruction. This would seem to bear out the remarks of Michael Ignatieff, in a recent commentary on Croats, Serbs, and Muslims. "The truth that matters to people," he wrote, is "not factual truth but moral truth; not a narrative that tells *what* happened but a narrative that explains *why* it happened and who is responsible." Truth, Ignatieff observed, is related to identity: "What you believe to be true depends, in some measure, on who you believe yourself to be."[14]

And indeed, the perception that Jews, especially those living in the Diaspora, are endangered victims has been particularly strong among Israeli Jews. In a 1965 survey conducted by Simon Herman, 65 percent of Israeli eleventh-graders (and 78 percent of their parents) felt certain, or thought it conceivable, that "in the foreseeable future" anti-Semitism was "likely to endanger the existence of Jewish communities abroad."[15] In a follow-up survey conducted soon after Israel's dramatic victory in the 1967 war, Herman found that 17 percent felt the Holocaust could recur in "all countries," 11 percent "in most countries," and 56 percent "in some countries." Almost 60 percent agreed completely with the statement "Every Jew in the world should see himself as a survivor of the Holocaust."[16]

Writing in the late 1980s, David Biale suggested that the impact of the Holocaust and the circumstances under which Israel has had to fight for its survival "dramatically colored the understanding of power and history held by most Jews today. As a result of the continuing conflict with the Arabs, the Zionist hope to create a 'normal' nation has receded and been replaced by . . . an 'ideology of survival.'" To those who hold this ideology and worldview, Biale continued,

> hatred of Jews remains a problem unsolved. Instead of sovereignty turning the Jews into a nation like all others, the Jewish state becomes a new expression of the separation between the Jews and the rest of the world. Instead of sovereignty bestowing a sense of security, it . . . led to contradictory feelings of inflated power and exaggerated fear.[17]

Since its inception, Israel's outward behavior has often appeared to its detractors to be aggressive and based on raw power. In Israel's defense, supporters have pointed to Arab aggressive intentions and a basic insecurity to explain or excuse the sabra (native-born Israeli) bravado and cult of the Israel Defense Force (IDF). Yet some of the harshest criticism of Israeli militaristic attitudes has been self-criticism. In his essay "The State as Reprisal," based on a talk given in 1962, Amos Oz noted a disturbing tendency to view the IDF's commander-in-chief as "a kind of bellicose Samson whose hands had been tied by the Elders of Zion with their diaspora mentality," their alleged cowardice and passivity. Oz detected a "reprisal" underside to the "ideology of survival" I outlined above, in the form of a

> desire to breed a race of sweat and blood that [would] be cruel and "non-Jewish" like the antisemites, not merciful and submissive like the diaspora Jews. In brief, a vision of the State of Israel as a great reprisal for our historical humiliation. According to this sentiment, the purpose of the State of Israel [was] not to save the Jews but to teach the non-Jews a lesson and vent our rage on them and particularly to show them how tough and warlike and cruel we too can be, and how much they ought to respect us for being as bad as they are if not more so. . . . The clichés are all taken from the old self-pitying stock: "Israel are scattered lambs," "a people dwelling on its own," "a sheep among seventy wolves."[18]

Two decades after uttering those words, Oz again attacked extreme expressions of macho militarism, echoing the outspoken Orthodox Jewish scholar, Professor Yeshayahu Leibowitz, in his critique of the militant brand of "Judeo-Nazism" that developed among fanatical West Bank settlers in the wake of the June 1967 war.[19]

3. *The Shadow of the Holocaust*

Many Jews today recall vividly the joyous, elated, and often boastful reactions of Israeli and Diaspora Jews following the IDF's swift military victory in the Six-Day War of June 1967. Yet even the lopsided military victory of June 1967 could not do away with the inability, within Israel's mainstream, to reconcile evidence of actual Israeli power with perceptions of historical Jewish powerlessness. Interviews with Israeli soldiers immediately following the war indicated that

> the consciousness of the Holocaust was even more strongly present in 1967 than in 1948[. . . .T]here are numerous references to the profound influence of the memory of the Holocaust as a background factor in their reaction to the

threats of the enemy. Into the minds of many of them came the thought that an Arab victory would mean another Holocaust.[20]

A number of writers have grappled with the question: Why did the Six-Day War victory not ease or erase deep-seated Jewish fears of annihilation? Certainly, in the months leading up to Israel's decision to launch its preemptive attack on June 5, 1967, Jews and Israelis experienced a disturbing repetition of the old feeling of being encircled by enemies while being abandoned by erstwhile allies. Probing the psychological dimension, Jay Gonen cited Amnon Rubinstein's characterization of "the schizophrenic coexistence of superstrength and mortal weakness in Israeli perceptions and actions." Writing in 1975, Gonen commented that

> [d]riven by shame and a sense of inferiority, the Jews felt the need to compensate and even overcompensate. By now they have already experienced massive doses of pride . . . [accompanied by] a switch from passivity to activity in both thoughts and deeds. . . . On the whole, Jews are no longer regarded by themselves or others as passive weaklings who sit on their behinds and wait for fate to overtake or overrun them.[21]

But Gonen and others sensed that, even while the *world's image* of them may have changed in this way, this was not how Jews and Israelis continued to *perceive themselves.* Rather than interpreting 1948 and 1967 as proofs that Zionism and Israel represented a revolutionary escape from Jewish history and an end to millennia of victimization, many Israelis came to reinterpret their Zionism, turning it instead into a modern variation of the same old lachrymose "Jewish fate."

Such thinking, with its potential for political and military overreaction, was one component of a vicious circle of violence involving armed Palestinian bands and occasionally the regular armies of the neighboring Arab states. Arab bellicose rhetoric, vowing not only to avenge a lost battle but to correct the "historic injustice" caused by Israel's very existence since 1948, provided ample justification of Israeli and Jewish fears.[22] These fears were further inflamed by sensational acts of international terrorism in the decade following the June 1967 victory. A spate of airplane hijackings during 1968–1971 and the murder of eleven Israeli athletes during the Munich Olympic Games in September 1972 were followed by several raids into northern Israel that killed dozens of Israeli civilians, many of them children, at Nahariya, Kiryat Shemona, and Ma'alot. At the same time, the apparent capitulation of many Western, African, and

Asian countries to the pressures of Arab oil suppliers and the 1975 passage of a UN General Assembly resolution equating Zionism with racism only helped to fuel the continued Israeli self-identification as victims facing "eternal isolation, unending antisemitism, and a continual threat to Jewish survival."[23] The Israeli commandos' daring rescue of hostages held at the Entebbe airport in Uganda by German hijackers working on behalf of the Popular Front for the Liberation of Palestine in 1976 seemed to restore Israeli and Jewish morale from a low point of alienation and victimization. But, for many Jews, the existence of Israel and recent examples of her military prowess proved only that "Jews now possessed the weapons to *resist* this fate, but *not* to *change* or *eliminate* it."[24]

In his seminal study, social psychologist Simon N. Herman has argued that Jewish and Israeli identity cannot be properly understood without a deep understanding of the impact of the Holocaust. "It is a constant background factor," Herman wrote in the early 1970s,

> Moving from time to time into the foreground—affecting the way Jews see themselves and the way they perceive their relationship with the non-Jewish world. The shadow which the Holocaust casts over the relationship between Jews and the non-Jewish world has lengthened across the years.[25]

Perhaps the most perceptive insights into the Israeli mood in the immediate wake of the 1967 war come from the best-selling *The Israelis: Founders and Sons,* in which veteran journalist Amos Elon called the Holocaust "a basic trauma of Israeli society" and noted that it was "impossible to exaggerate its effect on the process of nation-building."[26] When it came to Israel's unresolved conflict with the Arabs, Elon referred to a "latent hysteria in Israeli life that stems directly from" the Holocaust, whose "lingering memory" made "Arab threats of annihilation sound plausible." There was, he wrote, "an obsessive quality in such preoccupation; inevitably some Israelis, at certain times and places, have found it unduly morbid, burdensome, and even contrived."[27] Nonetheless, Elon stressed, an understanding of the Holocaust, helped to explain

> the fears and prejudices, passions, pains, and prides that spin the plot of public life [in Israel] and will likely affect the nation for a long time to come. . . . If, in Israeli eyes, the world at large has tended to forget too soon, Israelis hardly give themselves the chance. The traumatic memory is part of the rhythm and ritual of public life.

The Holocaust, Elon continued, "accounts for the prevailing sense of loneliness, a main characteristic of the Israeli temper since Independence. It explains the obsessive suspicions, the towering urge for self-reliance at all cost in a world which permitted the disaster to happen."[28]

The Holocaust's contribution to a wider tendency to focus on Jewish tragedies rather than on Jewish achievements was evident in the 1980s. When asked to list the most important events in the history of the people of Israel, writes Shulamith Hareven, most Israeli schoolchildren included the destruction of the First Temple, the destruction of the Second Temple, the expulsion from Spain, the Holocaust, the establishment of the state, [and] the Yom Kippur War, but not, Hareven stresses, the building of the First Temple, the existence of the Second Temple, "the magnificent, lengthy construction of the Mishnah and the Talmuds," the Golden Age of Jews in Spain; and the Jewish contribution of ethical monotheism to world civilization.[29]

4. *The "New Zionism" and Menachem Begin's Likud Party*

What became known in the 1970s as the "New Zionism" abandoned the utopianism and optimism that had characterized the pioneering and socialist brand of Zionism in the earlier part of the century. According to the ideology of the New Zionism, the creation of Israel had

> failed to solve the problem of anti-Semitism because anti-Semitism [was] endemic to the non-Jew. Moreover, the world [would] never allow the Jews to leave the center-stage of history. Jews [would] continue to have the status of pariahs, but now as a pariah state among the nations of the earth.[30]

The rise of the New Zionism was accompanied by a marked increase in the use of Holocaust rhetoric in Israeli political discourse, both at home and abroad. In the decade following the election of a Likud government in June 1977, Jews were portrayed, like Isaac in the Book of Genesis, as "the sacrificial victims on the altar of their own history. . . ." Their "eternal destiny" was to play the role of history's victims.[31] As Michael Goldberg has recently observed, "[w]hen it came to exploiting Jews' victimization, Menachem Begin, Israel's first Holocaust-survivor prime minister, had no peer."[32]

Begin seemed to embody more than his own personal history—not the typical subservient "ghetto mentality," but the rebellious variant. He also reflected a public mood uniting all Jews in Israel in the common belief that "Zionism was not so much a negation of the Diaspora as a continuation of its fate in a new way. With Begin, the experience of the Holocaust survivors became the ethos of the state."[33] As one American Jewish observer remarked in 1982,

> the Prime Minister and the issue of Israel's safety are not so easily separated. Begin gained much of his power by appealing to his people's fear of national annihilation, a fear that is genuine in him, and not a political expedient. Indeed, the reason its expression carries such weight in Israel is that it is not an idea of the moment, but one that lies so deep in Jewish thought it is often inexpressible. Begin understands Jewish thought. What he understands specifically is that a great many Jews live with their eyes on the past, for good reason; and when they are called upon to make fundamental choices, they will turn to the past for guidance, though it contains all the hell of their history.[34]

Begin's appeals resonated not only (predictably) for Jews of Ashkenazi-European origin, but (unexpectedly) even for those of Sephardi-Mediterranean background whose identity and traditions were not so intuitively intertwined with the lachrymose reading of Jewish history.[35]

Perhaps the most public international display of Begin's Holocaust ethos came during the signing ceremony for the Israeli-Egyptian peace treaty on the White House lawn in March 1979. At that time, the Israeli prime minister felt obliged to inject what many considered a sour note, setting the joyous occasion of signing the treaty into a more somber context. It was, he declared, not exactly the happiest, but the *third* happiest day of his life (after Israel's independence on May 14, 1948 and the reunification of Jerusalem in June 1967). On this occasion, he felt obliged to "bring back to memory" and recite in Hebrew a biblical psalm known as *Shir hama'alot* (Song of Degrees), which he had learned in his parents' home before it was destroyed,

> because they were among the six million people, men, women, and children, who sanctified the Lord's name with their sacred blood, which reddened the rivers of Europe from the Rhine to the Danube, from the Bug to the Volga—because, only because they were born Jews, and because they didn't have a country of their own, neither a valiant Jewish army to defend them, and because nobody, nobody came to their rescue, although they cried out: save us! save us! de profundis, from the depths of the pit and agony[.][36]

During the early 1980s, Menachem Begin again made explicit use of the Holocaust in Israeli foreign policy when justifying the high-risk bombing by the Israeli air force of the Osirak nuclear reactor in Baghdad, raising the cry "Never again!" against the preparation of weapons of mass destruction aimed at the Jewish people and against the possibility of a second Holocaust in his lifetime. The Holocaust motif also figured in the Israeli prime minister's portrayal of his 1982 "Operation Peace for Galilee" as a war in which valiant Israeli soldiers were making up for past Jewish passivity by rescuing helpless Lebanese Christian civilians from Muslim Nazi hordes. Similarly, the IDF's siege of and attack on the headquarters of the Palestine Liberation Organization (PLO) in Beirut was seen as a reenactment of the 1945 bombardment of Hitler's Berlin bunker.[37]

As David Biale has observed, the "ideology of survival" espoused by Menachem Begin and his minister of defense, Ariel Sharon, fed "at one and the same time feelings of power, represented by Jewish sovereignty, and feelings of impotence, represented by the Holocaust . . . oscillat[ing] between these extreme feelings of power and powerlessness."[38] While some Jews and Zionists may still be expecting the Jewish state to develop one day into a normal state "like all the other nations," Israel became for many Jews in the 1970s and 1980s just another "embodiment of persecuted and desperate Jewry. The Jew remained a victim," Biale wrote, "but now a victim with an army."[39]

5. *"Never Again"—"No Jewish Guilt"*

Much of the complicated gut feelings of Jews and Israelis have been reduced to a simple cry: "Never again!" This slogan was popularized by the late Rabbi Meir Kahane, first in the Diaspora through the Jewish Defense League and later in Israel, where he served as the leader of the extremist Kach Party and a member of the Knesset. The main thrust of the slogan was that only a strong and militant Israel could ensure that never again would Jewish victims passively accept their fate at the hands of murderous oppressors. Along with "Never again!" came another call: "No Jewish guilt!" Begin, Kahane, and others used this cry to claim immunity against criticism leveled not only by unworthy non-Jews and outsiders, but even by those whom they defined as "self-hating" members of the Jewish community. The "no-Jewish-guilt" theme was used, for example, to deflect criticism of the Israeli invasion of Lebanon in 1982 and again during the early years of the Palestinian Intifada in 1987–88, with Kahane defending the behavior of the IDF against Palestinian rioters and stone-throwers at that time. "If the only way to survive," he declared in a

Kach Party paid advertisement in the *New York Times,* was "to take the lives of people who attack us, we have no choice." There was "nothing immoral in winning and nothing necessarily noble in a loser," the ad continued. Arguing that the best way to end the Arab-Israeli conflict was to remove all Arabs from Israel and "let them live with their brothers and sisters in any of the twenty-two Arab states," the statement went on to say:

> And let us not fear the world. Those who stood by during the Holocaust and when Israel faced destruction in 1948 and 1967 have nothing to tell us. Faith in the G-d of Israel and a powerful Jewish army are the only guarantors of Jewish survival. Let us not fear the world. Far better a Jewish State that survives and is hated by the world, than an Auschwitz that brings us its love and sympathy.[40]

Changing the Jewish and Israeli Self-Image

About ten years ago, David Biale observed that the continuing war with the Arabs

> brought the Holocaust home to Israel in a way never imagined by the founders of the state. . . . Anti-Zionism [became] the new form of [the centuries-long] anti-Semitism, and Israel [felt] herself to be a ghetto among the nations. Between the Jew as victim and the Jew as military hero, the ideal of the Jew as a normal human being [began] to disappear. A legacy of powerlessness [became] the justification for the exercise of power.[41]

Biale also put his finger on the important irony that

> the sense of impotence that mark[ed] one pole of the ideology of survival [was] the mirror image of how Israel's enemies perceive[d] the conflict: they typically [saw] themselves as impotent and Israel as omnipotent. Thus, there [was] a symmetry between the views of Jews and Arabs: each suffer[ed] from the same disjunction between images of itself and the other.

It is, he added wisely, "out of such illusory perceptions of oneself and one's enemies that political conflicts become mythologized and their resolution grows increasingly remote."[42]

Certainly, as I have tried to illustrate, it is difficult to imagine much progress in Israeli-Palestinian reconciliation—individual to individual, people to people, society to society—until such perceptions and self-images of victimhood are subjected to critical reevaluation and revision. The Israeli self-identification as victim provides a number of complex psychological obstacles to reconciliation with Palestinians. For many Israelis, it means, ipso facto, that they have no moral accounting to do before any outsiders. "If I am a victim—and not just any victim but an eternal victim—then I am excused from many things," writes Shulamith Hareven. But, as Hareven goes on to argue, there comes a time "when it is no longer possible to use this victimhood as an excuse for everything. As every educator knows, it creates a great residue of cynicism, if only because of the obvious gap between what children are taught by rote and what they see with their own eye."[43]

The Israelis' self-concept as victim is an obstacle to reconciliation with the Palestinians also because it sharply reduces the potential for empathy towards others. "If I am the sole and eternal victim," continues Hareven, "then I create around and within myself and raise my children to an inability to see anyone who is not me."[44] Writing during Menachem Begin's premiership, A. B. Yehoshua had similarly argued that "[h]aving suffered such a horrendous experience, we are liable to grow indifferent to any lesser suffering. He who has suffered greatly may become inured to the suffering of others. That is completely natural." However, the Israeli writer went on to admonish his Jewish and Israeli readers,

> as the bearers of the anti-Nazi message we must whet our sensitivity, not dull it. We must bear in mind that our having been victims does not accord us any special moral standing. The victim does not become virtuous for having been a victim. Although the Holocaust inflicted a horrible injustice on us, it did not grant us a certificate of everlasting righteousness. The murderers were amoral; the victims were not made moral. To be moral you must behave ethically. The test of that is daily and constant.[45]

The prevailing attitude, against which Yehoshua, Hareven, and others have fought, has not been eliminated even in our own day. To the extent that the political manipulation of victimhood continues, it leaves no room, either intellectually or emotionally, for Israelis to consider the possibility that their peace-process partners, the Palestinians and other Arabs, also have grievances and also view themselves as victims. Such use of victimhood in the construction of present-day identity and in the determination of future policy options can be dangerous and self-destructive. "In the longer run," writes Hareven, "the perpetuation of the victim identity causes complete severance from reality, utter dependence on the past and the past alone, and distortions of all proportions and emphases to the point of warping the personality."[46]

The problems of selective memory can have deeper consequences. In raising the question "How much past is enough?" columnist Roger Rosenblatt wondered: "At what point does a devotion to history cease to be a weapon against present and future error, and begin to cripple those who seek its protection?" Rosenblatt suggested there might be "another side to Santayana's excessively quoted aphorism, [namely,] that those who *only* remember the past are *also* condemned to repeat it. To live exclusively with the past is to become the past."[47]

Decades of real-life experience of "the other" as belligerent and menacing have been reinforced by an unhealthy (but all-too-normal) dose of propaganda demonizing the enemy. This process has left generations of Israelis and Palestinians convinced that, when all is said and done, only brute force will ensure their basic physical survival against determined and bloodthirsty opponents. It has reached the point where an almost-impossible series of mental gymnastics would be required for most Israelis and Palestinians to imagine "the other" as victim rather than aggressor. No amount of well-intentioned love-thy-neighbor peace propaganda can cause a reversal of such self- images and images of "the other."

Questions remain. Can the parties ever hope to break out of this vicious circle? Can opinion-makers in both communities generate convincing alternative master stories and self-concepts to replace the overriding, competing, and often mutually exclusive images of Jew-as-victim and Palestinian-as-victim? Can academic and journalistic critiques of accepted myths become transformed into popular countermyths capable of winning a wide following? Are there any such signs of change?

In attempting to answer these questions, we should be reminded that there are scholars and people involved in Jewish and Israeli public life who, like Israeli author Shulamith Hareven, have questioned

> whether it is possible to raise a generation on nothing but traumas that were caused by others, exclusively on a sense of perpetual destruction and deterministic hatred, or whether there are some other things about Judaism, not necessarily related to victimization, that define us both as a people and as individuals. Does being a Jew only mean being a victim, defined by the actions of others? Or does it also mean being a people that established an elaborate judicial system, created a language to be proud of, built a state and established a social order . . . ?[48]

While acknowledging that "under no circumstances are we to forget our tragedies," Hareven warns that "whoever bases our identity on them and them alone, distorts the greatness of this people and keeps from its sons not only pride, but sanity itself."[49]

The American scholar Michael Goldberg argues that victimhood and vulnerability are not the only lessons of history that can inform Jewish, Zionist, or Israeli identity. As a modern religious thinker, Goldberg laments the dominance of the Purim and Holocaust master stories at the expense of building Jewish identity and a Jewish future on what he argues is a more worthy narrative: the Passover Exodus story of the liberation of the children of Israel from slavery in Egypt. On the surface, the story of Moses and the ancient Hebrews seems consistent with the Jewish self-concept as victim, and Pharaoh's role of victimizer seems no different from that of Haman or Hitler. Yet, the Exodus narrative contains important *universal* and *supernatural,* and not only tribal, ingredients. Orthodox Jews, for example, stress that the children of Israel were liberated not merely for territorial conquest or for a safe homeland in which to be free, but in order to serve their God in accordance with the Covenant at Sinai. At the other end of the Jewish spectrum, many Reform and Reconstructionist Jews participate in adapted and updated Passover rituals that transpose many lessons of the Exodus story into Jewish solidarity with calls for freedom from oppression for all peoples.

We may well be, as Michael Goldberg argues, living in an absurd age when "virtually anybody could claim to be a victim."[50] This raises another question: Have we perhaps reached the point where the currency of victimhood has become so debased that it may be losing its effectiveness in local, national, and international politics? If this is so, then prescient leaders should be actively considering alternative master stories, myths, and legends on which to base their people's self-image, with which to motivate their followers, and on which to base their claims to justice and a place in the sun.

Recent Signposts

Let us conclude by examining some of the recent signposts indicating possible changes in contemporary Israel. In another chapter in this volume, Gershon Shafir and Yoav Peled describe the forces of liberalization that have left their mark on Israeli society in the late 1980s and 1990s. Correspondent Glenn Frankel, in *Beyond the Promised Land,* has characterized the new realities as follows:

> Quietly, hesitantly, painfully, [Israel] is making the transition from a small, collectivist, mobilized garrison-state under siege to a more open, pluralistic, bourgeois and democratic country. The old Zionist state, for better or for worse, is dying; a new post-Zionist Israel is being born.[51]

Even more pointed is the observation by Adam Garfinkle in a new textbook entitled *Politics and Society in Modern Israel* that, after honing its national character on decades of a reality-based "sense of siege,"

> [t]oday, by contrast, Israel is strong and prosperous. Few military experts doubt that the IDF could defeat all its immediate neighbors simultaneously in war, and its economy is larger than those of Egypt, Syria, Jordan, Lebanon and the Palestinians put together. It has the world's greatest power, the United States, as its closest ally, and the Soviet Union no longer even exists. . . . [T]he psychic cohesion afforded by the Holocaust is receding before the passage of time and memory, as it must. Efforts to use the Holocaust for various purposes, too, . . . have—rightly or wrongly—irritated more than a few who believe that the subject has been overplayed for less than fully sincere purposes.[52]

Most analysts point to the beginnings of an abandonment of the Israeli self-image as victim as an elite phenomenon marked by the ascendancy of the new technocratic class and the return to power of the Labor Party in June 1992.[53] Yitzhak Rabin's election was accompanied by some interesting shifts in the leadership's rhetoric about Israel's place in the world. In presenting his first Cabinet to the new Knesset in 1992, Rabin declared that it was

> our duty, to ourselves and to our children, to see the new world as it is now—to discern its dangers, explore its prospects, and do everything possible so that the State of Israel will fit into this world whose face is changing. No longer are we necessarily "a people that dwells alone," and no longer is it true that "the whole world is against us." We must overcome the sense of isolation that has held us in its thrall for almost half a century.[54]

Indeed, in the two years following the October 1991 peace conference convened in Madrid, thirty-four countries established (or reestablished severed) diplomatic relations with the Jewish state, while in December 1991 "a completely different correlation of forces at the United Nations" voted to revoke the infamous 1975 "Zionism-equals-racism" resolution.[55]

Reflecting this new spirit of international acceptance, Rabin's appeals to his countrymen began to incorporate some of the discourse previously confined to marginalized peace activists and liberal spokesmen such as former Foreign Minister Abba Eban, who had for years been arguing that Israelis should stop thinking like outnumbered and beleaguered ghetto fighters, but should rather visualize themselves as strong and secure enough to take some calculated risks for peace.[56] At one point, the prime minister went so far as to dismiss then-opposition leader Binyamin Netanyahu as a frightened boy whose ideas were unworthy of serious discussion. "I'm embarrassed when I hear leaders in the Likud and extreme right compare our situation today to the period of the Holocaust," Rabin told one audience. "For Jews who have an army like this, how is it possible to talk about a threat to our existence from the Palestinians? What are they blabbering?"[57]

Some, like political scientist Yaron Ezrahi, claim that a significant transformation had taken place among Israelis—"nothing less than the recovery of the Jewish people from the Holocaust." Elaborating upon Ezrahi's views, Glenn Frankel describes "the nation that journeyed to the White House to shake Yasser Arafat's hand" in September 1993 as being "not Yitzhak Shamir's fearful and paranoid Israel, but a proud and self-confident country."[58] Perhaps one manifestation of this new self-confidence is that visiting foreign dignitaries are no longer obliged to stop at the country's Holocaust memorial, Yad Vashem, although most continue to make the recommended pilgrimage.

Frankel and Ezrahi, however, may well be overstating their case. Deeply ingrained attitudes, perceptions, and self-images are not changed so radically overnight, and one cannot be too sanguine about how lasting or profound such signs of openness or optimism may be. Much depends on the degree of safety (or vulnerability) of Jews both in Israel and in all the lands of their dispersion. While it does seem as if some Israelis may be ready, under the impact of openings caused by the Oslo peace process, to modify their worldview somewhat along Labor's liberal lines away from a self-concept as the world's permanent victims, others are not sure whether it is yet time to herald the good news that peace has come. Reporting on the bloody Palestinian-Israeli clashes of April 1997, an American journalist was reminded that "[r]enewing old grievances and nursing self-images of victimhood, decisive blocs of Israelis and Palestinians in opinion surveys have turned against their attempt at coexistence or concluded that it has no prospect of success."[59] Indeed, many Israelis still cannot let their guard down, and they cling to the cautious and defensive attitude reflected in Binyamin Netanyahu's arguments against returning to what he once termed Israel's pre-1967 "Auschwitz borders." Others may subscribe to Ariel Sharon's warning that the Oslo agreements would lead to the gas chambers, or to Rafael Eitan's comparison of the pact with Arafat to capitulation to Hitler.[60]

It is never easy to combat such fear-driven rhetoric; yet efforts on both sides do—and must—continue in an effort to break away from the enduring and self-fulfilling sense of victimization felt by both Israelis and Palestinians. Small improvements in the chances of reconciliation might follow if leaders could bring their people's perceptions of power more into line with the realities of power. Addressing only the Israeli side of this equation, David Biale wrote a decade ago that "Jews must find a way of navigating a middle course between dreams of boundless power and nightmares of historical powerlessness." Applying these perceptive words to both parties today, we might conclude by saying that peace and reconciliation will come only after successful efforts to convince both Israelis and Palestinians that they are neither as powerless as they might fear, nor as powerful as their patriotic impulses might lead them to believe.[61]

Notes

* The author wishes to thank Usher Caplan, Professor Laura Zittrain Eisenberg and Ms. Lital Levy for sharing their criticisms and insights with him.

1. Isaac Deutscher, "The Israeli-Arab War, June 1967" (from an interview given to the *New Left Review,* June 23, 1967), in *The Non-Jewish Jew and Other Essays* (London: Oxford University Press, 1968), 136–37.
2. Amos Oz, *Under this Blazing Light: Essays,* trans. Nicholas de Lange (New York: Cambridge University Press, 1995), 8–9.
3. In his recent, penetrating study of Palestinian identity, Rashid Khalidi does not focus on a Palestinian equivalent to this Jewish Israeli sense of victimhood. The closest concept to the latter would be Khalidi's focus on the common Palestinian identity forged by overwhelming external threats and a long history of failures and defeats. These setbacks became portrayed as triumphs and victories, in the sense of *sumud* (steadfastness) in confronting daunting odds and surviving as a people. See Rashid Khalidi, *Palestinian Identity: The Construction of Modern National Consciousness* (New York: Columbia University Press, 1997), chapter 2 and 177–78, 191–95, 263.
4. Michael Goldberg, *Why Should Jews Survive? Looking Past the Holocaust Toward a Jewish Future* (New York: Oxford University Press, 1995), 153–58.
5. *Jewish Book News,* March 1997: 40–41.
6. Jackie Mason, with Ira Berkow, *How to Talk Jewish,* (New York: St Martin's Press, 1990), 6–7.

7. Jay Y. Gonen, *A Psychohistory of Zionism* (New York: Mason/Charter, 1975), 37.
8. Goldberg, *Why Should Jews Survive?* 125.
9. Shulamith Hareven, "Identity: Victim" (1986), in *The Vocabulary of Peace: Life, Culture, and Politics in the Middle East* (San Francisco: Mercury House, 1995), 148.
10. Goldberg, *Why Should Jews Survive?* 124.
11. *The Israel-Arab Reader: A Documentary History of the Middle East Conflict,* 5th rev. & updated ed., eds. Walter Laqueur and Barry Rubin (New York: Penguin, 1995), 66–67; Yehuda Bauer, *From Diplomacy to Resistance: A History of Jewish Palestine, 1939–1945* (Philadelphia: Jewish Publication Society, 1970), chapter 6.
12. For a recent reexamination, see David Arnow, "The Holocaust and the Birth of Israel: Reassessing the Causal Relationship," *Journal of Israeli History* 15, no. 3 (Autumn 1994): 257–81.
13. David Biale, *Power and Powerlessness in Jewish History* (New York: Schocken, 1986), 172.
14. Michael Ignatieff, "Articles of Faith," *Harper's Magazine* (March 1997): 15.
15. Simon N. Herman, *Israelis and Jews: The Continuity of an Identity* (Philadelphia: Jewish Publication Society, 1971), 251.
16. Herman, *Israelis and Jews,* 78–80, 284–85. The same questions were posed in 1974 and 1985 follow-up surveys, with similar results. See: Simon N. Herman, "In the Shadow of the Holocaust," *Jerusalem Quarterly* 3 (Spring 1977): 95–96; Simon N. Herman, *Jewish Identity: A Social Psychological Perspective,* 2nd ed. (New Brunswick NJ: Transaction Books, 1989), 8, 11.
17. Biale, *Power and Powerlessness,* 146.
18. Oz, "The State as Reprisal" (based on a talk given in 1962), *Under this Blazing Light,* 65–66.
19. Amos Oz, *In the Land of Israel,* trans. Maurie Goldberg-Bartura (New York: Harcourt Brace Jovanovich, 1983), 87–100.
20. Herman, *Israelis and Jews,* 211–12; also Herman, "In the Shadow," 89.
21. Gonen, *Psychohistory of Zionism,* 145–47.
22. Y. Harkabi, *Arab Attitudes to Israel* (Jerusalem: Keter, 1972).
23. Biale, *Power and Powerlessness,* 159.
24. *Ibid.* (emphasis added).
25. Herman, "In the Shadow," 85–86. Cf. Herman, *Jewish Identity,* chapter 6.
26. Amos Elon, *The Israelis: Founders and Sons* (New York: Holt, Rinehart & Winston, 1971), 198–99.
27. *Ibid.,* 199, 203.
28. *Ibid.,* 199.
29. Hareven, "Identity: Victim," 148.
30. Biale, *Power and Powerlessness,* 162.
31. *Ibid.,* 163.

32. Goldberg, *Why Should Jews Survive?* 125.
33. Biale, *Power and Powerlessness,* 160.
34. Roger Rosenblatt, "Israel: How Much Past Is Enough?" *Time,* Sept. 20, 1982: 47.
35. In Herman's 1974 survey of eleventh-grade students in Israel, a significant 46 percent of students of Oriental backgrounds (as opposed to 53 percent of those of Ashkenazi origins) "completely agreed" with the statement "Every Jew in the world should see himself as a survivor of the Holocaust." See Herman, "In the Shadow," 95.
36. Speech by Menachem Begin at the treaty-signing ceremony, Washington, DC, March 26, 1979, doc. 251 in *Israel's Foreign Relations: Selected Documents 1977–1979,* vol. 5, ed. Meron Medzini (Jerusalem: Ministry of Foreign Affairs, 1981), 720. For a balanced and thoughtful critique, see Michael R. Marrus, "The Use and Misuse of the Holocaust," in *Lessons and Legacies: The Meaning of the Holocaust in a Changing World,* ed. Peter Hayes (Evanston: Northwestern University Press, 1991), 106–19.
37. Press conference with Prime Minister Begin, IDF Chief of Staff Eitan, IAF Commander Ivri and DMI Saguy, June 9, 1981, doc. 28 in *Israel's Foreign Relations: Selected Documents 1981–1982,* vol.7, ed. Meron Medzini (Jerusalem: Ministry of Foreign Affairs, 1988), 76; Ze'ev Schiff and Ehud Ya'ari, *Israel's Lebanon War* (New York: Simon and Schuster, 1984), 39, 220; Sheldon Kirschner, "Israel and the Holocaust," *Canadian Jewish News,* April 6, 1995: 11.
38. Biale, *Power and Powerlessness,* 163.
39. *Ibid.,* 161.
40. Kach International Advertisement, *New York Times,* February 2, 1988.
41. Biale, *Power and Powerlessness,* 164.
42. *Ibid.,* 163–64.
43. Hareven, "Identity: Victim," 150.
44. *Ibid.,* 151.
45. A.B. Yehoshua, "The Holocaust as Junction," in *Between Right and Right,* trans. Arnold Schwartz (New York: Doubleday, 1981), 17.
46. Hareven, "Identity: Victim," 149.
47. Rosenblatt, "How Much Past," 47 (emphasis added).
48. Hareven, "Identity: Victim," 148–49.
49. *Ibid.,* 154.
50. Goldberg, *Why Should Jews Survive?* 125.
51. Glenn Frankel, *Beyond the Promised Land: Jews and Arabs on the Hard Road to a New Israel* (New York: Simon & Schuster, Touchstone, 1996), 11.
52. Adam Garfinkle, *Politics and Society in Modern Israel: Myths and Realities* (Armonk, NY: M.E. Sharpe, 1997), 236, 270.
53. See, for example, Michael Keren, "Israeli Professionals and the Peace Process," *Israel Affairs* 1, no. 1 (Autumn 1994): 149–63.

54. "Presentation of the New Government, Address to the Knesset by Prime Minister Yitzhak Rabin, 13 July 1992," in Laqueur and Rubin, *Israel-Arab Reader,* 590. Cf. similar remarks in a Rabin address to the Knesset, June 27, 1993, Information Division, Israel Ministry of Foreign Affairs, website: www.israel-mfa.gov.il.
55. Aharon Klieman, "New Directions in Israel's Foreign Policy," *Israel Affairs* 1, no. 1 (Autumn 1994): 98–99.
56. For example, Abba Eban, "Why Hysteria on a Mideast Parley?" *New York Times,* April 3, 1988.
57. Quoted in Frankel, *Beyond the Promised Land,* 370.
58. *Ibid.,* 368.
59. Barton Gellman, *Washington Post* article reproduced in *The Gazette* (Montreal), April 9, 1997.
60. Quoted in Kirschner, "Israel and the Holocaust," 11; Frankel, *Beyond the Promised Land,* 389.
61. Biale, *Power and Powerlessness,* 174–76.

5

Citizenship and Stratification in an Ethnic Democracy*

Gershon Shafir and Yoav Peled

The 1990s have witnessed a dramatic transformation in the structure of ethnic relations in Israel. By recognizing the Palestine Liberation Organization (PLO) as the legitimate representative of the Palestinian people and beginning to withdraw from Palestinian territories it occupied in 1967, Israel began to emancipate the most subjugated of its ethnic groups. This about face was all the more unexpected since the Israeli-Palestinian conflict was long considered one of the world's most intransigent. A more careful look at Israeli society would reveal, however, that Israel's policy change on the Palestinian issue was part and parcel of a profound and wide-ranging process of economic, social, political, and cultural transformation.

In the first half of the 1990s the Israeli economy was growing at a pace similar to that of the East Asian tigers. Especially impressive was the number of gainfully employed people in Israel, which rose by 40 percent in the decade between 1986 and 1996, compared to 16 percent in the United States, 11 percent in Japan, and about 5 percent each in Britain, France, and Germany.[1] Between 1975 and 1995, Israel's GDP itself grew sevenfold and its "dollar product" increased by about 600 percent. By the end of 1996 these high growth rates brought the per-capita income of Israelis to $16,690, which ranked them number twenty-one on the international income scale. In April 1997, in recognition of its rapid growth,

Israel was added by the IMF, together with Singapore, South Korea, Hong Kong, and Taiwan, to its list of developed countries.

But economic change, impressive as it may be, is only one indicator of the emergence of a "new Israel." Among the multiple and interlocking changes in the society one can list the decline in the prestige of the military and in the motivation to perform military service; the rush of students to business and law schools; the adoption of an embryonic bill of rights in the form of two constitutional laws dealing with civil rights; the disappearance of the Histadrut—the all-encompassing political-economic umbrella labor organization—and its replacement with a much-weakened trade union-type structure; and the rise of an autonomous and self-confident business community.

The peace process is deeply embedded, then, in a broader liberalization process, and the opposition to peace reflects, to a large degree, people's apprehensions about liberalization. Any serious attempt to comprehend the character of ethnic relations in the "new Israel" requires, therefore, a broad-based theoretical framework that would encompass both past and currently contending socio-economic models and their corresponding cultural visions. Such a framework can be provided, we argue, by examining Israel's competing and evolving discourses of citizenship. By citizenship discourses we mean political and linguistic strategies of membership fashioned out of alternative combinations of identities and claims. Citizenship, conventionally conceived of as a civic mechanism of incorporation, is locked in battle in multiethnic societies with identity politics that seek to use particular criteria of membership as the basis for claim-making. Thus citizenship discourses are employed in competition over access to rights allocated by state and para-state institutions. As a result, citizenship, instead of solely leveling status differences, can actually function as a tool of stratification.[2]

Theories of citizenship form a rich intellectual and political tradition in the history of Western political thought. Through the two and a half millennia of its evolution, the concept of citizenship has adapted to multiple social transformations, so that it now comprises alternative conceptualizations of membership and the rights that accompany it.[3] This heterogeneity, we will show, is the key to the usefulness of the concept of citizenship for the analysis of ethnic relations in Israel. Our argument will proceed as follows: a theoretical discussion of different citizenship discourses will be followed by an examination of the discourses prevailing in Israel and their resultant "incorporation regime." We will then outline the ways in which Israel's citizenship structure and ethnic relations have been changing over time and will conclude with an assessment of the dilemmas that are facing Israeli society in the context of these changes.

Citizenship Discourses

Three important discourses of citizenship can be identified in the tradition of Western political thought: liberal, republican, and ethno-nationalist. The liberal conception of citizenship accents personal liberty: it views individuals, and only individuals, as the bearers of universal, equal, and publicly affirmed rights. Individuals, in either the utilitarian or contractual liberal view, are the sovereign authors of their lives who pursue their private rational advantage or conception of the good and are not beholden to the community. The role of politics in this approach remains negative: only to aid and protect individuals from interference by governments in the exercise of the rights they inalienably possess. In return for this protection, individuals undertake certain minimal political duties—pay taxes, vote periodically, obey the law, and serve in the military. Consequently, citizenship, in the liberal view, is an accessory, not a value in itself. What citizenship actually consists of, in this account, is a bundle of rights designed to protect each individual's private sphere from encroachment by her/his fellow citizens and, especially, by the state.

Liberalism's strength lies in its ability to tolerate religious, cultural, and political diversity by creating a self-limiting political realm respectful of individual rights and an institutional framework within which polarizing disputes are avoided by permitting the political expression of only those conceptions of the good that are not monopolistic. Even the more socially conscious liberal theorists, such as Rawls, emphasize that no notion of liberal justice may be viewed as a comprehensive moral doctrine but only as a practical modus vivendi that allows the emergence of an overlapping consensus of moral principles between opposing doctrines.[4]

The liberal notion of citizenship is currently being challenged on two fronts. In the United States, a civic virtue-based, republican, or communitarian critique contends that citizenship should be seen as constituting a moral community. Communitarians retain the ancient Greeks' view of politics as the hub of human existence and as life's supreme fulfillment. Politics is a communal affair, and citizenship is an enduring political attachment. Citizens are who they are by virtue of participating in the life of their political community and by identifying with its characteristics.

Members of this community experience, or should experience, their citizenship not intermittently, as merely protective individual rights, but rather as active participation in the pursuit of a common good. If we amplify political life by demanding more from the citizen, as Oldfield's emphasis on duties indicates, her existence will be richer and she will lead a more fulfilling and morally inspired life. Active participation is the core of the citizen's civic virtue and the criterion entitling her to a differential share of the community's material and moral resources.[5]

A third version of citizenship, one that originated in German romanticism and spread to Eastern Europe, roots membership in a special kind of community: the nation or ethnic group. In the ethno-nationalist, or *völkisch,* approach, citizenship is not an expression of individual rights but of membership in a homogenous descent group.[6] This notion of citizenship expands the concept's purview outside the realm of politics. Nations, in romantic nationalism, are all radically different from each other because their members possess distinct cultural markers, such as language, religion, and history. Since, in this view, nations are inscribed into the identity of their members, ethnic nationalism denies the possibility of cultural assimilation.[7]

Of these three conceptions of citizenship, the individualist liberal one is the most inclusive. It has been pointed out, however, by critics such as Giddens, Held, Tilly, and Gorham,[8] that even the meaning of liberal citizenship is not immediately revealed by its formal characteristics alone: civil, political, and social rights, with their corresponding institutions, establish not only entitlements but mechanisms of surveillance and control and arenas of political contestation as well. Thus the precise meaning of citizenship and noncitizenship in each social context, that is, the extent to which either of them empowers or disempowers individual and collective members of society, is subject to political negotiation and struggle. Moreover, while the liberal discourse of citizenship, being the most universal, is commonly the one put forth for legitimational purposes, the actual practice of citizenship in each particular society may consist of two or more discourses of citizenship, superimposed on one another.[9]

The coexistence, not only of multiple citizenship rights but also of alternative citizenship discourses within the same society, poses a number of sociological questions. For example, how does the multiplicity of citizenship discourses affect social stratification in a particular case? And, given the conflicting views of these discourses on the issues of inclusion and exclusion, what is left of the universalist claims made on behalf of citizenship as full membership in society? These questions can best be answered, we submit, if by "citizenship" we understand not only a bundle of formal rights, but the entire mode of incorporation of individuals and groups into the society. For such an understanding directs our attention to a whole gamut of specific social institutions and raises meaningful empirical questions as to the method, variety, scope, and dynamics of memberships and incorporation.

The mode of incorporation, combining both formal, written principles as well as informal social practices, has been termed by Yasemin Soysal "incorporation regime," a pattern of institutional practices and more or less explicit cultural norms that define the membership of individuals and/or groups in the society and differentially allocates entitlements, obligations, and domination.[10] Incorporation regimes, in general, can be thought of as forming concentric circles, in which the boundaries become more rigid as one moves toward the periphery: inclusion in internal circles is based on the force of habit or custom, whereas in the outer ones it is based on force and the sanction of law. Movement towards the center indicates social mobility, since it implies more rights and greater access to resources.

Israel's Incorporation Regime

Historically, Israel's incorporation regime was constituted through a combination of all three citizenship discourses discussed above: a collectivist republican discourse, based on "pioneering" civic virtue; an ethnonationalist discourse, based on Jewish descent; and an individualist liberal discourse.[11] The combination of the three discourses in Israeli political culture was the effect of a number of social processes that intersected at critical historical turning points: the politicization of Jewish ethnicity in the Pale of Settlement, the legitimization of Zionism's territorial vision by the secularization of part of Judaism's legacy, the separatist Jewish colonial settlement in Palestine, the voluntarily elected institutions of the Zionist movement and the *yishuv* (the Jewish community in pre-statehood Palestine), the 1948 war and the flight and expulsion of the majority of the Palestinian inhabitants, and the massive Jewish immigration from North Africa and the Middle East in the state's early years. The political culture that emerged from the intersection of these social processes may be analyzed as a pattern of interaction between the exclusionary dimensions of Israel's colonizing and nation-building practices and the inclusionary aspects of its democratic state institutions.

In many ways Zionist discourses of national redemption resembled Eastern European romantic nationalism.[12] Seeking to nationalize an ancient religious community and to legitimize its settlement project in Palestine, secular Zionism forged the solidarity of the *yishuv* around ethnic Jewish identity. Israel's Law of Return (1950) has guaranteed automatic citizenship to any Jew upon immigration to Israel, without any length-of-residence or language requirement. This law became the most important legal expression of Israel's self-definition as a Jewish state. It established ethno-nationalist citizenship that, in principle, encompassed all Jews, and only Jews, by virtue of their ethnic descent. This citizenship discourse also guaranteed the privileged position of the true keepers of the faith—religiously Orthodox Jews—in Israeli society.[13] By the same token, it ensured the secondary status of Israel's non-Jewish citizens.

Israel's constitutional definition as a Jewish state precluded the possibility of adopting one of the key identifying features of a liberal state—the separation of state and religion. Instead, Jewish religion, or more accurately, Orthodox Jewish religion, is guaranteed an important role in the country's public life. This is manifested primarily in four important areas: legal sanctioning of the observance of the Sabbath and of Jewish holidays in the public sphere; the almost exclusive jurisdiction granted religious courts over matters of family law; state support of religious educational institutions that are largely autonomous of the general educational system; and various privileges granted Orthodox individuals, most importantly the exemption from military service granted Orthodox women and Orthodox yeshiva students.

The privileged status of Jews and of Orthodox Jewish religion makes the question "Who is a Jew?" an important political issue. Over the years, the official definition of "Jew" has become progressively restricted and more closely aligned with Orthodox thinking. However, this restriction came into conflict with the demographic aim of Zionism to produce, maintain, and increase the Jewish majority in Israel. As a result, the Law of Return was amended, in 1970, so that one Jewish grandparent is now sufficient to entitle a person and her/his spouse to the privileges provided by the law. Thus, it is estimated that up to 20 percent of the immigrants from the former Soviet Union in the early 1990s, and fully 60 percent by the mid-1990s, were not Jews by the Orthodox definition.[14] Similarly, the Jewishness of the Ethiopian immigrants is also questioned by the Orthodox rabbinic establishment, although in their case the questions do not refer to individuals but rather to the community as a whole. Since marriages, divorces, and burials are all under the exclusive jurisdiction of religious authorities (whether Jewish or non-Jewish), these non- and doubtful Jews run into problems when they come to need these services, unless they convert to Judaism. One paradoxical result of the amended Law of Return, then, is the development of a diverse new non-Jewish, non-Palestinian group. The influx of foreign workers into Israel, which began with the Intifada and was accelerated after the Oslo accords, is augmenting and fragmenting this diverse cluster even further.

Palestinians who had not fled or been expelled from the territory of the State of Israel during the 1948 war were either granted, or allowed to apply for, Israeli citizenship. They were placed, however, in a systematically dependent economic, political, and legal position.[15] Their secondary citizenship status was formalized in 1985 in an amendment to the law governing elections to Knesset. That amendment stated:

> A list of candidates shall not participate in elections to the Knesset if its goals, explicitly or implicitly, or its actions include one of the following:
> (1) Negation of the existence of the State of Israel as the state of the Jewish people;
> (2) Negation of the democratic character of the state;
> (3) Incitement of racism.

Ironically, the declared purpose of this amendment was to prevent racist and antidemocratic political parties from participating in Knesset elections. And indeed Meir Kahane's ultranationalist Jewish party was disqualified in 1988 for violating clauses (2) and (3). However, judicial interpretations of the amended law made the demand to turn Israel from a Jewish state to a state of all its citizens, that is, to equalize the citizenship status of Jews and Palestinians, a violation of clause (1). Thus the amended law reaffirmed the liberal citizenship rights of Israel's Palestinian citizens as individuals, but excluded them as a group from the core, ethno-republican citizenship reserved for Jews only.[16]

While Zionist ethno-nationalism resembled other Eastern European nationalist discourses, Zionism, unlike them, needed to seek out a territory for immigration and colonization. Thus, as a settlement movement Zionism bears important similarities to other European overseas colonial societies established through territorial struggle with native peoples.[17] Like other "pure settlement colonies" with their own immigrant laboring classes,[18] Zionist bodies aimed at creating a relatively homogeneous settler-immigrant population. To overcome the competition of lower-paid Arab workers, who successfully displaced Jewish workers accustomed to a

"European standard of living," a subsidized economic sector, settling and employing only Jews, was formed. The main institutions of this vertically and horizontally integrated cooperative community were the Jewish National Fund and the Histadrut. These became the two pillars supporting the political predominance of Labor Zionism in the *yishuv* and in Israeli society. The "redemptive" pioneering activities necessitated by this new economic sector—physical labor, agricultural settlement, and military service—became the core of a new, republican conception of virtue. Thus out of the Jewish-Palestinian conflict over land and labor there emerged a second citizenship discourse, which established those committed to the moral purpose of state-formation through colonization as a virtuous republican community. Labor Zionism, located at the overlap between the Jewish ethno-national and the republican citizenship discourses, enjoyed the benefits of both and constituted an ethno-republican community.

Whereas the ethno-nationalist citizenship discourse encompassed all Jews, the republican discourse divided and stratified them. Around the core of the virtuous immigrant-settlers, who actively participated in the labor movement's colonizing and military activities, there formed a periphery of passive citizens entitled to a smaller share of societal resources. The latter's contribution to Zionist redemption was viewed as quantitative, rather than qualitative: by immigrating to Palestine they helped bring closer the day when Jews would form a majority there.[19] Most Ashkenazi (European) immigrants, but especially those from Russia, Lithuania, and Poland, had institutional or family ties to the core and were able to share in its aura of "pioneering," whether or not they actually participated in pioneering activities;[20] most Mizraḥi (Middle Eastern and North African) immigrants were relegated to the periphery.[21] An "ethnic gap" in political power, income distribution, occupational status, and educational attainment between Ashkenazim and Mizraḥim has persisted and, in some respects, even widened, to this day.[22]

The republican citizenship discourse has discriminated between Israeli Jews not only on the basis of ethnicity, but also on the basis of gender. In addition to the well-known general factors that make for women's subjugation in Western democratic societies, Israeli Jewish women have suffered from specific burdens imposed by two characteristics of Israeli society as a colonial society: the close linkage between civic and military virtue, typical of the republican discourse, which is enhanced by the Arab-Israeli conflict; and the numerical inferiority of Jews in the Middle East that has infused Israeli Jews with demographic anxiety. While military service is mandatory for both men and women, only men are considered to possess military virtue. Women, regardless of their occupational status, are under pressure to excel in the "battle of the cribs" against Palestinian women. As a result, individually Jewish Israeli women enjoy fewer rights than male members of their social group in the civil and social spheres and, collectively, they are denied full membership in the republican political community. The emphasis on maternity as women's primary contribution to the common good has had a devastating effect on women's struggle for equality, even in the most egalitarian sector of Jewish society, the kibbutz.

Jewish Israeli women have been marginalized not only by the republican discourse but also by the discourse that claims the unity of all Jews as its highest value—the ethno-nationalist discourse. The most significant aspect of the non-separation of state and religion in Israel is the fact that religious courts enjoy almost exclusive jurisdiction over all matters of family law. As Jewish (and Muslim) religious law treats women as a subordinate class of persons, Israeli family law has a pronounced pro-male bias. This is manifested in marriage and divorce laws that discriminate against women, in a restrictive (though not prohibitive) abortion law, and in an unquestioned acceptance of the traditional patriarchal model of the family as normative.[23]

Thus, although the ethno-national discourse has provided the strongest glue for the nation-building project of Zionism, it has also harbored a powerful principle of division and stratification. Mizraḥim and Jewish women, regarded as fulfilling the demographic task of procuring a numerical Jewish majority, were accorded a diminished citizenship status. On the other hand, Jewish religious Orthodoxy, viewed as a crucial legitimator of Zionist aspirations, was privileged in many respects. Orthodox Jews have not only been accepted as full citizens of the state, but their corporate cultural rights, typical of the premodern notion of citizenship, have also been guaranteed. These guarantees should not be confused, however, with the recognition of minority or multicultural rights. The cultural autonomy granted to Orthodox Jews allows them not only to lead their own autonomous life but to control key aspects of the life of all Jews in the country.

Israel's liberal citizenship discourse also has its roots in the *yishuv* period. The *yishuv* was a democratic republican community in which individual liberal rights and the formal, procedural rules of democracy were respected. This was mandated by its semivoluntary nature and the need to keep all Jewish social sectors within its bounds, for demographic and legitimational purposes.

When the State of Israel was founded in 1948, a new republican civic virtue, *mamlakhtiyyut,* was invoked to legitimate the transition to statehood. This ethos emphasized the shift from sectoral interests to the general interest, from semivoluntarism to binding obligation, from foreign rule to political sovereignty. Equal application of the law was of paramount importance if the state was to assert its authority over the various Jewish social sectors, which had enjoyed a large degree of autonomy in the *yishuv,* but also over the Palestinians, who had become a minority in Israeli territory at the conclusion of the 1948 war and who under this principle were granted Israeli citizenship.

As understood in the context of *mamlakhtiyyut,* the uniform rule of law did not entail, however, a neutral, liberal state or a universal, liberal citizenship structure. The state was to continue to be committed to the values of *ḥalutsiyyut* (pioneering) and to demand such commitment from its citizens. *Mamlakhtiyyut,* then, was not meant to displace the pioneering mobilizing ethos or abandon the settlement project; quite the contrary, it was meant to endow them with the organizational and political resources of a sovereign state. Thus, under the legitimational guise of universal liberal citizenship, individuals and social groups continued to be treated by the state in accordance with their presumed contributions to the common good as defined by the Zionist project.[24]

In sum, this process of differential incorporation proceeded in a number of stages. First, the liberal idea of citizenship functioned to separate citizen Jews and Palestinians from the noncitizen Palestinians in the occupied territories and abroad, whether these were conceptualized as refugees or as stateless, rightless subjects of Israel's military occupation. Then the ethno-nationalist discourse of inclusion and exclusion was invoked to discriminate between Jewish and Palestinian Arab citizens within the sovereign State of Israel. Lastly, the republican discourse was used to legitimize the different positions occupied by the major Jewish groups, Ashkenazim and Mizraḥim, men and women. The innermost group, consisting of Jews, enjoyed not only liberal and ethno-nationalist rights but also the privileges of republican citizenship: participation, to a greater or lesser degree (Ashkenazim more than Mizraḥim, men more than women), in the definition of the common good of society. Thus the tension between the exclusionary and inclusionary categories of membership in the *yishuv* and in Israeli society has been expressed in a hierarchical and fragmented citizenship structure. The state and related institutions (most importantly the Histadrut) have been mobilizing societal resources and dispensing rights, duties, and privileges in accordance with this multilayered and complex index of memberships.

The Transformation of Israeli Citizenship

The historical trajectory of Israel's development since 1948 has consisted of the gradual decline of the republican discourse and the gradual transformation of the society from a colonial to a civil society. This transformation has accelerated significantly since the mid-1980s, to the point where it might be thought of as a "bourgeois revolution." Its parallels in Great Britain and the United States, the Thatcherite and Reaganite "revolutions," were presented as revival movements returning to a period that had preceded massive state intervention. In Israel, however, there never was a period approximating free enterprise. The change there is more radical, therefore, even though it is not likely to go as far as it did in Great Britain or the United States, because it has shallower roots and the opposition to it is more potent. In this section we will briefly review the interlocking changes making up this revolution, in the areas of economic organization, ethnic relations, social welfare, and constitutional law.

Historically, Israel's Jewish, Ashkenazi, state-building elite had utilized the republican conception of citizenship in order to legitimize the privileges it derived from its association with colonial settlement and its consequent control of the state and of other public institutions, most notably the Histadrut. In the mid-1960s, however, some members of this elite began to call for liberalization of the economy and the society, in order to remove the political and social impediments that, they felt, were placed on economic activity by its subjugation to the Zionist nation-building agenda. In 1976, the Democratic Movement for Change (DMC), a political party representing the professional, the academic, and part of the business segment of this elite had seceded from the Labor Party and gained fifteen Knesset seats (out of 120) in the general elections held in the following year. This party drew most of its votes from the ranks of Labor, thus allowing Likud to take power for the first time. (Labor lost nineteen Knesset seats in 1977, Likud gained four seats, and the DMC won fifteen.)

Initially, Likud's efforts to liberalize the economy failed and resulted in hyper-inflation, because it could not secure the cooperation of the Histadrut, still controlled by Labor. Only when Labor joined Likud in a government of national unity in 1984, was an effective policy of disinflation and economic liberalization, known as the Emergency Economic Stabilization Plan (EESP) of 1985, put into place. This plan not only aimed at stabilizing the economy by bringing down the triple-digit inflation but went much further in transforming the Israeli economy from a protectionist and state-centered system to a much more open, neo-liberal one. Additional actions taken in subsequent years were the paring back of the government's role in the capital market, the easing of foreign currency regulation, the elimination of many import quotas, a slow process of privatization, and so on. These measures tilted the balance from public to private interests and concerns and from workers' organizations, first and foremost the Histadrut, to organizations representing employers and financial institutions.[25]

The background to the radical change was provided by the desire to terminate the drawn-out stagnation of the Israeli economy following the 1973 Arab-Israeli war. The momentum that allowed the process of economic liberalization to go further than originally intended had its roots in the "peace dividend" that ensued from the peace accord with Egypt, signed in 1979. The reduction of inflation, of the budget deficit, and ultimately of some aspects of the state apparatus and state control became feasible in large measure with the reduction in the share of military expenditures in the GNP, from 20 percent in 1979 to 10 percent in the 1986–88 period and close to 8 percent in 1991 and 1992. The Iran-Iraq war and the recasting of U.S. aid from loans to grants bolstered this process even further.[26]

Whereas reduced military expenditures permitted budgetary cuts and lowered inflation, they also had a significant impact on the military-industrial complex. This complex had been built up after the 1973 war and had acted, since the late 1970s, as the driving force of Israel's economic growth and as a disseminator of knowledge for advanced high-technology industries. The complex of military industries became the main source of export growth, moving Israeli industry from import-substitution industrialization to genuine export orientation. The defense industry included three of Israel's top five corporations and had become a major earner of foreign currency. Not only did military production produce relatively high added value but it also helped pry open doors for Israeli civilian products.

The turn toward peace and reduced purchase schedules by the Israeli military has adversely affected the military industries, the profitability of many private and Histadrut-owned companies producing for the military, and finally the status of the military itself and of the republican citizenship discourse with which it was associated. While the military-industrial complex declined, it left a legacy of a new economic direction. The accelerated differentiation of military and civilian high-tech production began in Israel about half a decade before the end of the Cold War, when some of the military-trained and -recruited technological and managerial manpower moved to private and/or civilian industry as employees and entrepreneurs. The cumulative result of all of these changes was that a new model of socioeconomic development became both possible and necessary.

One of the most important aspects of this new model of development has been the emergence of a self-confident business community and of a cohort of politicians, academics, journalists, and civil servants with similar views. This new elite has adopted values that are more consonant with a liberal discourse of citizenship than with the ethno-republican discourse of pioneering virtue. They have been promoting liberal reforms in various areas of social life, in addition to the economy: civil rights, the electoral system, health care, education, mass communications, and so forth. Thus the emergence of a "new Israel" is a multifaceted phenomenon, manifested not only in the economy but in the cultural, legal, political, and social spheres as well. No area of social life seems to be immune now from sweeping changes that question the legacy of the formative colonial era and its tradition of republican values and citizenship practices.

The most telling outcome of this transformation has been the reduction of the Histadrut from an all-encompassing political-economic umbrella organization that embodied the values of pioneering republican citizenship into a weak trade union federation. The practice of collective bargaining, performed mostly through the Histadrut, which ensured a measure of equality in the distribution of income, is declining and being replaced with personal contracts. As a result, poverty is on the increase and various indicators point to a growing disparity between the social classes.[27] A growing segment of the working class has come to depend on government transfer payments in order to reach the minimum wage. The method adopted for privatizing Histadrut- and state-owned firms is their sale on the stock market. Notwithstanding Israel's socialist traditions, according to which the Histadrut's companies were owned by its members, few creative ways were sought to transfer part of these properties to the membership or to public institutions.

In the sphere of social welfare there is a powerful thrust to make the provision of social services means-tested, rather than universal.[28] The reduction in the 1980s of the national budget share that goes to education has led to the emergence of "gray education"—privately funded courses on school premises in neighborhoods where parents can afford to pay for them. Privatization of public land (currently comprising 90 percent of the country's land area) is being considered, and the use of land leased to kibbutzim and moshavim to pay off debts seems a first step in that direction. Politically, the power of political parties and their authority over their Knesset members is declining, due to increasing reliance on intraparty primary elections and the direct election of the prime minister. These new electoral methods have added to the political clout of business people and concerns that can contribute to politicians' election campaigns at the expense of political parties and the Histadrut. Since in Israel social class correlates very strongly with ethnicity, the growing class inequality that has resulted from these developments translates into growing disparity between the main ethnic groups: Ashkenazi Jews, Mizraḥi Jews, and citizen Palestinians.[29]

The capstone of liberal reform was the adoption in 1992 of two constitutional laws ("basic laws"): Freedom of Occupation and Human Dignity and Freedom, designed to give pride of place to civil rights within the legal edifice. This legislation was appropriately viewed by legal observers as a "constitutional revolution" because it expressly established the two basic laws as standards by which future legislation (and in the case of the Freedom of Occupation law, past legislation as well) should be evaluated. In this way the principle of judicial review of primary legislation was introduced into Israel's constitutional system.[30]

It is indicative of the direction of these changes that the freedom of economic activity was grounded in a constitutional law while other, but equally basic, civil rights and liberties (such as the right to equality before the law and the freedoms of expression, religion, association, and assembly) are yet to be constitutionally guaranteed. Efforts to introduce basic laws that would guarantee these rights have faltered on the opposition of the Jewish religious parties to any constitutional legislation. Their concern is that such basic laws could be used to nullify much of the religious legislation that has been passed over the past fifty years.[31] The same fate was met by a proposal to enact a basic law guaranteeing social rights, introduced by the Histadrut. As a result, it is quite possible that the Freedom of Occupation law would be used to undermine many of the rights currently enjoyed by Israeli workers, as well as much of the country's progressive social legislation.[32]

This process of economic, legal, and cultural transformation is still partial and is riddled with contradictions and occasional reversals. Three developments that seem to contradict the diminishing role of the state have been: the nationalization of health insurance in 1994, the renewed underwriting by the state of fixed-interest non-tradable bonds for pension funds, and the increase of state subsidies to Jewish religious institutions. This appearance may be misleading, however. Nationalizing health insurance was a crucial measure in the effort to undermine the Histadrut, which had owned the largest health-care system and provided medical services to over 70 percent of the population. This has led to the decline of publicly supplied health care and to its partial privatization and is likely to lead to much more widespread privatization in the future. The rescue of the pension funds by the state was an emergency measure, done under the threat of serious economic dislocations. Increased subsidies to Jewish religious institutions were a political payoff to Prime Minister Netanyahu's coalition partners, a standard Israeli practice.

In sum, the final decline of the republican discourse has stemmed from changes in the global and Israeli political and economic realities, such as the peace accord with Egypt, the world-wide economic liberalization and the opportunities it offered to Israeli industries, the growth of legal and cultural elites that wish to express their new influence through a vibrant civil society, and so on. These changes have rendered the collectivist incorporation regime based on the republican discourse economically counterproductive. The Ashkenazi core group, old beneficiaries of the republican discourse, have shifted their allegiance, therefore, to the liberal discourse and to civil society. The resources they accumulated under the collectivist regime enable them now to act independently of the state and of the corporatist structures that they have come to regard as obstructing rather than supporting their interests.

This shift, starting as a response to the inflationary crisis and general malaise of the 1980s, but more profoundly to the economic stagnation that set in after the 1973 war, resulted in the adoption of a policy of wide-ranging economic liberalization. Coupled with the Intifada, liberalization reduced the willingness of the core Ashkenazi group to pay the material and moral price for the repression necessitated by the continued existence of the Israeli control system as constituted in 1967 (encompassing Israel and the occupied territories). Furthermore, although for many years the beneficiaries of state-driven and protected industrialization, the Histadrut's job-creation schemes, and the high-tech military-industrial complex, many industrialists have become enthusiastic supporters of the peace process, which promised to end the Arab boycott and open up the world market for Israeli products.[33] Thus the synergy of military and moral difficulties in putting down the Intifada and the desire for economic expansion has resulted in the Oslo accords and the onset of decolonization in the occupied Palestinian territories.[34]

Dilemmas of Citizenship

Since the signing of the Declaration of Principles with the PLO in Oslo in September 1993, the tactical conflict between doves and hawks over the means of attaining security has given rise to a profound conflict between neo-Zionists, who have replenished old Zionism with a fundamentalist religious and anti-Western twist, and post-Zionists, who view the stage of conquest, colonization, and state-building as over. These competing perspectives are articulated most clearly in competing citizenship discourses that structure, stratify, and provide ideological expression to the hopes and fears of all social groups: Ashkenazim, Mizraḥim, Orthodox Jews, citizen and noncitizen Palestinians.

The Ashkenazi elite has outgrown the confines of its colonial phase of development and now seeks to venture out into the world. It thus lost much of its interest in maintaining the primacy of republican citizenship with its emphasis on a strong state and on communal public-spiritedness. The declining influence of the republican citizenship discourse has caused fierce competition for hegemony between the adherents of the other two discourses. These discourses—the liberal and the ethno-nationalist—now appear not as subordinate or secondary to the republican discourse, as they had been through most of Israel's history, but as comprehensive alternatives in their own right.

A central dilemma of the mostly secular Ashkenazi Jews who pursue the promise of liberal citizenship is how to address the conflict between their individual rights and the role played by Judaism in the public sphere. The option of separating state and religion is rarely raised because it would mean doing away with Israel's character as a Jewish state. Instead, a piecemeal approach of gradually eroding the religious status quo through liberal legislation and judicial action is favored. For example, a major struggle has emerged over Supreme Court rulings that established the right of women and non-Orthodox Jews to serve on religious councils, the municipal bodies that provide Jewish religious services at the local level.

The Palestinians, both citizens and noncitizens, are also keenly interested in the liberal discourse. Between 1967 and the institution of the Palestinian autonomy in the mid-1990s, the Palestinian Arab population in the West Bank and Gaza enjoyed only heavily circumscribed rights. Officially, two systems of law operated in the occupied territories: military law for the Arab residents and Israeli civil law for the Jewish settlers. In fact, arbitrary and discriminatory application of the military regulations was combined with a generally permissive attitude toward violations by settlers.[35] The Palestinian residents, who were in fact, but not in law, part of Israeli society, were deprived of most legal means of struggle by being defined as lying outside even the liberal conception of citizenship. Their actual or potential emancipation from direct Israeli rule has been the result of their armed uprising, the Intifada, together with the liberalization of Israeli society.[36]

Palestinians who are Israeli citizens possess individual civil and political rights, including the right to vote. In many other areas, however, such as employment, social and educational rights, and, most importantly, membership in the core republican community, they have remained second-class citizens. If the liberal discourse replaces the republican one as the primary narrative of Israeli citizenship, this would go a long way toward equalizing the citizenship status of Jews and Palestinians. One key issue, however, still divides citizen Palestinians from Jewish liberals, namely, the latter's continued commitment to the preservation of Israel's character as a Jewish state.[37] This has led many citizen Palestinians to demand national-cultural autonomy, that is, to recast the Israeli state as a consociational or multiculturalist democracy.

Consociationalism, of course, is a communal rather than a liberal arrangement. Moreover, since many aspects of Palestinian culture are informed by Islam, the Palestinian demand for cultural autonomy could lead to an unbridgeable rift between Palestinians and Jewish liberals, who have become very impatient with religion. The key issue now between the Jewish majority and Arab minority, then, is whether the latter will gain the option of liberal citizenship, integrating as individuals into the state that will be redefined as belonging to all of its citizens, or else be recognized as a national minority with corresponding effective multicultural citizenship rights.

As long as the republican discourse predominated, the political efficacy of groups that were excluded or marginalized by it was necessarily limited: they could tilt the political balance by providing the support needed by a particular section of the core group to prevail politically (religious Zionists and Mapai in 1948–77, Mizraḥim and Likud in 1977, citizen Palestinians and Labor in 1992), but they could never become dominant themselves. Consequently, these outer groups could not take the political initiative, and the rewards they gained from supporting sections of the core group were inevitably frustratingly small.

The coalition that elected Binyamin Netanyahu prime minister in May 1996 was made up of such excluded and marginalized Jewish groups: Mizraḥim, religious Zionists, and *ḥaredim* (ultra-Orthodox Jews). This coalition, which had crystallized around the ever more religiously articulated ethno-national discourse, narrowly defeated the rival coalition, made up primarily of Ashkenazi and citizen-Palestinian adherents of liberalism.

Some adherents of the ethno-national discourse, primarily the religious Zionist settlers of Gush Emunim, have been trying to claim the republican mantle of "pioneering" and drape it in a religious garb. However, since the Intifada they have come to be regarded by most of the original bearers of republican virtue, who had been quite ambivalent about them in the past, as usurpers. The battle over decolonization of the occupied territories, which rages primarily between these two groups, has already claimed the life of Yitzhak Rabin, an archetypal representative of the original beneficiaries of the republican discourse.

For Mizraḥim, the state, which has traditionally treated them as secondary to Ashkenazim, is assuming ever growing importance now, as the republican discourse continues to decline. They seek in the state protection against the adverse effects of economic liberalism and an affirmation of their privileged status as Jews in the society. They cling ever more strongly to the ethno-national discourse of citizenship, increasingly infusing it with religious content and, to a lesser extent, with the demand for the protection and extension of social citizenship rights. It is not clear whether a Mizraḥi secular cultural alternative to religious identification is available, but it is obvious that the fulfillment of social rights through membership in religious institutions, in a manner similar to fundamentalism in other Middle Eastern countries, does not allow class interests to be properly expressed or defended. This was strikingly attested to when, in July 1997, Shas, the religious Mizraḥi party, cast the crucial votes against the proposed Basic Law: Social Rights.

While the settlers and the Mizraḥim share an essentially traditionalist outlook and oppose liberalization, the former are interested primarily in keeping the occupied territories, whereas the latter are more eager to preserve the state as both a provider of welfare services and the primary avenue of social mobility open to them. Their *ḥaredi* allies are interested neither in territory nor in the state, but rather in maintaining the Jewish character of public life in Israel, which is the basis of their privileges and which they see being threatened by liberalization and by the use of civic criteria of membership. Thus, this ethno-national coalition, no less than the liberal one, is subject to internal tensions and contradiction.

Given the acrimony of the normative struggle and the conflict over the centrality of the institutions that dispense citizenship rights and duties—the marketplace and judicial system for the liberals, the welfare state and religious institutions for the proponents of ethno-nationalism—the battle between them appears sometimes to assume the character of a total war. The question is whether a single universal and "assimilationist" liberal citizenship, extended to groups that previously did not enjoy its full benefits, would become the dominant model, or ethno-nationalist citizenship, by absorbing themes previously associated with the competing discourses, such as republican pioneering and social citizenship, would prevail. The most likely outcome is that another incorporation regime of multiple citizenships will emerge. But how fragmented this regime will be depends mostly on the future of the peace process.

The peace process, especially the future of the occupied Palestinian territories, is the axis around which liberals and ethno-nationalists contend. The outcome of their struggle will therefore affect not only Israeli society itself and the respective identity, membership, and rights of Ashkenazim, Mizraḥim, Orthodox Jews, women, and citizen and noncitizen Palestinians, but also the future of the entire Middle East. As the forces that shape Israeli society are becoming more global, the prospects of the liberals to win out are improving. For the more minimal demands of liberal citizenship cohere better with international trends than either the republican or the ethno-national discourses. Even the ethno-nationalist camp is led by those who are committed to a liberal economic vision. It would be very difficult to square this vision with the interventionist state and repressive military practices required for maintaining the occupation and defending Jewish settlers on the West Bank.

Notes

* This paper is based on our forthcoming book, *The Dynamics of Israeli Citizenship: Between Colonialism and Democracy.* We would like to thank Boaz Neumann, Meir Shabat, and Amit Ron for their research assistance and the Israel Science Foundation, the Joint Committee on the Near and Middle East of the Social Science Research Council, and the American Council of Learned Societies for their financial assistance.

1. Arie Caspi, "Data of the Week" [Hebrew], *Ha'arets,* Weekly Supplement, July 25, 1997.
2. Yoav Peled and Gershon Shafir, "The Roots of Peacemaking: The Dynamics of Citizenship in Israel," *International Journal of Middle East Studies* 28 (1996): 391–413; Gershon Shafir, *The Citizenship Debates: A Reader* (Minneapolis: University of Minnesota Press, 1998).
3. Shafir, *The Citizenship Debates.*
4. John Rawls, *A Theory of Justice* (Cambridge, MA: Belknap Press, 1971); John Rawls, *Political Liberalism* (New York: Columbia University Press, 1993).
5. Michael J. Sandel, *Liberalism and the Limits of Justice* (Cambridge: Cambridge University Press, 1982); Charles Taylor, "Cross-Purposes: The Liberal-Communitarian Debate," in *Liberalism and the Moral Life,* ed. Nancy L. Rosenbaum (Cambridge, MA: Harvard University Press, 1989); Adrian Oldfield, *Citizenship and Community: Civic Republicanism and the Modern World* (London: Routledge, 1990).
6. Liah Greenfeld, *Nationalism: Five Paths to Modernity* (Cambridge, MA: Harvard University Press, 1992).
7. Rogers Brubaker, *Citizenship and Nationhood in France and Germany* (Cambridge, MA: Harvard University Press, 1992).
8. Anthony Giddens, *The Nation-State and Violence* (Cambridge: Polity Press, 1985); David Held, *Political Theory and the Modern State* (Cambridge: Polity Press, 1989); Charles Tilly, *Coercion, Capital and European States: AD 990–1992* (Cambridge, MA: Blackwell, 1992); Eric Gorham, "Are Citizens Becoming Subjects? Irony in the Discourse of Neoliberalism," a paper delivered at the annual meeting of the American Political Science Association, Chicago, 1992.
9. Rogers M. Smith, "The 'American Creed' and American Identity: The Limits of American Citizenship in the United States," *Western Political Quarterly,* no. 41 (1988): 225–51.
10. Yasemin Nuhoglu Soysal, *Limits of Citizenship: Migrants and Postnational Membership in Europe* (Chicago: The University of Chicago Press, 1994).
11. Yoav Peled, "Ethnic Democracy and the Legal Construction of Citizenship: Arab Citizens of the Jewish State," *The American Political Science Review* 86 (1992): 432–43.
12. Benedict Anderson, *Imagined Communities* (London: Verso, 1983), 136.
13. Yonathan Shapiro, *Politicians as an Hegemonic Class: The Case of Israel* [Hebrew] (Tel Aviv: Sifriat Poalim, 1996), 46–69.
14. Yossi Bar-Mooha, "The 16th Tribe Discovered" [Hebrew], *Ha'arets,* Weekly Supplement, August 8, 1997; Yossi Bar-Mooha, "Third Generation, Second Reading" [Hebrew], *Ha'arets,* August 11, 1997; "The Halacha vs. the Law of Return'" [Hebrew], *Ha'arets,* August 11, 1997.
15. Ian S. Lustick, *Arabs in the Jewish State* (Austin: University of Texas Press, 1980); Sammy Smooha, "Minority Status in an Ethnic Democracy: The Sta-

tus of the Arab Minority in Israel," *Ethnic and Racial Studies* 13, no. 3 (July 1990): 389–413; David Kretzmer, *The Legal Status of the Arabs in Israel* (Boulder, CO: Westview, 1990); Noah Lewin-Epstein and Moshe Semyonov, *The Arab Minority in Israel's Economy: Patterns of Ethnic Inequality* (Boulder, CO: Westview Press, 1993).

16. Yoav Peled, "Ethnic Democracy and the Legal Construction of Citizenship: Arab Citizens of the Jewish State," *The American Political Science Review* 86 (1992): 432–43.
17. Gershon Shafir, *Land, Labor and the Origins of the Palestinian-Israeli Conflict, 1882–1914* (Cambridge: Cambridge University Press, 1989).
18. George Fredrickson, "Colonialism and Racism: The United States and South Africa in Comparative Perspective," in *The Arrogance of Race* (Middletown, CT: Wesleyan University Press, 1988), 218–21.
19. Gershon Shafir "Ideological Politics or the Politics of Demography: The Aftermath of the Six Day War," in *Critical Essays in Israeli Society, Politics, and Culture,* ed. Ian S. Lustick and Barry Rubin (Albany, NY: State University of New York Press, 1991), 41–61.
20. Yonathan Shapiro, *The Formative Years of the Israeli Labor Party: The Organization of Power, 1918–1930* (London: Sage, 1976).
21. Shlomo Swirski, *Israel: The Oriental Majority* (London: Zed Books, 1989).
22. Vered Kraus and R.W. Hodge, *Promises in the Promised Land* (New York: Greenwood, 1990), 66, 68; Uziel O. Schmeltz, Sergio Della Pergola, and Uri Avner, *Ethnic Differences Among Israeli Jews: A New Look* [Hebrew] (Jerusalem: The Hebrew University, Institute of Contemporary Jewry, 1991), 109–12; Sammy Smooha, "Class, Ethnic, and National Cleavages and Democracy in Israel," in *Israeli Democracy Under Stress,* eds. Ehud Sprinzak and Larry Diamond (Boulder, CO: Lynne Rienner, 1993), 309–42; Yaacov Nahon, "Educational Expansion and the Structure of Occupational Opportunities" [Hebrew], in *Ethnic Communities in Israel—Socio-Economic Status,* eds. S.N. Eisenstadt, Moshe Lissak, and Yaacov Nahon (Jerusalem: The Jerusalem Institute for Israel Studies, 1993), 33–49; Yaacov Nahon, "Occupational Status" [Hebrew], in *Ethnic Communities in Israel,* 50–75; Yitzchak Haberfeld and Yinon Cohen, *Schooling and Income Gaps Between Western and Eastern Jews in Israel, 1975–1992* (Tel Aviv: Tel Aviv University, Golda Meir Institute for Social and Labor Research, 1995); Noah Lewin-Epstein, Yuval Elmelech, and Moshe Semyonov, "Ethnic Inequality in Home-Ownership and Value of Housing: The Case of Immigrants in Israel," *Social Forces* (forthcoming).
23. Dina Hecht and Nira Yuval-Davis, "Ideology Without Revolution: Jewish Women in Israel," *Khamsin,* no. 6 (1978): 97–117; Yael Azmon and Dafna N. Izraeli, eds., *Women in Israel* (Studies of Israeli Society, Vol. VI) (New Brunswick, NJ: Transaction Publishers, 1993); Iris Jerby, *The Double Price: Women, Status, and Military Service in Israel* [Hebrew] (Tel Aviv: Ramot, 1996); Nitza Berkovitch, "Motherhood as a National Mission: The Construc-

tion of Womanhood in the Legal Discourse in Israel," *Women's Studies International Forum,* no. 21 (1997).

24. Yoav Peled, "Ethnic Democracy and the Legal Construction of Citizenship: Arab Citizens of the Jewish State," *The American Political Science Review* 86 (1992): 432–43.
25. Nicholas Kochan, "Israel: Bidding to Be the Next 'Economic Dragon,' " *Multinational Business,* Spring 1992; Michael Shalev, *Labor and the Political Economy of Israel* (Oxford: Oxford University Press, 1992).
26. David Brodet, "Economic Might and Military Might" [Hebrew], *Rev'on lekalkalah* 41, no. 2, (July 1994): 225; Shmuel Ben-Zvi, "The Overt and Covert Security Burden" [Hebrew], *Rev'on lekalkalah* 41, no. 2 (July 1994): 227–28.
27. "Poverty and Inequality in Income Distribution in Israel" [Hebrew], in *Seqirah kalkalit* (Bank Hapoalim) 82, no. 1 (August 1996).
28. Avraham Doron, "The Marginalization of the Israeli Welfare State" [Hebrew], unpublished paper, 1994.
29. Shlomo Ben-Ami, *Combining the Elements: Society, Security, and Policy in Israel* [Hebrew] (Jerusalem: The Hebrew University, The Leonard Davis Institute for International Relations, 1997).
30. David Kretzmer, "The New Basic Laws on Human Rights: A Mini-Revolution in Israeli Constitutional Law?" *Israel Law Review,* no. 26 (1992): 238–49; Aharon Barak, "The Constitutional Revolution: Protected Fundamental Rights" [Hebrew], *Mishpat umimshal* 1, (1992): 9–35; Aharon Barak, "Human Dignity as a Constitutional Right" [Hebrew], *Ha'arets,* June 3, 1994.
31. David Kretzmer, "The New Basic Laws on Human Rights."
32. Ruth Ben-Yisrael, "Implications of the Basic Laws for Labor Law and for the System of Labor Relations" [Hebrew], *Labor Law Annual,* no. 4 (1994): 27–47.
33. "Soaring to Lofty Profits on the Wings of Peace, "*Money* (November 1993).
34. Yoav Peled and Gershon Shafir, "The Roots of Peacemaking: The Dynamics of Citizenship in Israel," 391–413; Yaron Ezrahi, *Rubber Bullets: Power and Conscience in Modern Israel* (New York: Farrar, Straus and Giroux, 1997).
35. Baruch Kimmerling and Joel Migdal, *The Palestinians: The Making of a People* (New York: Free Press, 1993), 253.
36. Yoav Peled and Gershon Shafir, "The Roots of Peacemaking."
37. Ruth Gavison, "A Jewish and Democratic State—Political Identity, Ideology and Law" [Hebrew], *Tel Aviv University Law Review* 19, no. 3 (1995): 631–82.

Part II

Israeli and Palestinian Identities in Literature

6

Patriotic Rhetoric and Personal Conscience in Israeli Fiction of the 1948 and 1956 Wars

David C. Jacobson

Participants in wars, whether of an offensive or defensive nature, are typically called upon to engage in acts of violence and control that violate the moral code to which they would normally subscribe in peacetime. To insure the willingness of soldiers to engage in acts of war governments tend to develop a patriotic rhetoric that justifies such departures from moral norms. Nevertheless, as so many war novels and memoirs have shown, certain individual soldiers may not be persuaded by patriotic rhetoric to set aside their moral commitments and are driven to dissent from their government's attempts to justify war. Sometimes this dissent takes the form of openly opposing a war or even of refusing to fight. Often it stays at the level of an inwardly felt discomfort with what one is called upon to do as a soldier.

A number of works of Israeli fiction portray the experiences of characters serving in the Israeli army in 1948 and 1956, when it occupied land inhabited primarily by Arabs. A fictional approach to the portrayal of such war experiences has allowed writers to critique the patriotic rhetoric that prevailed in Israeli culture at the time of each war. In so doing they have made good use of the power of literature to present, in the words of Jonathan Culler, "a commentary on the validity of various ways of interpreting experience; an exploration of the creative, revelatory, and deceptive powers of language; a critique of the codes and interpretive processes manifested in . . . language. . . ."[1]

Four works of Israeli fiction will serve to illustrate this critical approach to the language of patriotic rhetoric in the wars of 1948 and 1956. Two works portray the entrance of Israeli soldiers into largely abandoned Arab villages in the Galilee during the 1948 war: "Parʿoshim" (Fleas, 1948), by Yehoshua Bar-Yosef (1912–),[2] and "Ḥirbet Ḥizaʿah" (1949), by S. Yizhar (1916–).[3] Two others portray the period of Israel's occupation of the Gaza Strip in the 1956 war: "Al ḥudo shel kaddur" (On the Point of a Bullet, 1958, revised 1978), by Yitzhak Orpaz (1923–),[4] and "Haʿir halevanah" (The White City), a chapter in the novel *Miqreh hakesil* (Fortunes of a Fool, 1959), by Aharon Megged (1920–).[5]

Yehoshua Bar-Yosef's story "Fleas" begins with a description of the fierce battle fought by Israeli soldiers to conquer an Arab village in the 1948 war. In the narrator's portrayal of the aftermath of that battle we see a series of juxtaposed images that underline the tension between the feeling, reinforced by the language of patriotic rhetoric, that an important military victory is to be celebrated and the alternative perception that focuses instead on the ways in which so many have suffered on both sides as a result of the battle. In one passage the narrator notes the incompatibility of the joy of victory and its bloody consequences:

> By morning the trash containers of the hospital were filled with packages of bandages soaked in blood, parts of fingers and pieces of human flesh; and the hearts of the healthy and living were filled with the joy of victory and shouts of intoxication. The village was conquered. The enemy was defeated and had run for his life. (91)

While the "the healthy and living" soldiers have embraced the language of patriotic rhetoric so succinctly captured in the expression, "the village was conquered," the narrator calls attention to the bandages and body parts that are a part of the scene from which the soldiers are blinded by their triumphant perspective.

It is not only the suffering of their fellow Israeli soldiers that the jubilant victors ignore, but also the suffering of the enemy:

> [A]mong the sabra bushes was seen the dead body of an Egyptian spread out like a kind of rag, without the pleasing movement of a person who can walk, but no one paid attention to it nor to the dreams and fears that were buried in the flesh rotting in the heat of the day. (92)

The narrator contrasts the language of patriotic rhetoric in the expression "the enemy fled" with a description of the defeat of the village that sensitively captures all that is tragic in the experience for the villagers:

> The enemy fled. Residents who cried their first infant cries and married women and sired babies and buried their dead went; they're no more, scattered to the winds with eyes staring in horror and with fathomless curses on their lips. (93)

This perception is far from the minds and hearts of the Israeli soldiers, who are able to sleep "deeply, the sleep of conquerors" (93).

As the soldiers take up residence in the village that they have conquered, their blindness to human suffering is undermined by what the narrator refers to as "a plague of fleas" (*makkat par'oshim*). On a symbolic level, this plague would appear to represent an act of retribution brought upon the soldiers for their role in occupying the village and exiling its inhabitants, ironically recalling the biblical plagues (*makkot*) with which God inflicted the Egyptians to force them to release their Israelite slaves. The flea epidemic challenges the soldiers' self-perception as total victors. As one soldier declares, "The Arabs actually did not run away from here; they left these fleas behind for us" (94–95). At first, this challenge to their status as all-powerful victors is experienced by the soldiers on an individual level. Each soldier is ashamed to reveal publicly that he is suffering from fleas. After a while, however, it becomes clear to all that they are suffering from the same problem. The soldiers feel humiliated by the plague as it lowers them in their own eyes to the level of the defeated Arabs whom they disdain:

> The matter angered us. And more than it angered us it insulted us, and more than it insulted us it humiliated us. In less than a month's time the people underwent a total change. If their soldiers' uniforms were stripped off of them and they were dressed in the clothing of Arab villagers and they changed their language, there would be no more great discernible distance between them and those who fled from them; they too are smitten with bites and rolling in the trash and cursing for its own sake, out of enjoyment and out of idleness; they too look hungrily toward what they don't have and dream exciting and strange dreams saturated with desire and lust and blood and murder. (96)

The plague of fleas makes it impossible to portray the victory in the language of patriotic triumph that had been embraced by the soldiers at the beginning of the occupation. One soldier laments the fact that he can no longer glorify the victory in a romantic literary style:

> Now all his beautiful dreams are smashed to pieces. No courageous glory or romantic glory. Despicable fleas and fattened flies, and that's it. His wounded, humiliated pride burns in him mercilessly. He is like them all. He is less than them all. (97–98)

The only relief the soldiers get is when they are allowed to take turns visiting a nearby kibbutz to take showers. The kibbutz provides them with relief not only in a physical sense, but in a symbolic, moral sense as well, for the kibbutz as an institution represents all that is positive in the Zionist enterprise. Nevertheless, as soon as they walk back to the conquered village, they again start to sweat, they get dusty, and fleas left on their uniforms reappear to torture them.

In the end, one of the soldiers is driven, in defiance of standing orders, to burn down the village in a desperate attempt to rescue his fellow soldiers and himself from their humiliating defeat by the fleas. Ironically, the flames of the village alert the enemy Arab soldiers to their position, thereby thrusting them once again into battle. Nevertheless, this new battle succeeds in liberating them from their humiliation. Once again the language of patriotic rhetoric triumphs as "the soldiers shouted joyfully this time heading toward the firing that came from the enemy positions" (101).

The narrator of S. Yizhar's story "Ḥirbet Ḥizaʿah" is one of the soldiers engaged in the 1948 war in conquering and occupying an Arab village with the name in the story's title. Near the beginning of the story the narrator recalls the order issued to him and his fellow soldiers to conquer this village. By means of quotation marks, he calls attention to euphemistic expressions in the order that are central to manipulating the soldiers' perception of war. In one section the order

> warned immediately of a growing danger of "infiltrators" and of "core groups of gangs," and of (and this is a beautiful expression) "emissaries with enemy purposes;" and also the paragraph after it, which was even more important, . . . said explicitly that we are "to collect the residents . . . to load them on the vehicles and to transfer them onto the other side of our lines; to blow up the stone houses and to burn the mortar huts; to arrest the young and the suspicious, and to purify the area of "hostile forces. . . ." (38)

The narrator comments with irony on what appears to be an attempt to present this order of destruction and expulsion as a relatively normal activity to be approached in a civilized manner:

> [F]or now it will be clear with how many good and honest hopes were the departing [soldiers] armed when they received all this "burn-blow-up-arrest-load-send-off" that they will arise and burn and blow up and arrest and send off with utmost etiquette and especially with cultured moderation, and this is a sign of refreshing winds, of a good education, and perhaps of the great Jewish soul. (38)

As the Israeli soldiers proceed to take control of the village, the narrator feels increasingly uneasy. At one point, when the Israeli soldiers are firing at fleeing villagers, the narrator becomes caught up in the hunter-like drive to which his fellow soldiers have succumbed, but at the same time a countervoice of moral revulsion emerges within him. He is, however, too intimidated by the group mentality to openly protest:

> "Look there!" I roared and pointed to Gabi: ". . . to the right of the tree standing by itself! You can catch them beautifully!" And at the same moment I trembled somewhat, and while my hand was pointed in intoxicated enthusiasm toward the ones running away that I discovered, I felt that someone shouted differently in me, like a wounded bird. (50)

When a soldier firing at the fleeing Arab villagers misses, the narrator is surprised to realize that he is secretly relieved, and he thinks to himself, "Let them not hit, ah, not hit them" (50). He then quickly looks around to see if anyone has caught him in his feelings of mercy, which he sees as an embarrassing flaw not to be revealed in public.

In the course of the story the narrator becomes more open in his dissent from the acts of destruction and expulsion in which he and his fellow soldiers are engaged. At one point he argues with another soldier about the connection between their actions as Israeli soldiers and Jewish historical experience. When the narrator raises the question of whether they have the right to expel the villagers, one soldier declares to him, "You listen to what I say! To Ḥirbet, whatever its name is, will come [Jewish] immigrants, do you hear, and they will take this land and will work it and it will be great here!" (86). The narrator, however, refuses to celebrate the moment as the prelude to the national growth and development of the State of Israel. Instead he connects it with the Jewish historical experience of exile:

> I tried to control myself. My insides cried out. Colonists, my insides cried. It's a lie, my insides cried. Ḥịrḅeṭ Ḥịẓạ"ạḥ is not ours. . . . What didn't they tell us about refugees. Everything, everything for the sake of the refugees, their welfare and saving them—and of course our refugees. Those whom we expel—that is a completely different matter. Wait: two thousand years of exile. . . . They kill Jews. Europe. Now we are the masters. (86–87)

As he imagines the future suffering of the exiled Arab refugees and contemplates the quiet that has come to the valley in which the village sits as a result of the Israeli soldiers' successful operation, the narrator expresses his discomfort by alluding to the biblical story of the corrupt cities of Sodom and Gomorrah:

> And when quiet encloses all, and no one breaks the silence . . . God will go out and descend to the valley to move around and see about its cry. (88)

The Hebrew word used to refer to the valley's cry, *haketsaʿaqatah,* alludes to the cries of the oppressed in the city of Sodom that God decides to investigate (Genesis 18:21). Here, the oppressed about whom God is concerned are the Arab villagers who cry out in protest against the Israeli army's abuse of its power.

In "On the Point of a Bullet" the narrator, an Israeli soldier, tells of his capture of an Arab prisoner during Israel's occupation of the Gaza Strip in the 1956 war. For this soldier the tension between patriotic rhetoric and alternative moral ways of viewing his actions in war is reflected in the ways he goes back and forth between viewing his prisoner as a dangerous enemy and as a fellow human being with whom he has much in common.

Detecting possible signs of life in a cave, the narrator enters only to be surprised by an Arab who leaps out, crying in Arabic, "God is great!" (240). The narrator's instinctive reaction is to shoot at the Arab with his Uzi, but the weapon does not fire. His next instinct is to flee, but he stays glued to the spot. As he stares at the whites of the Arab's eyes, he thinks to himself, "Here is the enemy... you or he" (240). Thus, the narrator's first perceptions of the Arab are as an anonymous threat. His relationship with the Arab is simple and direct: he is an object to kill in self-defense.

The narrator has an opportunity to enter into a more complex set of relationships with the Arab when the latter throws down his rifle and prostrates himself on the ground in surrender. As long as the Arab is under his control, the narrator keeps shifting his perceptions of him. At first, his prisoner appears to be a typical Arab freedom fighter. Later, as they walk toward the army camp, the narrator notes to himself that the Arab strongly resembles one of the Jewish *shomrim* (guards) of the early Zionist settler days. That modification of the sense of estrangement between Jew and Arab is suddenly interrupted when the narrator notices that the Arab is starting to lower his hands from his head. Immediately, the narrator reverts to stereotypical images of his prisoner as a crafty and untrustworthy Arab:

> Son of a bitch, whore, crafty and hypocritical bastard! Make friends with him and he pulls out a knife from a secret hiding place and stabs you in the back. Filthy Arab nature. (241)

In the aftermath of this incident the Israeli soldier develops an attitude toward his Arab prisoner that combines condescension with a strong desire to be able to relate to him as he would to a fellow Israeli. As he conducts a body search of the Arab he notes the "generations of yellow filth on his dark skin," and he thinks, "if he washed well with soap he would appear lighter and more understandable" (241). Upon learning the prisoner's name and seeing pictures of him and members of his family, the narrator begins to view the Arab more as a human being. When the Arab reveals blackened teeth upon smiling, however, the narrator notes that those teeth "ruined the smile, which was really warm" (241). Later the narrator returns to his earlier observation of how dirty the Arab is, when he imagines that if he could just give this prisoner a good bath, feed him, dress him "like a human being," and give him a profession, he would really become "a human being" (243).

The Israeli soldier thinks of the Arab as having national traits that are inferior to those of Israelis:

> So, what in the end is the difference? It seems that you think and challenge, while he accepts and surrenders and believes that all is from Allah. (244)

He recognizes, however, that these inferior national traits are not immutable. Perhaps, he considers, the Arab's inability to think for himself is the result of his being without freedom and without hope, and if the circumstances of his life would change, he could develop more desirable traits. The soldier imagines the possibility of standing the prisoner up straight, calling him *ḥaver* (comrade) and transforming him into a thinking person.

The notion that a human connection could be established between the Israeli soldier and his prisoner is almost destroyed when the Arab suddenly leaps forward. The narrator assumes that the prisoner is trying to attack him. The Arab trips, and then the soldier realizes that the reason the Arab moved was that he had spotted a viper and was trying save the soldier from being bitten by it.

At the army camp the narrator, convinced that the Arab will bring no harm to the occupying Israeli troops, suggests to an officer that he be freed. The officer tells him that if the Arab's rifle does not fire, they can return it to him and release him. Another soldier takes the Arab and his rifle outside, and a shot is heard. It turns out that the shot was directed at the Arab who had fled, presumably because he thought he was going to be killed. As the narrator and his fellow soldiers move on, he hears them singing "Hevenu shalom aleikhem," a song traditionally sung in connection with youthful field trips to parts of Israel. For the other soldiers, war is just another Israeli group experience as harmless as a children's outing. The narrator's perception, however, is very different. As he looks at the grave of the dead prisoner he thinks of him as the friend who was betrayed by his fellow Israeli soldiers.

"The White City" is a chapter in a novel composed of loosely connected stories about an antiheroic narrator in Israel in the mid-1950s. The stories leading up to this chapter portray the narrator as a "fool" in the sense that everyone else in the society (including his wife) seems to know more about reality than he does. At the beginning of the chapter the narrator is emotionally swept away by the sense of belonging that his participation in the battle to conquer the Gaza Strip in the 1956 war gives him. This connection with a patriotic goal contrasts for him in a refreshing way with his usual sense of alienation from society. Nevertheless, in the course of the war it is actually this fool, apparently so ignorant of the ways of the world, who displays the greatest wisdom of all when he dissents from what he sees as the arbitrary use of power by the Israeli occupying forces in the Gaza Strip.

The Israeli patriotic justification for the 1956 war is made clear to the narrator and his fellow soldiers in the words of their commanding officer:

> Our task is to shatter [the enemy's] offensive positions which threaten the integrity of our land and its very existence and to foil once and for all the enemy's aggressive plans . . . No country can put up with a state of permanent threat to its borders and unceasing attacks on its settlements. War is an unpleasant business, which involves suffering and sacrifice. But it is more unpleasant to live in constant fear, when at any moment the enemy is liable to flourish his naked sword and cut off your head. (Hebrew, 226; English, 81–82)

During the battle, however, the narrator is shaken from this patriotic rhetoric when an Israeli soldier he knows is killed. Immediately following that he severely twists his ankle. As a result, when he marches into Gaza, while the surrendering residents appear to be completely submissive to the other soldiers, the narrator is convinced that as he limps he is being mocked by those residents.

While walking on his own around Gaza, the narrator has another experience that undermines the patriotic rhetoric of his commanding officer:

> I saw a little [Arab] girl, about eight or ten, carrying on her back a torn mattress twice as big as herself, which was slipping all over her body in all directions and covering her head. Her bare legs were sunk in the sand, and her back was bent like a bow, until it seemed that her head was touching the ground . . . . She was so small compared to the mattress that I wanted to take her to wherever she wanted to go. (Hebrew, 241; English, 98)

The narrator lowers his gun and approaches the girl. Seeing the Israeli soldier approach her, the little girl panics, lets the mattress slip off of her back, and runs away. Unfortunately, even as the narrator lets down his guard and tries to relate to the Arab as simply a little girl in need, his uniform and his gun keep her from seeing him as a human being. She can only see him as a monster bent on her destruction.

Whenever the narrator in "The White City" dissents from abuses of power, he is answered with the rhetoric of euphemism and self-justification that seeks to shield the soldiers from the unpleasant aspects of being a conquering army. At one point the narrator is asked to participate in the rounding-up of suspected members of a dangerous Arab gang. The officer makes clear to the soldiers he is ordering that it is essential that the members of the gang be wiped out, "not only as a punishment but in order to prevent disasters, clashes, murder" (Hebrew, 254; English, 114). With trembling lips, the narrator naively says to the officer, "You said we have to finish them off. . . . Do you mean to kill them?" (Hebrew, 254; English 114). When in response the officer only grimaces, the narrator feels humiliated for asking what he now realizes is to the others such a foolish question.

Nevertheless, in the larger context of the story the questioning attitude of the narrator maintains its moral force. Each defense of the Israeli army's occupation practices comes across to the reader as morally questionable. When at one point the narrator calls for better treatment of the residents of Gaza, he is told, "War is war" (literally in the Hebrew: "occupation is occupation," Hebrew, 260; English, 122). When the narrator declares his belief in a story that some Israeli soldiers killed surrendering Arabs with their hands up, he is berated with the declaration by a fellow soldier that the story could not possibly be true: "I know our boys. Pure gold, that's what they are. No army in the world would have treated the inhabitants as we have at a time of occupation" (Hebrew, 261; English, 122).

In all four of these stories the authors have made clear that there is a problematic relationship between the behavior of an occupying army and the moral code by which most people live in peacetime. The authors call attention to the way in which the language of euphemism and simplistic self-justification attempts to prevent members of an occupying army from coming to terms with the moral implications of their treatment of the residents of the occupied territory. Such declarations as "occupation is occupation" can be reassuring to a soldier until he begins to realize that the same event that brought his people victory has brought suffering to those whom they have defeated.

The authors raise moral questions about these occupations by presenting an alternative perspective expressed by the narrator, who in three of the stories is a participant in the events. In "Fleas," while the third-person narrator is not a direct participant he, too, presents the alternative perspective. This alternative perspective includes several points endorsed by the authors of these stories: it is inhumane to ignore the real human suffering that both Israelis and Arabs undergo in wartime; the enemy is at times less dangerous than he is imagined to be by other Israeli soldiers; the Arab enemies share with the Israelis a common humanity that makes them closer to Israelis than is usually supposed; and Israeli soldiers should relate to the conquered Arabs in ways that are as close as possible to the moral code that prevails when one is not at war.

In each story, the perspective expressed in the language of patriotic rhetoric is a formidable force that is not easily shaken by this alternative perspective. The process of questioning patriotic war rhetoric is at first experienced on an individual level, and when it is, there is a tendency to be ashamed to dissent from the national consensus. When the soldiers in "Fleas" first have their perspective changed by the plague of fleas, they are too self-conscious to tell each other about their suffering. Then, after admitting their sense of humiliation they eagerly embrace the new battle that will redeem them from their shame, without having learned anything from their suffering. In "Ḥirbet Ḥizaʿah," "On the Point of a Bullet," and "The White City," the first-person narrators remain solitary protesters who do not succeed in convincing the other soldiers to see beyond patriotic euphemisms and self-justifications.

One gets the sense from these stories that what is particularly disturbing to the authors is the contrast between Zionist ideals and the experience of military occupation. It would appear that the authors had hoped for a less morally troubling existence than the one they experienced in the wars of 1948 and 1956. The flea-infested soldiers in "Fleas" seek refuge in the showers of the idealistic Zionist institution the kibbutz. In "Ḥirbet Ḥizaʿah" the declaration that the occupation of the village prepares the way for the fulfillment of the Zionist ideal of providing a refuge for Jews is presented in ironic contrast to the price paid by the Palestinian refugees in order to fulfill that dream. In the story "On the Point of a Bullet," when the narrator identifies his Arab prisoner as looking like the early Zionist guards, one senses his discomfort with the fact that his role as an occupier is less palatable than the role once played by the early Zionist pioneers defending their settlements against attack. In "The White City" the call to defend the territorial integrity of Israel does not fit well with the image of a little Arab girl running in panic from an Israeli soldier.

Each writer conveys to his readers that while political and military leaders will always try by means of language to paper over the difference between the moral code of peacetime and the conduct of soldiers in wartime, voices of dissenting Israelis have emerged to challenge the language of simplistic patriotic self-justification. This challenge is not necessarily accompanied by a denial of the overall goals of Israel as a nation. It calls, however, for Israelis to judge the actions of their army by the highest moral standards.

Notes

1. Jonathan Culler, *The Pursuit of Signs: Semiotics, Literature, Deconstruction* (Ithaca, NY: Cornell University Press, 1981), 35.

2. "Parʿoshim" may be found in *Nikhtav betashaḥ: mivḥar shirim vesippurim shenikhtevu bymei milkhemet haʿatsmaʾut,* ed. A. B. Yoffe (Tel Aviv: Reshafim, 1989), 91–101. The page references are from that anthology. Yoffe does not identify the date and place of publication of the story. He does indicate that the majority of works in this anthology of literature of the 1948 war were published in newspapers, periodicals, and collections between the years 1947 and 1952. The story may also be found in *Erets merivah: hariv al haʾarets bereʾi hasifrut haʿivrit,* ed. Aharon Amir (Tel Aviv: Israel Ministry of Defense, 1992), 143–54. The translations of passages are mine.
3. S. Yizhar, *7 Sippurim* (Tel Aviv: Hakibbutz Hamuechad, 1971), 35–88. The page references are from that anthology. Yizhar records the date of writing the story as May 1949. The translations of passages are mine.
4. "Al ḥudo shel kaddur" was published in Yitzhak Orpaz, *Esev pere* (Tel Aviv: Hakibbutz Hameuchad, 1979), 59–69. The story may be found in *Erets merivah,* 239–45. The page references are from that anthology. The translations of passages from this story are mine.
5. Aharon Megged, *Miqreh hakesil* (Tel Aviv: Hakibbutz Hameuchad, 1959). The page references from the Hebrew text are from that edition. A version of "Haʿir halevanah" was also published as a separate story in the collection Aharon Megged, *Ḥatsot hayom* (Tel Aviv: Hakibbutz Hameuchad, 1973), 162–97. The translations of passages are by Aubrey Hodes in *First Fruits: A Harvest of 25 Years of Israeli Writing,* ed. James A. Michener (Philadelphia: The Jewish Publication Society of America, 1973), 80–138. The page references to the English translation are from that anthology.

7

Adumbrations of the Israeli "Identity Crisis" in Hebrew Literature of the 1960s

Arnold J. Band

> But is there a more terrible tyranny in the world than the tyranny of the saints? The wicked may condemn you to suffering, torment, terror. But the righteous don't let you live!

Towards the end of his 1965 novel, *The Living on the Dead* (208),[1] Aharon Megged has the plaintiff's lawyer, Evrat, read before the author-defendant, Mr. Jonas, a transcript of a brief statement the latter had made at a party. Jonas is being charged with breach of contract: he did not write a contracted book about the prototypical Zionist hero of the previous generation, one Abrasha Davidov. Jonas's own lawyer finally claims that he couldn't write it because of "a mental crisis" in his life. To disprove this claim, Evrat reads Jonas's statement that Davidov, in his heroic righteousness, was a tyrant and "if we want to live, it is our sacred duty to wipe out his memory for ever and ever!" The breach of contract was therefore deliberate. I cite this passage because it captures so vividly the matrix of the turbulent attitudes animating so much of Israeli fiction of the 1960s, fiction that so eerily adumbrates the so-called identity crisis of Israeli society discussed by social scientists in the 1980s and 1990s.

I refer to this identity crisis with hesitation because I think it is time to retire this tired cliché. Recent sociological studies (including one by James Clifford)[2] have taught us that identity is not stable and reifiable, but rather a flexible concept contingent upon changes in a person, his circumstances, and those he interacts with. Rather than speak of identity crises, we would be better advised to talk of transformations over a period of time, occurring at times very rapidly. In literary criticism the reification of identity crises is normal and frequent; what we often view as an identity crisis in fiction, for instance, is really the product of the conflict necessary to heighten the interest in plot. What we see is transformation structured and condensed to yield tense drama.

The transformation that interests me in this chapter is one that has been developing for some time in Israeli society, namely the gradual moving away from the so-called Zionist narrative that reigned supreme in the Jewish society of pre-Israel Palestine and subsequently in Israel through the 1950s. This was the narrative that educated generations of students and mobilized Jewish society to create the state and its many institutions. Viewing the past with the hopefully dispassionate eyes of the historian, we can indeed trace the crystallization of this narrative and its transformations. A fine example of this type of study is Yael Zrubavel's *Recovered Roots.*[3] Frequently when contemporary sociologists or political scientists study the state of Israeli society in the 1990s, a society in which ideals of the founders are notably attenuated, perhaps noticeably absent, they tend to attribute this dissipation to specific political events. Reaching backward from the present, they offer as candidates such events as the Lebanese War of 1982, or the decline of the Labor Party after the Yom Kippur War of 1973, or, at most, the problems engendered by the battlefield successes of the Six-Day War of 1967. The last is a favorite candidate for speculation especially since it fits in with the pressing political issues of the 1990s, the Intifada, and the peace negotiations between Israelis and Palestinians.

Anyone familiar with the developments in Israeli literature in the past two generations is fully aware that these political markers are inadequate for the task of tracing these transformations for two reasons: first, many aspects of the Zionist narrative began to change shortly after the establishment of the state in 1948; and, second, there are many facets of Israeli life—or of any human existence—that are not necessarily the products of political conflict.[4] Yizhar's early stories "The Prisoner" (1948) and "Ḥirbet Ḥizaʿah" (1949) are obvious literary articulations of the rejection of the optimism and triumphalism of the period, as are several novels portraying the disenchantment with kibbutz life.[5] Works of fiction written by Moshe Shamir, Aharon Megged, Nathan Shaham, and others in the 1950s reflect a brooding meditation over the failures of the state to fulfill the dreams of its founders.[6] This disappointment is not unique to Israel: it is characteristic of most writers who are sensitive to the inevitable gap between the dreams they had inherited and the realities they must live with. It is most acute in the early years after a revolution or the establishment of a new political entity. If we do not find this expression of disappointment, we can usually expect to discover that the regimes in which the writers live do not tolerate public expressions of criticism.

Israeli literary critics noticed this critique embedded in Israeli fiction long ago. In the 1960s it was obvious, as one can see from Gershon Shaked's essays on the literature of this period,[7] that a new generation with new perspectives had appeared, and this has subsequently been more fully documented by Nurith Gertz,[8] among others. It is now abundantly clear that in the imagination of the writers of Israeli fiction, the transformations often attributed to the 1967 war were well developed in the decade before that war.

This is the subject of a much later article by Hannan Hever (1990), which I deliberately cite because it is replete with brilliant readings, but also because, in my opinion, it is fundamentally flawed. In its cultural critical, postcolonialist mode, it reduces everything to the tensions between the majority and minority cultures, leaning heavily on the theories of Deleuze and Guattari as evident even in its title, "Minority Discourse of a National Majority: Israeli Fiction of the Early 1960s."[9] The majority/minority pair refers in Hever's writing to the Jewish-Arab tension which, he suggests, defines much of what one might call the Israeli identity. In doing so he joins forces with the "New Historians" and "Critical Sociologists," whose work is found, among other places, in the periodical *Te'oryah uviqqoret.*[10] These scholars, however, in their sweeping effort to reinvestigate and rewrite Israeli history, connect the repression of the Arab voice with the repression of other voices, including those of Mizraḥim (Middle Eastern and North African Jews) and women. Hever is far more reductive. Obviously deeply influenced by the publication of Anton Shammas's novel *Arabesqot* (1986), the first impressive book in Hebrew by an Israeli Arab, Hever reduces his focus to this one aspect of Israeli life and seeks to find manifestations of the Arab theme twenty years earlier, in the literature of the 1960s.[11]

Here, as elsewhere, I reject the attribution of any complex human event to any one cause or set of causes, such as the definition of self by the suppression of the other. Identities in both real life and in sophisticated literature are much too complex for this reductionism. While I agree that there are radical and new perspectives that inform the literature of the

1960s, I will offer an alternative—and, in my mind, less reductionist—rubric. Instead of limiting my focus to the Arab-Israeli tension, which, I believe, is still a minor theme in the literature of the period, I will expand it to include the entire range of intergenerational conflict, between that of the founding fathers of the nation and that of the first generation of Israeli writers. To do so I will deliberately use a different set of examples. I will use one of Hever's three examples, but will change the other two. Hever deals in his article with A. B. Yehoshua's "Facing the Forests" (1963), Amos Oz's "Nomad and Viper" (1964), and Amalia Kahana-Carmon's, "Heart of Summer, Heart of Light" (1965).[12] I will examine the Yehoshua story, too, but will replace the Oz story with his longer novel, *My Michael* (1968), and begin my study with Aharon Megged's novel *The Living on the Dead* (1965).[13] Like Hever, I select my examples to support my thesis, but I would argue that my thesis and examples are more representative of the literature of the 1960s as experienced by the readers of that period. I believe that my selection of specimens and the attendant analytic strategy will yield a more varied and authentic picture.

We begin with Megged's *The Living on the Dead* (1965), not because it is the best novel of the period—it is far from that—but because it captures the generational transition more clearly than any other book of the period (in fact, it captures it too clearly) . Though now relegated to a deserved secondary position among fictional works of the 1960s, it was, upon its publication, hugely successful and influential. As mentioned above, it purports to be the story told by a young writer, Jonas, of his inability to write a contracted book about Davidov, a hero of the previous generation, the typical hero of Labor Zionist fiction from the 1920s to the 1950s. In the process of telling how his life has disintegrated since he signed the contract, he actually records the story of this hero as background to his present problems. His narration is set in three different situations: his interviews with friends and relatives of the deceased hero; court scenes from the trial in which he is charged for breach of contract after he declares his inability to write the book; and his dissolute carousing with artist friends, mostly in a Tel Aviv night club. The stories he records in his notebook are hagiographic tales of devoted hard labor and prodigious heroism characteristic of the literature of the Third Aliyah and of Israeli school textbooks, so characteristic in fact that they border on parody.

We learn, of course, as the story progresses that Davidov was far from an ideal family man. He was rarely home, often sought out other women, was excessively demanding of his son, and frequently beat his daughter.

But precisely because Jonas was contracted to tell a hagiographic tale of the Zionist hero, he couldn't write it. The Oedipal relationship is obvious: the saintly reputation of the dead Davidov repressed Jonas. Jonas, on his part, portrays his own life as the antithesis of the public image of Davidov's life. A writer who could not write, he is often drunk, and after divorcing his caring wife, he pursues several different women. So while he claims he must wipe out Davidov's memory, he cannot do it and has nothing to replace it. We must deduce that part of the failure of the founders' generation lies in their failure to rear worthy sons and daughters. The bleakness of the picture that Megged paints here has nothing to do with the Holocaust, or with the Arab problem, or with the exploitation of Mizraḥi Jews by Ashkenazi Jews. The heroes here are defined not by these three crucial moments in Israeli history, but rather by the internal dynamic of Zionist efforts of state building and social engineering. While other motifs adhere to this matrix and complicate it, I would submit that without a clear understanding of this matrix, no reliable reading of Israeli literature is possible.

Megged's novel is particularly poignant since it was written not by a member of the generation that appeared on the scene in the 1960s, but by a veteran writer, a longtime member of a kibbutz who earned his reputation in the early, more heroic years of the state. When he wrote *The Living on the Dead,* Oz and Yehoshua were already rising stars in the literary pantheon. Megged's novel provides an interesting and illuminating backdrop for Amos Oz's first novel, *My Michael,* which appeared three years later and may help us fill what I consider a gaping lacuna in the many interpretations of the novel I have read.

At the end of his novel, Oz is careful to indicate that the date of its completion is May 1967, that is, before the outbreak of the Six-Day War. Clearly, he does not want the reader to confuse the issues of the novel with anything having to do with that war. The story, in fact, takes place in the 1950s and purports to be a memoir written by an unhappy woman, Hanah Gonen, in 1961 after ten years of her marriage to Dr. Michael Gonen, a geologist. Though she claims she is writing this memoir "because people I loved have died" and she wants to recapture and revitalize her power to love, one senses that she also may be motivated by revenge.

She traces the story of her marriage to Gonen from their first encounter as students, their meetings with future in-laws, their wedding, his grinding away at his doctorate, her pregnancy, all of which are the normal stages of a young couple in a bourgeois society, an ambiance that she, in her vague aspirations for an ideally romantic union, detests. She seeks to escape bourgeois mediocrity by fantasizing about scenes of domination and violence. In anger at her responsible husband, she goes on wild shopping sprees. Her refusal to accept reality is often so acute and provokes such outbreaks of violence that it easily borders on psychosis, for while one can sympathize with her disdain of bourgeois acquisitiveness and careerism, one cannot condone her wild fantasies about violence and rape. At the end of the novel, Hannah is furious at her husband, who seems to be having an affair with a student, an outrage she cannot tolerate since she has always considered him so dull and unimaginative. In her rage she fantasizes that the twin Arab brothers she had befriended in childhood are slipping across the Jerusalem border as terrorists to blow up a symbolic water tower. The description of their deed in her fantasy is conveyed in an orgy of verbal realization, and its consummation seems to bring her temporary psychic calm.

What is missing in the standard interpretation of the novel is any interrogation of the possible cause of Hannah Gonen's sense of *shemamah* (desolation), her acute malaise fueling her wild fantasies. If this were merely a novelistic portrait of a psychotic young lady, all the detailed social scenes and references to politics—the Sinai War, for instance—would be unnecessary. If Hannah were merely an Israeli version of Emma Bovary, seeking erotic excitement as an escape from humdrum bourgeois life, we would have her involvement in routine adulterous affairs rather than her violent fantasies. The heroine's family background is not sufficiently delineated to allow us to determine a specific source of her psychosis. There is no hint of anything in her childhood or adolescence that might motivate her adult behavior. We know that upon her father's death in 1943, when Hannah was thirteen, the family broke up and Hannah was sent to a religious boarding school. We have little information about the crucial years between 1943 and 1950, when she turns up as a student at the Hebrew University in Jerusalem where she meets Michael.

I suggest that this powerful, relentless malaise, this sense of alienation from society and even from nature, is an expression of the collapse of the ideological certitudes of the Zionist narrative in the 1950s and 1960s. Once the state had been established and people had to turn to the normal routines of making a living, buying household goods, and raising families, the dreams had become obsolete and even absurd. The days of the *ḥalutsim* (Zionist pioneers) were over, but their rhetoric lingered on; the gap between language and reality was palpable, a rich subject for satire. Michael Gonen adapts to this new, unromantic reality, because he was never a romantic figure; he had not, for instance, served in the pre-state Jewish fighting force, the Palmaḥ. Hannah Gonen, in contrast, had been a student of literature at the Hebrew University in Jerusalem, and her aspirations for fulfillment are boundless, hence unrealistic. She could never adapt to the realities of the "day after the revolution." As her communication with reality collapses, she turns to violence in a futile attempt to recapture a sense of existence and identity.

We turn, finally, to the Yehoshua story, "Facing the Forests" (1963), precisely because it contains the most obvious pairing of Jew and Arab and is interpreted by Hannan Hever as centering on the adoption by the majority figure, the Israeli, of the discourse of the minority, the Arab. In this story a peculiar, alienated Israeli graduate student takes a job as a forest watcher for the Jewish National Fund, and at the end of his six-month tour of duty the forest is burned down, apparently by a mute Arab employed by the same Jewish reforestation agency. As the forest burns down, one can detect the ruins of the Arab village that the forest, planted by the Jews, had covered. The author is obviously criticizing the violence done to the indigenous Arab population of the country by the Zionist enterprise, which prided itself on the reforestation of the desolate land. This aspect of the story is undeniable, as is the adoption by the unnamed forest-watcher of some of the characteristics of the aged Arab; one can therefore understand why Hever found the schema of Deleuze and Guattari helpful.

Yet there is much more to the story than this; the Jewish-Arab relationship is, at best, only one of many interlocking themes, and a secondary one at that. The story centers on the nameless hero, one of the typical passive, pathetic men who populate Yehoshua's fiction in the 1960s and even later. This type of rootless hero is the inverse image of the purposive, active hero of Zionist fiction of the previous period who had become a tiresome cliché by the early 1950s. The entire story, as Yael Zerubavel has demonstrated, is the inverse of a story, "Anshei bereshit" (The Founders), published by Eliezer Smolly in 1933.[14] In that story, an archetypal *ḥaluts* named Hermoni heroically tends a forest that is burned down by a malevolent Arab. Pushing Zerubavel's statement one step further, I would argue that the intertextual comparisons are so striking that one must read the Yehoshua story as a parody of the Smolly story, and, most important, the listless Yehoshua hero as a parody of the dynamic Smolly hero. Following the pattern discerned by Shaked and Gertz, among others, we note that in Yehoshua's story the hero seeks to revive his sense of being and belonging by an act of violence, such as the burning of a cherished forest. While he does not actually start the forest fire, he seems to tacitly inspire the Arab to do so. The act of violence, however, does not succeed in redeeming the hero from his ennui; he returns to the city as forlorn and depressed as he was before. Though the story does impart a greater sense of realism than Yehoshua's previous stories, we are, I would argue, still in the genre of magic realism; the consciousness of the narrator is often so close to that of his hero that we often wonder whether the story is actually taking place in any identifiable reality or just in the mind of this very peculiar character. Certainly, there are many scenes—the stillness of the forest, the relationship to the aged Arab and his pre-adolescent daughter, even the fire itself—that make more sense and are, indeed, more compelling if seen as figments of the hero's fervid imagination.

The Hebrew reader can easily recognize the place of such a character in the evolution of the Hebrew literary hero, which has been fully described by Simon Halkin in several seminal works.[15] European Hebrew writers of the nineteenth century had imagined an enlightened, westernized hero, a *maskil,* who would bring redemption to his benighted brethren of Eastern Europe. The *maskil* type was mostly discredited after the pogroms of 1881–82; he was replaced in the late nineteenth and early twentieth centuries by romanticized traditional pious Jewish hero types or by the *talush,* the deracinated, alienated hero found in works by Yosef Hayyim Brenner, Uri Nisan Gnessin, and S.Y. Agnon, fused, perhaps, with echoes of Camus and Sartre. The *talush,* in turn, was replaced, at least in the prestate literature of Palestine, by the *ḥaluts* of the Zionist narrative. Following this evolutionary pattern, we can say that with the disintegration of the Zionist narrative, we can discover in Israeli literature of the 1960s the reemergence of the *talush,* albeit in an Israeli guise. Yehoshua's *talush* is thus defined not so much by the other, the "minority" figure that he tries to emulate, as Hever would see it, as by the lack of any authoritative model, now that the *ḥaluts* model is passé.

In rejecting Hever's majority-minority model in favor of the collapse of the *ḥaluts* model understood broadly as the literary manifestation of the dissipation of the ideals of the Zionist narrative, we are not substituting one reductionism for another, but are rather offering a complex, multifaceted explanation for a wide array of transformations in what we might call the evolving Israeli identity. Certainly, the abundant evidence marshaled by Shaked and Gertz supports our contention that we are dealing here with a gradual transformation of many aspects of Israeli life, not merely of the attitude of Israeli writers to the Arab minority. We should place Israeli fictional heroes in the broader context of Hebrew literature as it has undergone significant transformations over the past century. These transformations are manifold and involve the constant shifting of centers and peripheries, the emergence of new, hitherto repressed voices such as those of women, Mizraḥi Jews, and Arabs. Societies are not static; they change, at times with greater velocity than at other times. The velocity of change in the first years of any state or revolution are so understandably intense that radical, wrenching displacements should be accepted as the norm, not the exception. The literary historian should comprehend these changes, however bewildering and chaotic, as the normal process of history.

Notes

1. Aharon Megged, *The Living on the Dead,* trans. Misha Louvish (New York: McCall, 1971).
2. James Clifford, *The Predicament of Culture: Twentieth-Century Ethnography, Literature, and Art* (Cambridge: Harvard University Press, 1988).
3. Yael Zerubavel, *Recovered Roots: Collective Memory and the Making of the Israeli National Tradition* (Chicago: University of Chicago Press, 1995).
4. This transformation is traced in Gerson Shaked, *Hasipporet haʿivrit: 1880–1980,* vol. 4 (Tel Aviv: Keter, 1993).
5. See Shaked, *Hasipporet haʿivrit* and Nurit Gertz, *Hirbet Hizaʿah vehaboqer shlemoḥorat* (Tel Aviv: Porter Institute, 1983).
6. Shaked, *Hasipporet haʿivrit.*
7. Gershon Shaked, *Gal ḥadash basipporet haʿivrit* (Merhavyah: Sifriat Poalim, 1971).
8. See both Gertz, *Ḥirbet Ḥizaʿah* and, more recently, Nurith Gertz, *Shevuyah baḥalomah* (Tel Aviv: Am Oved, 1995).
9. Hannan Hever, "Minority Discourse of a National Majority: Israeli Fiction in the Early Sixties," *Prooftexts* 10, no. 1 (January 1990): 129–48.
10. The emergence of the "New Historians" and the "Critical Sociologists" in Israel over the past decade has generated a broad literature in both books and periodicals. For a tentative summary and bibliographies see *History and Memory* 7, no. 1 (Spring-Summer 1995) and, more recently, *Teʾoryah uviqqoret* 8 (Summer 1996). For literary criticism in the light of the "New Historians," see Yitzhak Laor's *Anu kotvim otakh moledet* (Tel Aviv: Hakibbutz Hameuchad, 1995). This collection of essays has been critiqued in Gerson Shaked, "Aḥer: al *Anu kotvim otakh moledet* (1995) meʾet Yitzhak Laor" in *Alpayim* 1 (1996): 1–72.
11. Hever's reliance on the theories of Gilles Deleuze and Felix Guattari as presented in their *Kafka: Towards a Minor Literature,* trans. Dana Polan (Min-

neapolis: University of Minnesota Press, 1986) are standard for "cultural critics," particularly those who follow the postcolonialist theories of Edward Said. The applicability of these theories are convincing in Hever's article on Shammas's *Arabesques,* "Hebrew in an Israeli Arab Hand: Six Miniatures on Anton Shammas's *Arabesques,*" *Cultural Critique* 7 (1987): 47–76, reprinted in *The Nature and Context of Minority Discourse,* eds. Abdul R. JanMohamed and David Lloyd (New York: Oxford University Press, 1990), 264–93. They become less convincing as he attempts to apply his ideas to the entire corpus of Israeli literature. In a subsequent article, "Lehakot baʿaqevo shel Achilles," in *Alpayim* 1 (June 1989): 186–93, [English version in *Tikkun* 4/5 (Sept./Oct. 1989): 30–33], Hever considers the new openness of Israeli literature to Palestinian writers, usually translated from Arabic, as a major cultural breakthrough, an attack on the "Achilles heel" of the Zionist narrative that has dominated Israeli Hebrew literature. The theories of Deleuze and Guattari, especially "deterritorialization," support Hever's argument only if inverted, only if the features of the minority culture are appropriated—consciously or unconsciously—by the majority literature.

12. The first appearances of these stories are noteworthy: A.B. Yehoshua's "Facing the Forests" (Mul hayaʿarot), *Qeshet* 5 (Spring 1963):18–45; Amos Oz's "Nomad and Viper" (Navvadim vatsefa), *Haʾarets,* Feb. 7, 1964; Amaliah Kahana-Carmon's "Heart of Summer, Heart of Light" (Lev haqayits, lev haʾor), *Molad* 23 (dated Dec. 1965; actually appeared in Sept. 1966): 576–613.
13. Aharon Megged, *Haḥay al hamet* (Tel Aviv: Am Oved, 1965); Amos Oz, *Mikhaʾel shelli* (Tel Aviv: Am Oved, 1968).
14. Yael Zerubavael, "The Forest as National Idiom," *Israel Studies* 1, no. 1 (Spring 1996): 60–99.
15. Simon Halkin, *Mavo lasipporet haʿivrit: reshimot lefi hartsaʾot* (Jerusalem: Mifal Hashikhpul, 1958), 339–43; Simon Halkin, *Derakhim vetsidei derakhim besifrutenu,* vols. 1–3 (Jerusalem: Akademon, 1969). For an expansion and updating of Halkin's thesis, see Oz Almog, *Hatsabbar: deyoqan* (Tel Aviv: Am Oved, 1997).

8

Arabic and/or Hebrew: The Languages of Arab Writers in Israel*

Ami Elad-Bouskila

Most literature is written by residents of a particular country or homeland, and its language is usually the native tongue of the writers. Contemporary societies are not homogeneous, however, but made up of those who speak and write in the language of the majority and those who speak and write in other languages. Thus, when a group of writers that is not part of the majority chooses to write in the language of the majority, the question of motivation arises. Why do they do it? One must also distinguish between those who write only in the majority language, which is not their native tongue, and those who write in both languages—their native tongue and the language of the majority. These categories encompass a host of very different cases, and these differences are reflected in the attitudes toward the writer of both the surrounding majority culture and the minority language group.

One of the most fascinating subjects in the study of modern Palestinian literature concerns the language used by Palestinian Arab writers who live in Israel. Palestinian writers who reside in the other two Palestinian locales, the West Bank and the Gaza Strip, as well as those who emigrated to the Diaspora in Arab countries and elsewhere, have clearly chosen to write in Arabic. A few writers, such as Jabrā Ibrāhīm Jabrā (1919–94), wrote in both Arabic and English and composed many translations from English to Arabic.[1] Most Palestinian writers who were born in the various diasporas, especially in North America (like Arab writers in general), no longer write in Arabic but write instead in English.[2] One prominent example is Naomi Shihab Nye (1952–), who has published books of poetry and prose and has also composed translations (mostly of poetry) from Arabic to English.[3] In addition to Arabic or one of the languages of North or South America, Palestinian literature is also written in European languages, especially French and German. One prominent Palestinian writer in France is the prolific writer, playwright, and critic Afnān al-Qāsim, who generally writes in Arabic, with some of his criticism also produced in French.[4]

This twentieth-century phenomenon of emigration to another country with some writers continuing to write in their mother tongue, some writers beginning to write bilingually, and the younger generation born in the new community writing only in the new language, is not unique to Arab or Palestinian writers. This phenomenon, which produces bilingual writing, is related to economic, cultural, and social elements that are factors in the immigration process.

There is an additional universal phenomenon in which authors write not only in their native tongue or the local language, but also in an additional language, the language of the conqueror. This takes place, of course, in countries that were under an extended period of foreign rule, such as African and Asian countries controlled at one time by European or American colonial powers. One dramatic example is India, in which, under the impact of British rule, English became the official language. The primary reason for the dominance of English in India has been the competition among the various Dravidian languages, such as Tamil. To avoid granting "cultural imperialism" to Hindi, the use of English has been maintained.

Writers in Arab and North African states have chosen at various times to write in the languages of the colonial powers that ruled them, either English or French. In countries like Algeria, for example, the choice to write in the language of the conqueror has typically progressed through four stages. In the first stage, the local writers composed in the language of the conqueror, which was considered the language of "culture." In the second stage, when the colonial power left, a reaction set in and the local writers began composing in their own language. In the third stage, some writers again began composing in the language of the former conqueror, this time as a deliberate choice in the new circumstances. And in the fourth stage, writers returned to composing in the local language following the increased religious climate and the rise of fundamentalist Islam.

The above examples from both the Arab and the non-Arab world sharpen the uniqueness of the phenomenon to be explored here and also provide context and insight into it. Within the singularity of Palestinian literature in the corpus of modern Arabic literatures, Palestinian literature written in Israel stands out.[5] This literature is unique by definition, since most Arabic literature is written in Arab lands or where a local Arab community demands it. Egyptian literature, for example, is written only in Egypt, while modern Palestinian literature lacks a state and is written in various locations. Modern Palestinian literature from its inception was written not only in historical Palestine, but also outside it, in Arab capitals such as Cairo and Damascus. Palestinian literature written in Arabic in Israel is different from its sisters in that it is written in a Middle Eastern country where Hebrew is the main language and Arabic is only the second official language. Which language will be used for their writing by Arab Palestinians in Israel is an open question; while this is one of the fundamental issues related to the literary endeavor, it also belongs to the realm outside literature. The issue of the language of writing is related not only to language, but also to territory, the target audience, the goals of the writer, and the period of writing. No Arab writers in Israel choose to write only in Hebrew, but some write in both Arabic and Hebrew. It is important to examine when and why Arab writers in Israel choose to write in either Arabic or Hebrew or in both languages.

Israeli Jews Writing in Hebrew and Arabic

A parallel phenomenon exists among Jewish writers who lived in Arabic-speaking countries and wrote in Arabic. Their contribution to the development of modern Arabic literature in the early twentieth century is well known, especially in Iraq.[6] Some Jews living in Arab states felt that Arab culture was an inseparable part of their own culture. They saw no contradiction between being Jewish and being members of the Arab culture. Therefore these Jews, especially in Iraq and Egypt, were part of the literary movements of the nineteenth and twentieth centuries. The Jewish writers wrote in Arabic for an Arabic-speaking public, without differentiating between Jewish and Arab readers, as they shared the same territory and the same Arab culture.

When most of the Jews in the Arab states immigrated to Israel, the writers among them for a short while continued to write both fiction and nonfiction in Arabic, especially during the 1950s and 1960s.[7] Some of these writers stopped writing in Arabic in response to the conflict between Jews and Arabs and, in addition, out of a desire to contribute to the revitalization of modern Hebrew literature. Others continued to write in Arabic and to contribute to Arab journals and newspapers works of fiction, literary criticism, and writings in other genres.

Shimon Ballas (Adīb al-Qāṣṣ), born in Iraq in 1930, and Sami Michael (Samīr Mārid), born in Iraq in 1926, are two of the most notable examples of Jewish writers who began writing in Arabic, but in the early 1960s shifted their literary activity to Hebrew.[8] There is no fundamental difference between Ballas and Michael in terms of their Hebrew writing careers. Both underwent the same process, at first writing Arabic fiction and nonfiction in Iraq, then making the move to Israel, while continuing to write primarily in Arabic, and gradually making the transition to both languages, until their decision to use Hebrew as their literary language. Ballas published *Hamaʿabarah* (The Transit Camp), his first Hebrew novel, in 1964, and since then has published many Hebrew novels and short stories. He has not, however, completely stopped writing in Arabic. While he uses Hebrew for his literary works, his academic work about modern Arabic literature is in Arabic as well as in Hebrew and European languages. He is the editor of the Arabic journal *al-Karmil,* which is published by Haifa University. Like many of his colleagues, he is also a translator from Arabic to Hebrew, especially of Palestinian writing.[9]

Michael began his career in the Israeli Communist Party and published articles in Arabic in *al-Jadīd* and *al-Ittiḥād.*[10] His first novel, *Shavim veshavim yoter* (Equal and More Equal), appeared in 1974, and since then he has published more than half a dozen novels in Hebrew. *Viqtoryah* (1994),[11] his most recent novel, has won popular acclaim and seems to have installed him in the canon of modern Hebrew literature, while giving legitimacy to his Israeliness. In contrast to Ballas, Michael has chosen, in his words, to cut himself off from writing in Arabic. He has not, however, completely broken his ties to Arabic literature, as evidenced by his translation into Hebrew of the Cairene trilogy of Najīb Maḥfūẓ (1911–),[12] as well as by the fact that he continues to follow the developments of literature that appears in the Arab world.[13]

In general, Jewish writers who immigrated to Israel in the 1950s from the Arab states and Iraq in particular underwent a process of Israelization. During the course of this process, the Jewish writers aspired to become part of Israeli Jewish society and hence consciously chose to abandon their mother tongue partially or completely for the sake of the language of their nation.[14]

There are, however, two outstanding exceptions to this process: Yitzhak Bar-Moshe and Samīr Naqqāsh. Yitzhak Bar-Moshe was born in Baghdad in 1927 and after immigrating to Israel has held various jobs, primarily in journalism. He has continued to write mainly in Arabic, beginning with his first anthology of stories *Warā' al-Sūr* (Beyond the Wall), published in 1972. Since then Bar-Moshe has published many books in Arabic and is currently the editor of the Arabic-language publication of the Israeli Foreign Ministry. Despite Bar-Moshe's many jobs in the service of the government, which ostensibly would indicate his integration and acceptance into Israeli society, he has always preferred to write in Arabic. Interestingly, Bar-Moshe's writing in Arabic commands attention not just in the local Arab press, but also in the foreign Arab press, especially in Egypt.[15]

Samīr Naqqāsh represents this phenomenon of continuing to write in Arabic to the extreme. Born in Baghdad in 1936, Naqqāsh immigrated to Israel as an adolescent in 1951. Although he is one of the younger Iraqi Jewish writers, if not the youngest, Naqqāsh insists on writing exclusively in Arabic. Moreover, most of his colleagues, such as Sami Michael and Yitzhak Bar-Moshe, Hebraicized their last names and sometimes their first names as well, while Samīr Naqqāsh has rejected this trend and almost never uses his Hebrew first name. Following the appearance of his first collection of short stories *al-Khaṭa'* (The Mistake), in 1971, Naqqāsh has published many short stories, plays, and novels. Like some of his Iraqi Jewish colleagues, Naqqāsh translates from Hebrew to Arabic, which is almost his only professional connection to Hebrew.

Why would someone who immigrated at such a young age prefer to create and live in an "Arabic bubble," deliberately cutting himself off from his Israeli Jewish, Hebrew-speaking environment? One would expect that since Naqqāsh moved to Israel at a relatively young age he would have made the transition to Hebrew fairly rapidly, but the opposite has been true. Naqqāsh has felt foreign, exiled, and alienated in the Israeli Jewish environment and has thus continued to cling to his Arabic cultural heritage. Indeed, Samīr Naqqāsh has even announced his desire to move to an Arab country, although he has not yet carried this out. Here we are witnesses to a conflict between, on the one hand, the territory and language of the community and, on the other hand, the desires and cultural heritage of the writer. The national barrier is difficult to surmount. As a Jew living in Israel and writing in Arabic, Naqqāsh has not achieved wide popularity, despite his formidable talents and critical acclaim.[16]

Naqqāsh addresses the question of language in his Hebrew article

"Mah attem rotsim mimmenni? ani shomer al ha'otonomyah shelli!" (What Do You Want From Me? I'm Protecting My Autonomy!):

> Arabic is the first language I grew accustomed to when I learned to speak; it became my second nature, I love it and am devoted to it even after having immigrated to Israel at age twelve, where I filled in my missing vocabulary, and it is my most powerful means of expression derived from an ardent love for it. Besides all that, it is a language known for its perfection and rich heritage; if we compare it to Hebrew, which was dormant for thousands of years, then revived and returned to development a short time ago, we find that it [Arabic] is more beautiful and richer by several fold.[17]

Naqqāsh testifies that there are four psychological, social, and economic factors that created a situation in which he writes in Arabic and distances himself from Israeli matters: (1) his uprooting from Iraq, which was a form of holocaust, in his words; (2) the social and economic humiliation to which he and his family were subject when they moved to Israel; (3) the death of his father a short time after their immigration to Israel; and (4) the fact that he still views himself as Iraqi for all intents and purposes. Naqqāsh is aware of the fact that he is expected to become absorbed in Israel and to begin, as part of a natural process, to write in Hebrew. Even the famed Egyptian writer Najīb Maḥfūẓ has expressed his opinion about this complex matter in a letter to Naqqāsh: "The next step that I expect from you is that in the future you will write in Hebrew and be translated into Arabic. . . ."[18] Naqqāsh, however, takes the position that it is not his job to meet the expectations of others.

Israeli Arabs Writing in Hebrew and Arabic

Most of the Arab writers who live in Israel write in Arabic, although a small number write both in Arabic and Hebrew. Why should this be unusual, given the existence of similar examples of bilingual writing not just in the world at large but even in other parts of the Arab world? There is a fundamental difference between the general phenomenon of writing in the language of the other and the phenomenon in Israel of Arab authors writing bilingually. The political situation in the Middle East, which has involved an extended conflict between the Arab and Israeli communities and an ongoing state of war between Israel and some Arab states, gives special significance to the fact that these authors write in Hebrew. These authors are acclaimed by the Hebrew reading community, although some, such as Naʿīm ʿArāydī, are regarded by the Arab world and some Israeli Arabs as traitors to Arab culture and are often condemned.

It is important to note that only a limited number of Arabs began writing in Hebrew, and these writers continued to write in Arabic, for example the veteran writer ʿAṭallāh Manṣūr (1934–) and the younger writers Naʿīm ʿArāydī (1948–) and Anton Shammas (1950–). Together with the Arab writers who write in Hebrew there is also a group of Israeli Arab writers who use Arabic for their literary work, but Hebrew for their nonfiction articles. This includes, for example, Imīl Ḥabībī (Emile Habiby) (1921–96) and Samīḥ al-Qāsim (1939–), who have achieved prominence not just in the Arab world, but also in the Hebrew-speaking world and media.

The conscious decision of Imīl Ḥabībī and Samīḥ al-Qāsim to use Arabic for fiction, in the case of Ḥabībī, and for poetry, in the case of al-Qāsim, was presumably based on cultural and political considerations, and not just because they are more fluent in Arabic than in Hebrew. Moreover, Imīl Ḥabībī, who is considered not just one of the major twentieth-century figures in Palestinian literature, but also in Arabic literature as a whole, wrote an autobiographical text in Hebrew. But this fact did not prevent one of the respected publishing houses in the Arab world from publishing it in Arabic and mentioning its linguistic roots.[19] The fact that both these authors write for the Hebrew press, give frequent interviews in Hebrew on Israeli radio and television, and appear in literary evenings and interviews on subjects broader than Arabic literature indicates beyond doubt their involvement in the spiritual, social, and political life of Israel. Moreover, Samīḥ al-Qāsim also translates from Arabic to Hebrew. His choice to edit and translate an anthology of Hebrew poets, as well as to edit an anthology of the Israeli Jewish poet Ronni Somek, demonstrates his significant connection to Hebrew literature.[20]

One of the most salient features of Israeli Arab authors who write in Hebrew is the fact that most of them are Christian or Druze, rather than Muslim. This is related to ongoing ethnic tensions between Muslims, on the one hand, and Christians and Druze, on the other, fanned by both the Lebanon War in 1982 and the growth of the Islamic revivalist movement throughout the Middle East.

Of the two groups of Arab authors who write in Hebrew, clearly the Druze, whose foremost writer is Naʿīm ʿArāydī, are more integrated into Israeli society, primarily as a result of their compulsory service in the Israeli army. This group is exposed to the Hebrew language during their compulsory service in the Israeli army (to which most other Arabs are not subjected), through university education in which the language of instruction is Hebrew, or through the media. The exposure to Hebrew of these writers accelerates the process of their integration into the life of Israeli Jewish culture and can account for the relatively large number of Druze who write in both Arabic and Hebrew.

It is also interesting to note which literary genres Arab writers choose for their writing in Hebrew. Israeli Arab authors use Hebrew to write poetry, novels, and short stories, as well as literary criticism and articles. But indisputably the most popular genre in Hebrew for Israeli Arab writers is poetry. This strikes me as evidence of their internalization of the Hebrew language, as poetry is the most personal medium for a writer. (When Jewish writers lived in Spain during the Golden Age of the medieval period, they used Arabic for all genres except poetry, which was generally written in Hebrew.) A small number of Arab writers write poetry in Hebrew as well as in Arabic. Among these, the two most prominent poets since the 1970s have been Anton Shammas and Naʿīm ʿArāydī.[21]

Israeli Arabs who write in Hebrew can be divided into two general categories: those who wrote from the birth of the State of Israel until the late 1960s and those who have been writing since then. There is a sharp delineation between these two periods. In the first period, following the recent birth of the State of Israel and the attendant animosities between Jews and Arabs, we know of two Arab writers who wrote in Hebrew, ʿAṭallāh Manṣūr (1934–) and Rāshid Ḥusayn (1936–77). During the second period there were social, political, demographic, economic, and cultural changes in Israel, including the lifting of Israeli military rule over the Arab sector, that accelerated the process of the Israelization of at least some Israeli Arabs. These changes allowed for the emergence of many Arab writers writing in Hebrew, most prominently Naʿīm ʿArāydī and Anton Shammas. In the first period mostly prose was written in Hebrew, while in the second period, Arabs wrote both prose and poetry in Hebrew.

The fact that in the first twenty years of the state Arab authors in Israel did not write in Hebrew (with the few exceptions noted above) points to the fact that efforts to relate Arab society to Jewish society in Israel were private rather than collective. The linkage took place primarily in the fields of journalism and fiction, especially in Arabic newspapers and journals that appeared in the 1950s, whether sponsored by the Israeli Jewish establishment, such as *al-Mirṣād, al-Yawm, Ḥaqīqat al-Amr,* or *al-*

Anbāʾ; or by the Israeli Communist Party, including *al-Ittiḥād* and *al-Jadīd.* In both types of periodicals, Arabs and Jews all wrote in Arabic. In between, attempts were made, some successful and others not, to found independent or quasi-independent newspapers and journals in the 1950s, such as *al-Wasīṭ* and *al-Mujtamaʿ*.

ʿAṭallāh Manṣūr was the only Arab writer who published a narrative text in Hebrew during the first period, namely, his novel *Beʾor ḥadash* (In a New Light), issued in 1966 by a minor publishing house.[22] To understand the background to the Hebrew writing of Manṣūr, a brief sketch of his life would be useful. Manṣūr, born in the village of Jish in 1934, completed high school in 1949, and moved to Kibbutz Sha'ar Ha'amakim, where he lived for a year when he was seventeen years old. Manṣūr then worked as a journalist for the anti-establishment weekly *Haʿolam hazeh* (1954–56) and wrote for the daily *Haʾarets* for many years. In 1983, Manṣūr was one of the founders of the Arabic newspaper *al-Ṣinnāra,* and is a member of the editorial board to this day.[23]

The very fact that as a young man Manṣūr chose to live in Jewish society reflects his tendency to flaunt conventions of Arab society that not many dared to defy. Manṣūr writes in an article that he was not the first Israeli Arab intellectual to publish in Hebrew, but was preceded by Rāshid Ḥusayn, who wrote Hebrew poetry and even translated poetry from Hebrew to Arabic, as well as Ṣabrī Jirias, who wrote a book in Hebrew about the Arabs in Israel.[24] Manṣūr, however, is aware of how strange it was for him to choose to write in Hebrew during the early years of the state. He relates this choice to the cultural, social, and political situation of the Arabs in Israel, who found themselves between a rock and a hard place. On the one hand, they were called traitors by the Arab states for not abandoning their land and, on the other hand, the Israeli government viewed them as a fifth column. Manṣūr asserts that when he wrote his first novel in Arabic, *Wa-Baqiyat Samīra,* published by the Histadrut in 1962,[25] he was harshly condemned by the Hebrew press and accused of hostility toward Israel and the Jews. He then decided to write a novel in Hebrew with only one motivation: vengeance. He wanted to take revenge on the most important Israeli Jewish ideal of the time, the kibbutz. Thus, he wrote in Hebrew out of anger and a desire to humiliate this ideal. To his amazement and bewilderment, the Hebrew novel not only failed to anger the Jewish critics, they generally heaped praise upon it. Manṣūr suggests two possible explanations for the good reviews. The first reason is that while his first book, *Wa-Baqiyat Samīra,* written in Arabic, was reviewed by so-called experts on Arab affairs who considered their role to be censors of the enemy, the critics who reviewed his Hebrew novel held liberal views that led them to have a positive reaction to it. The second reason was that his Jewish readers were amazed and impressed that a Gentile could use Hebrew as a literary medium.[26]

The writers of the second period, who have been active since the early 1970s, have contributed to three central spheres of writing: the media, fiction, and translations. They include both veteran authors and poets who wrote and published in the first period, such as Imīl Ḥabībī, Samīḥ al-Qāsim, Sālim Jubrān, and ʿAṭallāh Manṣūr, as well as younger writers who began publishing in the second period, such as Nazīh Khayr, Naʿīm ʿArāydī, Anton Shammas, Sihām Dāwūd, and Asad ʿAzzī. What have been the factors that led Arabs to write in Hebrew during this second period, and do these differ from the external and internal factors in the first twenty years of the State of Israel? The political considerations have remained, but they have markedly changed. There has been a political transformation following the confrontations between Israel and the Arab and Palestinian world in the 1967 and 1973 wars, the Lebanon War of 1982, the Intifada that erupted in 1987, the Declaration of Principles with the Palestinians in 1993, the peace treaty with the Jordanians in 1994, and the attempts at peace agreements with Syria and Lebanon. All have profoundly influenced the overall relations between Israel and its neighbors, as well as the web of relations between Jews and Arabs within Israel, as Israeli Arabs have taken an increasingly active role in the process, especially in the context of the Palestinian National Authority headed by Yasser Arafat.

There has also been a marked transformation in the media between the first two decades of the state and the most recent twenty-five years. Changes have occurred in all the media, especially newspapers and journals, not only quantitatively, but also in terms of their greater variety and openness. As for the electronic media, television did not even exist during the first era, having been introduced to Israel in 1968. Today there are two TV channels in Israel, as well as the option of tuning in to radio and TV broadcasts from various Arab states, which allows Israeli Arabs to be exposed to what is going on in the Arab and Muslim world.

During the first period, most of the Arab population in Israel was rural, with approximately 150,000 inhabitants. Today, the Arab minority in Israel is over 800,000 strong, some living in Arab cities such as Nazareth, Shafāʿamr (Shfaram in Hebrew), and Umm al-Faḥm (pronounced Umm al-Faḥim), as well as the mixed cities of Haifa, Ramle, and Jaffa. In addition, there is no question that education in Israel, both in the Jewish and Arab sectors, has also undergone a metamorphosis since the 1970s. Until then, the number of Arabs who had more than an elementary school education was limited, and among Israeli Arabs there were only a small number of writers and readers of journals and newspapers. The dramatic increase in the education of Israeli citizens, including the Arabs, in the past twenty-five years has brought about changes in employment and media-consumption patterns, increased the number of girls in school, raised the level of education of the writers, and improved the quality of periodicals.

In recent years more and more Arab writers have acquired their high school education in Jewish schools conducted in Hebrew, including Sihām Dāwūd and Naʿīm ʿArāydī, and some, such as Naʿīm ʿArāydī and Anton Shammas, also did their university training in Hebrew. The effect is that Arab writers in Israel have not only a greater command of Hebrew, but also a much more complex understanding of Jewish reality. Thus, we see more Arab writers translating literary texts from Hebrew into Arabic; striking examples of this phenomenon are Anton Shammas in the 1970s and 1980s and Samīḥ al-Qāsim and Nazīh Khayr in the 1980s.[27] Anton Shammas, Naʿīm ʿArāydī, and Salmān Maṣālḥa have also translated stories, poems, and novels from modern Arabic into Hebrew, mainly in the late 1980s and early 1990s.[28]

Other than Naʿīm ʿArāydī, the only example, to the best of my knowledge, of an Israeli Arab writer who began writing in Hebrew and then switched to bilingual writing is the poet Sihām Dāwūd. She was born in Ramle (1952–) and moved to Haifa. Dāwūd states that Hebrew and Arabic are both part of her culture, but that she first wrote in Hebrew because she had attended a Jewish school in Ramle.[29] In this, Dāwūd differs from her colleagues in the second period, most of whom began their literary careers in Arabic, from which they switched into Hebrew. Common to all is that these writers did not completely abandon Arabic, but rather added Hebrew as a language of writing. Anton Shammas is to some extent an exception as he not only wrote his most recent works in Hebrew, but afterwards he did not return to writing in Arabic. Unlike Shammas, Naʿīm ʿArāydī has taken pains to write in Arabic and be involved in the Arab literary world as well.[30]

This bilingual writing characterizes Arab writers in the second period, primarily those in fiction and translation. For some of these writers, there sometimes appears to be a confusion or a blurring of the differences between writing and translation, especially for ʿArāydī, Shammas, Dāwūd, and Nazīh Khayr. The latter writes not just for newspapers and journals, but also publishes anthologies and translates together with Samīḥ al-Qāsim, especially from Hebrew to Arabic.[31]

The Arab writers in Israel in the second period were born at about the time of Israeli independence or soon after. The period of the first decades of the state was a decisive one in shaping these writers, including ʿArāydī, Dāwūd, and Shammas, in their adolescence and young adulthood. These writers were influenced by the political, social, and cultural realities of the Arab world in the mid-1960s. Most Arab states had already achieved independence and were preoccupied with state-building. The glorification of Nasserism was past its prime and the process of urbanization in the Arab world had gathered momentum. As Israeli Arabs, these writers did not remain indifferent to the turning points of the 1960s and 1970s, which included the trauma that gripped the Arab world after the 1967 war and the perception in the Arab world that the 1973 war provided a restoration of Arab pride.[32]

In addition, this group of Israeli Arab writers were influenced by developments in Hebrew and Arabic literature as well as world literature during this period. In the 1960s, Hebrew literature abandoned, to some extent, its tendency from before Israeli independence until the late 1950s to recruit for the cause of the collective. Writers such as Amos Oz, A. B. Yehoshua, Amalia Kahana-Carmon, Pinhas Sadeh, Yehoshua Kenaz, and others enriched and varied the literary inventory in the 1960s.[33] As for world literature in the late 1960s, the influence of the major literatures in the United States and Europe diminished, while the literature of South America, until then considered marginal, burst upon the scene, thanks in large measure to the novel *One Hundred Years of Solitude,* by Colombian writer Gabriel García Márquez.[34] Arabic literature flourished in the 1960s, especially in the genres of the novel, novella, and short story. This development was led primarily by such Egyptian writers as Najīb Maḥfūẓ (1911–), Fatḥī Ghānim (1924–99), and ʿAbd al-Ḥakīm Qāsim (1935–90). In Lebanon, the major writer was Laylā Baʿlabakkī (1936–); and in Syria, Zakariyyā Tāmir (1931–) and Ḥannā Mīna (1924–) were the outstanding writers. From Iraq, we can cite Fu'ād al-Takarlī (1922–) and Muḥammad Khuḍayyir (1940–). In Sudan, al-Ṭayyib Ṣāliḥ (1929–) and Ibrāhīm Isḥāq Ibrāhīm (1946–) tower over the others. The influence of al-Ṭayyib Ṣāliḥ on Arab writers in Israel, such as Zakī Darwīsh (1944–), Muḥammad ʿAlī Ṭāhā (1941–), and Riyāḍ Baydas (1960–) was profound from the late 1960s on. Prominent Arab writers since the 1960s from Saudi Arabia, Kuwait, and the Gulf states have included

Laylā al-ʿUthmān (1945–) and Sharīfa al- Shamlān (1947–); and writers from the Maghrib have included Muḥammad Zifzāf (1945–), Muḥammad Barrāda (1938–), and others.[35] In short, the literary and cultural activity of the Arab world in the 1960s was at a zenith, and ripples of it reached Israel as well. We must keep in mind, however, that until 1967, books from Arab countries almost never reached Israel. This situation changed drastically in the wake of the 1967 war, when Israeli Arab writers were exposed to more Arab newspapers, journals, and books and could meet with Arab and especially Palestinian writers.

As for the influence of Hebrew writing on Israeli Arab literature, we cannot make a claim for a significant impact either on the Arabs writing in Arabic or on those writing in both Arabic and Hebrew.[36] Young Arab writers did, however, use literature in Hebrew translation to gain access to writing from around the world. In other words, Hebrew was influential as a bridge to other cultures, although language is never just a mediator, but functions as a cultural world with its own codes and indicators. Anton Shammas describes well the process in which Arab writers drew sustenance from both Arabic and Hebrew literature:

> Today the younger generation of writers and poets is trying to capitalize on the achievements of the generations that preceded it. But while discovering its ties to the culture of the region, it is also leaping beyond the fence, overcoming the barrier of the Hebrew language, and trying to reach other areas. Poets such as Sihām Dāwūd and Naʿīm ʿArāydī belong to this generation. The fact that I also belong to this generation seems to liberate me from the obligation of evaluating it and taking a stand. But I believe that the uniqueness of this generation is that it draws from two worlds; knowledge of the Hebrew language brings it into contact, both through Hebrew literature and world literature translated into Hebrew, with unfamiliar mappings of experience, and knowledge of Hebrew confronts it with the latest achievements of modern Arabic literature.[37]

In the second period, at least four writers stand out: Naʿīm ʿArāydī, Anton Shammas, Sihām Dāwūd, and Nazīh Khayr. Sihām Dāwūd is the only Arab woman to write in both languages. Efforts to understand why these authors chose to write also in Hebrew indicate that they did it less out of a desire "to strike the Achilles heel"[38] of Israeli culture and more out of a desire to be integrated in Israeli culture and its emerging identity, each author for his or her own reasons. We will focus on two writers, Naʿīm ʿArāydī and Anton Shammas, because they are the two most prolific Arab writers in Hebrew and because they have been active in the translation of writing from Hebrew to Arabic, and vice versa.

Naʿīm ʿArāydī began his writing career in Arabic at a rather early stage, in poetry and research, then tried his hand at Hebrew writing in 1972, and has ever since continued to publish in Hebrew, especially poetry and fiction, as well as in Arabic. Interestingly, ʿArāydī preferred to write his first novel in Hebrew (*Tevilah qatlanit,* 1992), while he writes poetry and stories in both Arabic and Hebrew. In general, ʿArāydī is more aware of his choice of language, with all his doubts, misgivings, and reservations, than is Anton Shammas. In a response to Shammas, ʿArāydī wrote, "I don't know if I, who write in Hebrew, am writing Hebrew literature. But I do know that I am not writing Arab literature in Hebrew. And I believe that this possibility exists, since I do write Hebrew literature in Hebrew."[39] ʿArāydī does not attempt to gloss over the difficult dilemma he faces as a bilingual writer. On the contrary, he is fully aware of it and struggles with it in a way that leaves him with both options: two languages and two worlds. ʿAraydī is aware that his choice of writing in Hebrew does not relegate Arabic to the background, for Arabic continues to serve him for lectures, poetry, and nonfiction. He consciously chooses this division between Hebrew and Arabic, entering and leaving the world of Hebrew not diminished, but enriched. He understands that the choice of two languages for his fiction and nonfiction is not just a matter of bilingualism, but is a choice that is bicultural, and binational.

Interestingly, both ʿArāydī and Shammas, each citing different reasons, reach the same conclusion, that there is no hope of creating a high-quality literature among Israeli Arabs. This is the common opinion among educated Israeli Arabs in general. It is a view that is not shared, however, by many critics from the West and from the Arab states, who sometimes take great interest in Arabic literature written in Israel. Their interest is not just politically motivated, but based also on the high quality of some Arab writing in Israel, in both poetry (Samīḥ al-Qāsim, Sihām Dāwūd, Michel Ḥaddād, Muḥammad ʿAlī Ṭāhā) and prose (Imīl Ḥabībī, Zakī Darwīsh). I am not trying here to defend Arabic literature written in Israel, but to assert that the statements by ʿArāydī and Shammas are fundamentally in error when one considers the Arabic literature written today and the small numbers of Arabs who live in Israel writing it. The best proof of the incorrectness of their view is the fact that both ʿArāydī and Shammas translate into Hebrew literary works by such Israeli Arab writers as Zakī Darwīsh, Muḥammad Naffāʿ, Sihām Dāwūd, and the extraordinary Imīl Ḥabībī.[40]

It was one writer only, Anton Shammas, and indeed, one novel only, his Hebrew work *Arabesqot* (Arabesques, 1986),[41] that brought about the revolutionary, problematic issue of Arab authors writing in Hebrew and exposed it to criticism and serious debate. Until now, Shammas has published only one book in Arabic, *Asīr Yaqẓatī wa Nawmī* (Prisoner of My Wakefulness and My Sleep, 1974), as well as poetry books in Hebrew. He has also translated five books, mainly of poetry, from Hebrew into Arabic and three books from Arabic into Hebrew.[42] This impressive literary output by Shammas is quite different from the literary output of his colleague ʿArāydī, although they are similar in quantity. First and most important, more than half the books published by ʿArāydī are in Arabic. And, second, ʿArāydī has published studies in Arabic and Hebrew about both Arabic and Hebrew literature.[43]

Both writers are active in the Hebrew literary community, while ʿArāydī, in contrast to Shammas, does not neglect his audience of readers in Arabic. And yet the reactions to Shammas in the press and among Hebrew critics have been much more intense, charged, and agitated than the reactions to ʿArāydī. Why is this so? Is ʿArāydī's literary activity considered more legitimate because he is a Druze who served in the Israeli army or because Hebrew critics feel threatened by the quality of Shammas's writing in Hebrew? Why is Shammas perceived by a wide range of critics and journalists to be a fig leaf for coexistence and cooperation between Arabs and Jews? Whatever the answers, beginning with Shammas's poetry collections *Kerikhah qashah* (1974) and *Shetaḥ hefqer* (1979), the reactions to his Hebrew works throughout the entire political and literary spectrum of the Hebrew press were above and beyond what other Arab writers who write in Hebrew had ever received in Israel.[44] But this critical assessment of the Shammas oeuvre in poetry was only a preamble to the flood of reactions that met the publication of his novel *Arabesqot.*

Hebrew criticism, which has drawn the literary map in the 1980s and early 1990s, wrote about the works of Shammas, and specifically his novel *Arabesqot,* in the context of the total literary output of Hebrew writing by Jewish authors including Yoel Hoffmann, Youval Shimoni, Orly Castel-Bloom, and others. For example, the Hebrew critic Avraham Balaban writes:

> One of the salient features of modern [Hebrew] literature is the shattering of accepted literary and cultural dichotomies, and the challenging of the princi-

ples of hegemony that accompany it. *Arabesqot* is typical of this new writing direction in this as well. What could be more postmodernist than the text of an Arab-Palestinian-Christian that describes the conquest of his village by the "Jewish army", a text written in spit-and-polish Hebrew and constructed like a mask upon a mask upon a mask.[45]

The question of the place of the novel *Arabesqot* in modern Hebrew literature is also addressed by Hannan Hever, who claims that:

> A double provocation was thrown into the Israeli arena with the appearance of *Arabesqot,* the Hebrew novel by Shammas that cleverly served to undermine several of the most accepted criteria that define the limits of Hebrew literature. To address this complex issue of cultural identity, Shammas exposed the Israeli duplicity over the vague and loose distinction between Israeli and Jew. These trends were strikingly confirmed by the fact that, for example, some found it hard to accept this as a novel that belongs organically to Hebrew literature.[46]

Dan Laor treats the novel *Arabesqot* as a "normal" book, barely dealing with the fact that the author is an Arab, and he expresses the view that the novel is a failure from a literary artistic point of view:

> The failure of Anton Shammas in the writing of the novel *Arabesqot* can be attributed, first and foremost, to the fact that the author lacked the determination, artistic maturity, and perseverance for writing a novel that focuses entirely on the unknown world of the Galilean village of his birth, Fassuta. This statement is made recognizing that the encounter between an author like Shammas and materials taken from his nearby childhood surroundings created an extraordinary opportunity for artistic exposure of a unique and unfamiliar geographic, social, and historical reality, that while existing on the periphery of Israeli reality, can singularly illuminate its center.[47]

Literary critics, in addressing the use of Hebrew by Shammas, saw this novel as a throwing down of the gauntlet to the acceptance of non-Jewish writers in modern Hebrew literature. The author, poet, and translator Aharon Amir, who praises the work profusely, makes the following observation about the language of the writing:

> It is sufficient for me to note that this is a multifaceted work, laden with talent, and from the point of view of language and style, it is a multi-faceted diamond, glittering, polished to perfection. I did not hesitate to tell the author

> himself that in my opinion, he returns to Hebrew writing the honor that it lost to a great extent in the past decade, as it became permeated with the haphazard, sloppy style of pen-pushers who are poseurs, arrogant, superficial, smart alecks, raucous, show-offs. What Shammas does for Hebrew literature can be compared, in truth, to what was done for English literature in this century by English-writing authors born in India, Poland, the West Indies, or Russia, just as this can be compared to the work of writers from the cultural periphery of France—in northern or equatorial Africa, Egypt, the Antilles, Lebanon, Belgium, or Romania—to contemporary French literature, without which these literatures would be far poorer and more boring than they are.[48]

While other critics were put off by Shammas's Hebrew, they could not fail to be impressed by the level and quality of the language in the novel. These critics, moreover, refused to include the works of Shammas or of any Arab writer into the Hebrew corpus of modern Israeli literature. Obviously, the considerations of those who take stands on this matter are not purely artistic or literary, but often political, rooted in the relations between the Jewish majority in Israel that writes in Hebrew and the Arab minority that writes in Arabic. Some critics suggest that by writing in Hebrew, Shammas is deliberately defying Israeli linguistic-cultural conventions and mounting a challenge to the dominant Zionist discourse to include Israeli Arab culture within it.

Arab critics have not viewed favorably, to put it mildly, the Hebrew writings of Israeli Arabs, and their attitude has been aggressive and expressed in crass, insulting terms, which have included the charge that these writers have betrayed Arab culture. But the case of Anton Shammas is exceptional in this regard. Criticism in Arabic on the novel *Arabesqot* has been based mostly on readings of its French translation, and we shall present two striking examples. The first, by the Lebanese poet and critic Sharbal Dāghir, who lives in Paris, appeared in the Arabic journal *al-Nāqid,* which is published in London. The critic praises the novel from an artistic point of view, but condemns the choice made by Shammas to write in Hebrew:

> Is it possible that Shammas, by using Hebrew, is provoking the rival in his own home with his very own weapons? It is possible, but this provocation seems to take the form of a demand to recognize the other in him. Shammas has the right and the freedom to write in any language he wants, and we have the right and the freedom to raise these sensitivities, especially since language—as we and others have learned—is the fundamental basis in shaping national identity.[49]

The second criticism was written by Yumnā al-ʿĪd, a prominent Arab critic, who analyzes the novel in a long and comprehensive article. In this article, she applies a structuralist approach to *Arabesqot,* dealing with poetics, thematics, and ideology in a general way. As far as the poetics of the work is concerned, al-ʿĪd praises the structure of the novel, the depiction of the characters, and the treatment of time and place. But she presents incisive criticism in two areas: the Christian dimension, which she feels is all-encompassing at the expense of the Palestinian element, and the writing of the novel in Hebrew. She attacks Shammas on this latter point, claiming:

> It's strange, Anton Shammas [is living] in Israel, or so he says, but he wants to learn the language of this country. Hence he is beginning to write in Hebrew. And the Hebrew writing is the writing of a novel that creates its own authority, i.e., from a foreign land, and from its own time, it shapes the biography of the family (or the biography of the relationships among a group of Christians) and makes from the original that it creates an original for the narrator to relate, to write.[50]

As noted, criticism in Hebrew and Arabic has often dealt at length with the question of why the novel *Arabesqot* was written in Hebrew and not in Arabic. And, indeed, why was the novel written in Hebrew and not Arabic? And no less important, why was this novel translated into English, French, and Dutch, inter alia, but not into Arabic? Shammas addressed this question by writing:

> One needs a lot of chutzpa to write Hebrew prose. And to have perfect chutzpa, one must work hard to hone one's tools. In retrospect, the [Hebrew] poems were my small battles with the language, to command and to grapple with the angel of the Hebrew language. Prose is the true battleground. Here all the possible forms of nakedness are exposed. I came to the language with a particular baggage and I did not forget my language. But when I wrote this book, I did forget my language, or otherwise I would have written it in my language. This forgetting is a kind of salute to the language, homage that I give the Hebrew language. I tried to treat the language with great cautiousness, with respect, like an Arab elephant in a china shop (without breaking anything), trying to preserve inside the new language all the side baggage that I brought from my other culture, from the other side, from a world that doesn't even exist for some Arabs. It's a kind of double redemption of a slice of life that has now vanished. When legend disintegrates and recedes, from beyond the horizon the new language appears, the one my father tried to command,

> knowing inside that he would have to bind the mouth of the Arabic language beast in order to conquer the Hebrew language. Now I return the honor and write in Hebrew.[51]

To the best of my understanding, the novel *Arabesqot* was written in Hebrew and not in Arabic because Shammas, who was active in the Hebrew literary world from the 1970s until the mid-1980s, saw it as natural that he would continue to write in the language in which he had published his two previous poetry collections. Moreover, at the time Shammas decided to write in Hebrew, he was not perceived to be writing in the language of the other, unlike the Maghrib writers who wrote in French and lived in France, such as al-Ṭāhir b. Jallūn, or the Mahjar writers in the American diasporas who wrote in the local language. What is common to these two groups of writers is that they wrote outside their homeland, their country, their land, and that there was a complete split between the writers and their home territory. Shammas, in contrast, wrote his novel in his homeland in Hebrew, a language in which he swims like a fish. He also made wonderful use of the Hebrew language in all its levels and nuances, thus delivering a double message to readers and critics. The first part of the message was: I, Anton Shammas, an Arab, am writing Hebrew that is not only no worse than your Hebrew, but even better. The second part of the message was: Whether you like it or not, I am part of your literature, your culture, and you; and this is my place at this stage of my life, my education, and my literary work.

Although he is one of the top translators from Hebrew into Arabic in Israel, Shammas has rejected the notion of having his novel translated into Arabic or of translating it himself for precisely one of the reasons that led him to write the novel in Hebrew in the first place, which was the greater freedom in Israeli Jewish society, in contrast to Israeli Arab society, to criticize not just the other, but also oneself. In this novel, Shammas offers some rather harsh criticism not only of Jewish society in Israel, but also of Arab society inside and outside Israel, and he was not willing to criticize his society in its own language:

> I write in Hebrew about the village. I'm not sure what story would emerge had it been written in Arabic. I would certainly have been more cautious had I written in Arabic about the village. The Hebrew language paradoxically seems to give me security. I would not have had this freedom had I written in Arabic, because what would my aunt and uncle have said? This is a conscious act of camouflage. I use Hebrew as camouflage cover. But all this is in my mind. The

> younger generation in the village will read it all [anyway], know what is true and what not, and will undoubtedly pursue me until my dying day.[52]

Nevertheless, perhaps in another time and place, Shammas will change his mind and allow the translation of his novel into the language of his people.

Shammas has understood that the debate over his identity as a writer has epitomized the debate over the identity of Arabs and Jews in Israel. The dialogues between him and the Israeli Jewish writer A. B. Yehoshua[53] and the reactions of writers from all shades of the political spectrum have only clarified and sharpened the nuances of the problem of identity, which is an existential problem of the individual, of Israeli Arabs, and of the Jewish community in Israel, about which he writes:

> Israel defines itself as a Jewish state (or as a state for the Jewish people) and demands that its Arab citizens invest their citizenship with content, but when they do, the state clarifies in no uncertain terms that this was meant to be a social partnership only, that they have to search elsewhere for the political content of their identity (i.e., national belonging—to the Palestinian nation), and when they do search for their national identity elsewhere, they are at once accused of undermining the foundation of the state, and one who undermines the foundation of the state cannot possibly be recognized as an "Israeli," and so it goes, a perfect catch.[54]

Three years later, when he was in the United States, at some distance of time and space, Shammas related both to the subject of having written *Arabesqot* in Hebrew and to the problem of defining the identity of the Israeli Arabs:

> In articles about *Arabesqot,* people didn't always know how to define me. "An Israeli author?" they would ask. Not exactly, I would respond, even though this is what I called myself for years. "An Arab?" Also not. I chose the impossible combination of "an Israeli-Palestinian", and this was an act of defiance against them all, even against myself: de-Judaization and de-Zionization of the Jewish state by bestowing Israeli, national meaning on the word "Israel" and at the same time, emphasis of the Palestinian as an ethnic dimension equivalent to Jewish. And this was somewhat of a self-fulfilling prophecy in our day: just as Israel exists, so too Palestine will exist. And it held something of the fleeting and innocuous despair of the Israeli idea that I wanted to define in my battles with the windmills of the literary world over the years. And it

> held something of the desire to deal with bilingual translation—-the identity of the Galilean Arab translated to Israeli-Arabic, and then translated to Palestinian in Hebrew letters, and finally to Israeli-Palestinian, in spite of it all and thanks to the Hebrew.[55]

It is not clear whether the identification of some Israeli Arab authors with the Hebrew language and culture of the majority have stamped these authors with the mark of Cain or have brought them honor and pride. Israeli Arabs have certainly felt a sense of pride with regard to *Arabesqot* by Anton Shammas and its successful incorporation into mainstream Hebrew literature. It is possible that Israel's peace agreements with some of the Arab states, the Declaration of Principles by Israel and the Palestinians, and Israel's peace contacts with Syria and Lebanon will neutralize some of the accusations flung at Israeli Arab writers who write in Hebrew. It is also possible that these writers and others will not continue to write in Hebrew if peace comes to the region, or perhaps the opposite will be true: peace in the region could relieve the resistance to writing in Hebrew felt by most Arabs inside and outside Israel. This would indicate not only an acceptance of Israel in the Middle East, but also acceptance of these Israeli Arab authors who write in Hebrew.

Notes

* This article is part of a larger project entitled *Portraits in the Mirror: Studies in Modern Palestinian Literature and Culture* (forthcoming).

1. On the writing of Jabrā Ibrāhīm Jabrā in English, primarily his poetry, see ʿAbd al- Wāḥid Luʾluʾ, "Ṣūrat Jabrā fī Shabābihi, Shiʿr bi l-Inklīziyya," in *al-Nāqid* 10 (April 1989): 26–31.
2. Salma Khadra Jayyusi, *Anthology of Modern Palestinian Literature* (New York: Columbia University Press, 1992), 333–66.
3. For more information, see Jayyusi, *Anthology,* 727–28 and also *Food for Our Grandmothers: Writing by Arab-American and Arab-Canadian Feminists,* ed. Joanna Kadi (Boston: South End Press, 1994), 279–80.
4. The better known works of Afnān al-Qāsim are, among his novels, *al-ʿAjūz* (Baghdad: Wizārat al-Iʿlām wa Ittiḥād al- Kuttāb wa l-Suḥufiyyīn al-Filasṭīniyyīn, 1974); among his short stories, *Kutub wa-Asfār* (Cairo: al-Hayʾa al-Miṣriyya al-ʿĀmma li l-Kitāb, 1990); among his plays, *Umm al-Jamīʿ* (Beirut: ʿĀlam al-Kutub); and in the field of criticism, *Masʾalat al-Shiʿr wa l-Malḥama al-Darwīshiyya: Maḥmūd Darwīsh fī Madīḥ al-Ẓill al-ʿĀlī: Dirāsa Sūsyū-Bunyawiyya* (Beirut: ʿĀlam al-Kutub, 1987).

5. Ami Elad[-Bouskila], "Sifrutam shel haʿaravim beYisraʾel (1948–1993)" in Ami Elad[-Bouskila], ed., *Hamizraḥ heḥadash* (special issue devoted to the literature of Israeli Arabs) 35 (1993): 1–4.
6. On the Arabic and Hebrew literature of the Jews of Iraq, see Shmuel Moreh, *al-Qiṣṣa al-Qaṣīra ʿinda Yahūd al-ʿIrāq* (Jerusalem: Magnes Press, 1981), 1–25 and Nancy E. Berg, *Exile From Exile: Israeli Writers From Iraq* (Albany: State University of New York, 1996). On the dilemma of choosing between writing in Arabic and Hebrew, see Berg, *Exile from Exile,* 43–66 and Ammiel Alcalay, *After Jews and Arabs: Remaking Levantine Culture* (Minneapolis: University of Minnesota Press, 1993), 235–47.
7. Reuven Snir, "We Were Like Those Who Dream: Iraqi-Jewish Writers in Israel in the 1950s," *Prooftexts* 11 (1991): 153–73. Also see Reuven Snir, "Petsa mipetsaʿav: hasifrut haʿaravit haPalastinit beYisraʾel," *Alpayim* 2 (1990): 247; Maḥmūd ʿAbbāsī, "Hitpatḥut haroman vehasippur haqatsar basifrut haʿaravit bashanim 1948–1976," doctoral dissertation (Jerusalem: The Hebrew University, 1983), 251.
8. Shmuel Moreh and Maḥmūd ʿAbbāsī, *Tarājim wa-Āthār fī l-Adab l-ʿArabī fī Isrāʾīl, 1948–1986,* 3rd ed (Shafāʿamr: Dār al-Mashriq, 1987), 31–33 and Moreh, *al-Qiṣṣa al-Qaṣīra,* 187–90.
9. Shimon Ballas, ed. and trans., *Sippurim palestiniyyim* (Tel Aviv: Eked, 1970). Ballas also served as editor and consultant for Arabic literature of the Mifras publishing house, which has published more Palestinian texts than any other publishing house in Israel.
10. On the life and works of Sami Michael, see Moreh and ʿAbbāsī, *Tarājim wa-Āthār,* 226–27; Moreh, *al-Qiṣṣa al-Qaṣīra,* 221–24.
11. Sami Michael, *Viqtoryah* (Tel-Aviv: Am Oved, 1994).
12. The Cairene trilogy by Najīb Maḥfūẓ was published in 1956–57. In Hebrew, the trilogy was published by Sifriat Poalim as follows: *Bayit beQahir* (Part 1), 1981; *Bayit beQahir: Kamal* (Part 2), 1984; *Bayit beQahir: dor shelishi* (Part 3), 1987.
13. Sami Michael, "Shylock beKartago," *Yediot Aḥaronot* (October 28, 1994): 28; Sami Michael, "Historyah qatlanit," *Yediot Aḥaronot* (August 18, 1995):24.
14. On the subject of the legitimacy and the Israeliness of writers of Sephardic origin in modern Hebrew literature, see Lev Hakak, *Peraqim besifrutam shel yehudei hamizraḥ bemedinat Yisraʾel* (Jerusalem: Kiryat Sefer, 1985), 8–9 and Alcalay, *After Jews and Arabs,* 227–34.
15. Moreh and ʿAbbāsī, *Tarājim wa-Āthār,* 26–28; Moreh, *al-Qiṣṣa al-Qaṣīra,* 233–36; and Shmuel Moreh, "Olamo hameyuḥad shel Yitzhak Bar-Moshe," *Shevet veʿam,* second series 3 (8) (1978): 425–44.
16. Moreh, *al-Qiṣṣa al-Qaṣīra,* 251–54; Moreh and ʿAbbāsī, *Tarājim wa-Āthār,* 236–37; Alcalay, *After Jews and Arabs,* 236–38.
17. Samīr Naqqāsh, "Ma atem rotsim mimmenni? ani shomer al haʾotonomyah shelli!" *Mifgash* 7 (Spring 1986): 34.

18. *Ibid.*, 35.
19. Imīl Ḥabībī, "Kemo petsa," *Politiqah* 21 (1988): 6–21. In an anthology that appeared in Arabic called *Mukhtārāt min al-Qiṣṣa al-Qaṣīra fī 18 Baladan ʿArabiyyan* (*Selections of Short Stories From 18 Arab Countries*) (Cairo: Markaz al-Ahrām li l-Tarjama wa l-Nashr, 1993), 239–51, a footnote in Arabic notes, "This chapter was first written by the author [Imīl Ḥabībī] in Hebrew in response to a request by the monthly *Politiqah* and appeared in its special issue 'Arabs in Israel—An Inside Look—Mid-1988'; the Arabic language version was translated by the author himself who also made additions to the text."
20. Samīḥ al-Qāsim and Nazīh Khayr, eds. and trans., *al-Dhākira al-Zarqāʾ* (Tel-Aviv: Mifras 1991); Samīḥ al-Qāsim, *Yāsmīn: mishirei Ronni Somek* (Haifa: Beit al-Karma, 1995).
21. Anton Shammas, *Kerikhah qashah* (Tel-Aviv: Sifriat Poalim, 1974); *Shetaḥ hefqer: shirim* (Tel-Aviv: Hakibbutz Hameuchad, 1979); Naʿīm ʿArāydī, *Eikh efshar leʾehov* (Tel-Aviv: Eked, 1972); *Ḥemlah ufaḥad* (Tel-Aviv: Eked, 1974–75); *Ḥazarti el hakefar: shirim* (Tel-Aviv: Am Oved, 1986). To this list can be added such works as Asad ʿAzzī, *Lemargelot hagoral hamar* (Haifa: Renaissance, 1976); *Onat haleḥishot* (Haifa: Renaissance, 1978); Asad ʿAzzī and Fāḍil ʿAlī, *Shirei reḥov* (Daliyat al-Karmil: Milim Publishing House, 1979); Fuʾād Ḥusayn, *Yom shishi* (Tel Aviv: Sa'ar, 1990); *Siaḥ pesagot* (Haifa: Defus HaVadi, 1995); and Maḥmūd Zaydān, *Ketovet beḥalal* (Tel-Aviv: Eked, 1992). Fārūq Mawāsī wrote his poem "Shenayim" in Hebrew. See *Haʿetsvonim shelo huvnu: shirim,* trans. Roge Tavor (Kufr Qaraʿ: al-Shafaq, 1989), 79–81.
22. ʿAṭallāh Manṣūr, *Beʾor ḥadash* (Tel-Aviv: Karni, 1966). This book was translated into English as *In a New Light,* trans. Abraham Birman (London: Vallentine and Mitchell, 1969).
23. Moreh and ʿAbbāsī, *Tarājim wa-Āthār,* 218–19.
24. ʿAṭallāh Manṣūr, "ʿArab Yaktubūn bi l-ʿIbriyya: al-Wuṣūl ilā al-Jār," *Bulletin of the Israeli Academic Center in Cairo* 16 (1992): 65; Rāshid Ḥusayn, *Ḥayyīm Naḥmān Biyālik: Nukhba min Shiʿrihi wa-Nathrihi* (Jerusalem: Hebrew University, 1966); Sabri Jirias, *The Arabs in Israel (*Haifa: self-published, 1966).
25. ʿAṭallāh Manṣūr, *wa-Baqiyat Samīra* (Tel-Aviv: Dār al-Nashr al-ʿArabī, 1962).
26. Manṣūr, "ʿArab Yaktubūn bi l-ʿIbriyya," 65.
27. Anton Shammas translated into Arabic the poems of David Avidan in his book *Idhāʿa min Qamar Iṣṭināʿ*ī (Acre: Maktabat wa-Maṭbaʿat al-Surūjī, 1982) and edited and translated the anthology *Ṣayd al-Ghazāla (*Shafāʿamr: Dār al-Mashriq, 1984). Samīḥ al-Qāsim and Nazīh Khayr translated into Arabic and edited the anthology *al-Dhākira al-Zarqāʾ (*Tel-Aviv: Mifras, 1991). Samīḥ al-Qāsim translated into Arabic a selection of poems by Ronni Somek under the title *Yāsmīn: Qaṣāʾid* (Haifa: Bayt al-Karma, 1995).
28. Naʿīm ʿArāydī edited and translated some of the works in Arabic as well as Hebrew texts that appeared in his anthology *Ḥayalim shel mayim* (Tel-Aviv:

Sifrei Ma'ariv and Hakibbutz Hameuchad, 1988). He also edited and translated a collection of poems by Adonis, *Tehiliyyot* (Tel-Aviv: Kadim, 1989). In the 1970s, Salmān Maṣālḥa translated into Hebrew Saḥar Khalīfa's novel *al-Subbār* (in Hebrew: *Hatsabbar* [Jerusalem: Galileo, 1978]). In the late 1980s, Maṣālḥa translated into Hebrew Maḥmūd Darwīsh's book *Dhākira li l-nisyān* (in Hebrew: *Zekher lashikhehah* [Jerusalem and Tel-Aviv: Schocken, 1989]).

29. In an interview with Sihām Dāwūd in the Jerusalem weekly newspaper *Yerushalayim,* February 19, 1990.
30. By Anton Shammas in Hebrew: *Hashaqran hakhi gadol ba'olam* (Jerusalem: Keter, 1982) and *Arabesqot* (Tel Aviv: Am Oved, 1986). By Na'īm 'Arāydī in Hebrew: *Eikh efshar le'ehov* (Tel Aviv: Traklin-Eked, 1972); *Hanozlim hamenaggnim bytsirat Uri Zvi Greenberg* (Tel-Aviv: Eked, 1980); *Ulay zo ahavah* (Tel Aviv: Ma'ariv, 1983); *Ḥazarti el hakefar: shirim* (Tel Aviv: Am Oved, 1986); *Beḥamishah memadim* (Tel Aviv: Sifriat Poalim, 1991); and *Tevilah qatlanit* (Tel Aviv: Bitan, 1992). By Na'īm 'Arāydī in Arabic: *Qaṣā'id Karmiliyya fī l-'Ishq al- Baḥrī* (Shafā'amr: Dār al-Mashriq li l-Tarjama wa l-Ṭibā'a wa l-Nashr, 1984); *Masīrat al-Ibdā': Dirāsāt Naqdiyya Taḥlīliyya fī al-Adab al-Filasṭīnī al-Mu'āṣir* (Haifa and Shafā'amr: Maktabat Kull Shay', Dār al-Mashriq li l-Tarjama wa l-Ṭibā'a wa l- Nashr, 1988); and *Maḥaṭṭāt 'alā Ṭarīq al-Ibdā': Dirāsāt Naqdiyya fī l-Adab al- Filasṭīnī al-Mu'āṣir* (Haifa: Maktabat Kull Shay', 1992).
31. Nazīh Khayr, ed., *Mifgash ve'immut bayetsirah ha'aravit veha'ivrit* (Haifa: Bayt al-Karma, 1993). This book has writings in Arabic and Hebrew and also translations from and to both languages, which is not always noted in the text and raises questions about the original language in which it was written. Interestingly, the Arab and Jewish writers who appear in this anthology in the original or in translation also appear in anthologies edited by Nazīh Khayr, Samīḥ al-Qāsim, and others.
32. Aharon Leish, "Kavvim umegamot aḥarei milḥemet sheshet hayamim," in *Ha'aravim beyisra'el: retsifut utemurah,* ed. Aharon Leish (Jerusalem: Magnes Press, 1981), 240–47.
33. Gershon Shaked, *Hasipporet ha'ivrit, 1880—1980,* vol. 4 (Tel-Aviv and Jerusalem: Hakibbutz Hameuchad and Keter, 1993), 97–188.
34. Gabriel García Márquez, *One Hundred Years of Solitude,* trans. Gregory Rabassa (London: Penguin Books, 1970).
35. For broad surveys of the modern Arabic literatures of the Mashriq and the Maghrib from the 1960s, see Ami Elad[-Bouskila], ed., *Writer, Culture, Text: Studies in Modern Arabic Literature* (Fredericton, N.B.: York Press, 1993); Ami Elad[-Bouskila], *The Village Novel in Modern Egyptian Literature* (Berlin: Klaus Schwarz Verlag, 1994); Ali Gad, *Form and Technique in the Egyptian Novel, 1912–1971* (London: Ithaca Press, 1983); Sabry Hafez, "The Egyptian Novel in the Sixties," *Journal of Arabic Literature (*1976): 68–84; Roger Allen, *The Arabic Novel: An Historical and Critical Introduction* (Manchester: University of

Manchester, 1982); Muhammad Mustafa Badawi, ed., *Modern Arabic Literature* (Cambridge: Cambridge University Press, 1992); ʿAbd al-Raḥmān Abū ʿAwf, *al-Baḥth ʿan ṭarīq Jadīd li l- Qiṣṣa al-Qaṣīra al-Miṣriyya: Dirāsa Naqdiyya* (Cairo: al-Hayʾa al-Miṣriyya al- ʿĀmma li l-Taʾlīf wa l-Nashr, 1971); Sayyid Ḥāmid al-Nassāj, *Bānūrāmā al-Riwāya al-ʿArabiyya al-Ḥadītha* (Cairo: Dār al-Maʿārif, 1980); al-Saʿid al-Warāqī, *Ittijāhāt al-Riwāya al-ʿArabiyya al-Muʿāṣira* (Cairo: al-Hayʾa al-Miṣriyya al- ʿĀmma li l-Taʾlīf wa l-Nashr, 1982); Ami Elad[-Bouskila], introduction to the anthology *Meʿever laʾofeq haqarov: sippurim arviyyim benei yamenu* (Jerusalem: Keter, Bidayat, 1989), 13–16; Ami Elad[-Bouskila], "Mitsrayim: meʾah veʿesrim shenot sipporet," *Apiryon* (1989): 68–71; Ami Elad[-Bouskila], *Sifrut aravit belevush ivri* (Jerusalem: Ministry of Education, Culture, and Sport, 1995), 11–65; Sasson Somekh, "Hasippur hadu-ʿerki shel Najīb Maḥfūẓ," *Hasifrut* 2 (1969–70): 565–79; Sasson Somekh, "Haromanim haḥevratiyyim shel Najīb Maḥfūẓ," *Hamizraḥ heḥadash* 21 (1970–71): 260–81; Menahem Milson, "Najīb Maḥfūẓ uveʿayat haḥippus aḥar tokhen laḥayyim," *Hamizraḥ heḥadash* 19 (1968–69): 1–8; Menahem Milson, "Beḥinot aḥadot baroman hamitsri hamoderni," *Qeshet* 47 (Spring 1969–70): 161–70.

36. In this context, it is interesting to note the possible influence of Hebrew poetry on Arabic poetry in Israel. For an analysis of the influence of the poetry of Bialik on the work of Maḥmūd Darwīsh, see Jamāl Aḥmad al-Rifāʿī, *Āthār al-Thaqāfa al- ʿIbriyya fī al-Shiʿr al-Filasṭīnī al-Muʿāṣir, Dirāsa fī Shiʿr Maḥmūd Darwīsh* (Cairo: Dār al-Thaqāfa al-Jadīda, 1994).
37. Anton Shammas, "Hasifrut haʿaravit beYisraʾel leʾaḥar 1967," *Skirot* (Tel Aviv University) 2 (June 1976): 7.
38. Hannan Hever, "Lehakot baʿaqevo shel Achilles," *Alpayim* 1 (June 1989): 186–93; Hannan Hever, "Ivrit beʿitto shel aravi: shisha peraqim al *Arabesqot* meʾet Anton Shammas," *Teʾoryah uviqqoret* 1 (Summer 1991): 23–38. For an entirely different point of view, see Reuven Snir, "Petsa mipetsaʿav," 244–68.
39. Naʿīm ʿArāydī, "Sifrut ivrit, mah naʿamt," *Moznayim* 65, no. 4 (1991): 41.
40. Imīl Ḥabībī, *al-Waqāʾiʿ al-Gharība fī Ikhtifāʾ Saʿīd Abī al-Naḥs al-Mutashāʾil,* 3rd ed (Jerusalem, Manshūrāt Ṣalāḥ al-Dīn, 1977); for the Hebrew version, see *Haʾopsimist: hakhroniqah hamuflaʾah shel heʿalmut Saʿīd Abī al-Naḥs al- Mutashāʾil,* trans. Anton Shammas (Jerusalem: Mifras, 1984). Imīl Ḥabībi, *Ikhṭayya* (Nicosia: Kitāb al-Karmil 1,1985). For the Hebrew version, see *Ikhtayya,* trans. Anton Shammas (Tel Aviv: Am Oved, 1988). The stories by Habībī—"Levasof paraḥ hashaqed," "Rūbābīkā," and "Qinat hasartan"—were translated by Naʿīm ʿArāydī in the anthology he edited, *Ḥayyalim shel mayim,* 57–71. Imīl Ḥabībi, *Sarāyā bint al- Ghūl: Khurrāfiyya* (Haifa: Dār Arābesk, 1991). For the Hebrew version, see *Sarayah: bat hashed hara, Khurafiyya,* trans. Anton Shammas (Tel Aviv: Hakibbutz Hameuchad, 1993).
41. This appeared in English translation as Anton Shammas, *Arabesques,* trans. Vivian Eden (New York: Harper & Row, 1988).

42. Moreh and ʿAbbāsī, *Tarājim wa-Āthār,* 122–23.
43. *Ibid.*, 155–56.
44. *Ibid.*, 123–24.
45. Avraham Balaban, "'Hagal heḥadish' neged 'hagal heḥadash,'" *Yediot Aḥaronot,* (June 5, 1992): 34–35.
46. Hever, "Lehakot baʿaqevo shel Achilles," 191. For a full discussion of the novel *Arabesqot,* see Hever's article, "Ivrit beʿitto shel aravi."
47. Dan Laor, "Hafasutaʾim: hasippur shelo nigmar," *Haʾarets,* May 30, 1986.
48. Aharon Amir, "Geʾulah vehitbolelut," *Beʾeretz Yisraʾel* (October 1986): 9.
49. Sharbal Dāghir, "Arabisk Filasṭīniyya," *al-Nāqid* 2 (August 1988): 75.
50. Yumnā al-ʿĪd, *Taqniyyāt al-Sard al-Riwāʾī fī Ḍawʾ al-Manhaj al-Bunyawī* (Beirut: Dār al-Fārābī, 1990), 149.
51. "Millim shemenasot lagaʿat," an interview of Anton Shammas conducted by Dalia Amit in 1988.
52. *Ibid.*
53. On the debate between Anton Shammas and Avraham B. Yehoshua and those who joined the debate, see Anton Shammas, "Avram ḥozer lagolah?" *Itton* 77 72–73 (February 6, 1986): 21–22; Anton Shammas, "Ashmat hababushqah," *Politiqah* 5–6 (February-March 1986): 44–45; Anton Shammas, "Rosh hashanah layehudim," *Haʿir* 1 (September 1985): 13–18; Anton Shammas, "Qitsh 22, o: gevul hatarbut," *Iton* 77 84–85 (January-February 1987): 24–26; and Avraham B. Yehoshua, "Im attah nishʾar—attah miʿut," *Qol haʿir* (January 31, 1986): 42–43. The latter article also appeared under the title "Avraham B. Yehoshua: teshuvah leAnton," *Haʿir* (January 31, 1986): 22–23. See also Herzl and Balfour Hakak, "Shammas eino makkir bemedinah yehudit," *Moznayim* 5–6 (November-December 1986): 80; Michal Schwartz, "Al ashmat A.B. Yehoshua vehababushqah shel Shammas," *Derekh hanitsots* (February 5, 1986): 6–7; and B. Michael, "Kosot ruaḥ, pitspon veAnton," *Haʾarets* (January 17, 1986): 9.
54. Shammas, "Qitsh 22," 25.
55. Anton Shammas, "Yitsu zemani shel ḥafatsim nilvim," *Haʾarets, Sefarim* (June 13, 1989): 11.

9

Maḥmūd Darwīsh: Identity and Change

Issa J. Boullata

Since Maḥmūd Darwīsh began publishing his poetry in the early 1960s, his life has undergone many drastic changes. Until 1971, he lived in Israel and, as an active member of Rakah, the Israeli Communist Party, he was in opposition to many aspects of Israeli policy, particularly its treatment of Arabs living in Israel. During this period he was put in prison or under house arrest by the Israeli authorities several times. After a year studying in Moscow, he decided not to return to Israel. He went to Egypt for a brief stay and then settled in Lebanon, where he supported the activities of the Palestine Liberation Organization (PLO). Following the 1982 Israeli invasion of the country, he left for Tunisia with the PLO fighters evacuated under the protection of multinational forces. After a few years of intimate involvement with the PLO in Tunisia, he left for Paris in disagreement with the policies of the Palestinian leadership.[1] After the Oslo accords, he wanted to return to Haifa, where he had originally lived, but was not permitted to do so by Israel.

These changes in his life conditions affected his poetic vision, no doubt. In this chapter, I will focus on their effect on his concept of identity as a young and rising Palestinian poet who gradually became a national figure whose words commanded public attention by their articulate expression of feelings and their aesthetic sophistication. In one of his earliest poems entitled "Identity Card," in his collection *Awrāq al-Zaytūn* (1964),[2] Darwīsh puts forth a forceful and very direct expression of his identity. Ostensibly written in response to an Israeli official's questions, the poem ends by saying:

> Register
> I'm an Arab
> Robbed of my ancestors' vineyards
> And of a land I used to till
> Myself and all my children.
> Nothing was left for us and my grandchildren
> Except these rocks.
> Will your government
> Take them away . . . as was alleged?
> If so, then
> Register . . . at the top of the page
> I don't hate people
> I don't rob anyone
> But if I'm hungry
> I'll eat my usurper's flesh.
> Beware then, beware of my hunger
> And my anger![3]

Darwīsh states here in very simple terms the basic predicament of the Palestinian, robbed of his land and livelihood, who warns Israel not to push him to violence by further injustice. Land is an essential part of his identity, even if he is forcibly limited to its rocks; but if these are also to be taken away from him, he will respond with anger at the usurper, although his nature is to hate no one.

In later poems, the land of Palestine, its rocks, its soil, its olive trees, its jasmines and roses, its oranges, its birds become conflated into one sweetheart. Darwīsh becomes "a lover from Palestine," which is the title of his next collection, *ʿĀshiq min Filisṭīn* (1966).[4] As he matures poetically and abandons direct language in his later collections, Palestine is metaphorically addressed as a woman, its physical features metamorphosed in imaginative personifications, as in his *Ḥabībatī Tanhaḍu min Nawmihā* (1970)[5] and *Uḥibbuki aw lā Uḥibbuki* (1972).[6] The latter collection opens with a poem entitled "Psalms," written after Darwīsh left Israel, in which he addresses his homeland:

> I love you or I don't love you—
> I go, I leave losable addresses behind me.
> And I wait for those who will visit;

They know the appointed times of my death and come.
  You whom I don't love when I love you, Babylon's walls
  Are narrow by day, your eyes are large,
  And your face is spread out in the rays
As if you were not yet born, and we not yet separated,
As if you did not kill me.
For on the roofs of storms all speech is beautiful,
And each meeting is a farewell.[7]

Darwīsh's poems become longer, and their lyrical tone diminishes as they adopt an epic dimension, especially when he joins the PLO in Beirut. His poem "Ode of the Land,"[8] in his collection *Aʿrās* (1977), is a good example:

I call the soil an extension of my soul
I call my hands the walkway of wounds
I call the pebbles wings
I call the birds almonds and figs
I call my ribs trees
And I pluck a fig branch from my chest
And throw it as a stone
And blow up the conquerors' tank[9]

The poet here identifies himself with his country's soil, which is an extension of his own soul. Parts of his body and of his homeland are unified in a struggle against the conquerors. These parts are blended and wound together to be used as defense weapons. His tropes or figures of speech become difficult to assimilate logically as they express an almost mystical union of the two terms of each metaphor or simile used. But they leave the impression of an entity consisting of two things that are identical and unified: the homeland and the poet are one. He ends the poem with the declaration:

I am the land
O you who are going to the wheat grain's bed
Plow my body
O you who are going to the Mountain of Fire
Pass over my body
O you who are going to the Rock of Jerusalem
Pass over my body
O you who are crossing over my body

You will never pass
I am the land in a body
You will never pass
I am the land in its wakefulness
You will never pass
I am the land.
O you who are crossing the land in its wakefulness
You will never pass
You will never pass
You will never pass![10]

The poet here is the land itself in its resistance to the conquerors. The enemies who intend to possess it will have to pass over his dead body, which means that they will meet with resistance and will never possess it really, because he, along with the land and its people, are wakeful.[11] He identifies with the modern history of his land, symbolized by the "Mountain of Fire," which is the name given to Nablus and its region in Palestine in commemoration of their heroic resistance to the British mandate's policies in the Palestinian rebellion of 1936–39. He also identifies with the religious Islamic history of the land, symbolized by the "Rock of Jerusalem," which refers to the Dome of the Rock in al-Ḥaram al-Sharīf, one of the holiest Islamic places after Mecca and Medina.

We should note that Darwīsh does not lament but seeks to resist and to instill resistance in others. His identity lies in an indestructible hope fired by deep love and a deep faith in his people. In one of his early poems entitled "On Resistance," in his collection *Awrāq al-Zaytūn,* he writes:

We love roses,
    But we love wheat more.
We love the fragrance of roses,
    But purer are the ears of wheat.
Defend then your ears of wheat against the whirlwind
With tawny chests,
Build up the hedge with chests.
With chests, how can it be broken?
Grip the neck of wheat spikes
    As you grip a dagger!
The land and the peasant and determination
    Tell me: how can they be defeated . . .
This trinity,
    How can it ever be defeated?[12]

This spirit of resistance as an element of identity remains constant in Darwīsh's later poetry, even when it sheds its direct didactic tone and is couched in more sophisticated imagery as in his long poems, "Ode of the Land,"[13] written to commemorate Land Day in 1976; "Aḥmad al-Zaʿtar,"[14] written to commemorate the Tal al-Zaʿtar massacre of Palestinians in Lebanon in 1976; or several others that were set to music and sung by the politically committed Lebanese populist singer Marcel Khalīfa, such as "Rītā and the Gun"[15] or "Promises from the Storm."[16] Despair does not enter Darwīsh's vision, even in dark hours when national heroes die or activist friends are assassinated. In his elegy for Gamal Abdel Nasser (Jamāl ʿAbd al-Nāṣir), "The Man with the Green Shadow,"[17] he celebrates the Egyptian leader's deeds that have given pride and hope to all Arabs, and he promises to live on and continue the struggle. In another poem, entitled "A Song to the Green [Color],"[18] he celebrates the color green in the midst of prevailing black as a call for renewed Arab life and continuing Arab hope.

However, it did not take Darwīsh long to realize that the Arab world for which he left Israel was far from ideal. In a 1986 interview with *al-Yawm al-Sābiʿ*, an Arabic magazine published in Paris, he states:

> I have often said that the Israeli repression transformed me into an Arab, and that disappointment with the Arabs transformed me into a Palestinian. What lay outside the window, the window of prison [Israel], was an easy hope. The Arab world in my imagination painted a blue picture for itself and an open expanse for Palestine. But my Arab shock was also severe when I experienced reality at a short distance and saw the absence of Palestine and the absence of democracy [in the Arab world] so that the [1967] defeat was no longer an incidental event or a surprise. It is natural that that would influence my way of expression.[19]

Although Darwīsh's latest poems retain a spirit of resilience and a constant call to resistance and dignity in fighting injustice, there is a deep existentialist concern that pervades them. Many of his poems have become even longer and contain pensive, confessional elements and a deep tragic sense not present in his earlier poetry. In a short poem entitled "Arabic Music" in his collection *Ḥiṣār li-Madāʾiḥ al-Baḥr* (1984), Darwīsh makes an oblique allusion to a verse in a poem by the pre-Islamic poet, Tamīm ibn Muqbil, wishing he were a stone without feeling:[20]

> "Would that man were a stone . . ."
> I wish I were a stone . . .[21]

Then he recalls recurring experiences of good and beautiful things in life, reminding him of his homeland and causing him only pain for being away from it. In another poem in the same collection, "The Earth Is Too Small For Us," he returns to the theme of resistance and dying for the Palestinian cause:

> Where will we go after the last frontiers?
> Where will the birds fly after the last sky?
> Where will the plants sleep after the last air?
> We will write our names in crimson-colored vapor
> We will cut off the song and let our flesh complete it
> Here in the last passage
> Here, or here our blood will plant its olives . . .[22]

Death here is not an end but rather a beginning. It is the death of the wheat grain in the earth so that it may live, as the poet says earlier in the poem.[23]

The reality of exile weighs heavily on Darwīsh, but he does not let it crush him or his memories, and he does not allow it to kill his hope of returning to Palestine and resuming a normal life on its soil. In a beautiful and powerful long poem he wrote in March 1989 titled "The Tragedy of Narcissus and the Comedy of Silver,"[24] he celebrates Palestinian life, its memories of the homeland and folk culture, and its dreams in exile of returning to the ancestral soil in which it is deeply rooted. In this poem he repeats, "One's land is inherited as one's language," to emphasize the closeness of Palestinian identity to the land of Palestine or, indeed, the inseparability of Palestine and the Palestinians, and the indivisibility of their unity.

When Palestinian conditions brought about the Intifada, spontaneously uniting frustrated Palestinians in a popular, grass-roots uprising against over twenty years of Israeli occupation, Darwīsh felt justified as the world then acclaimed the heroic attempts of unarmed people to fight with stones against a ruthless and heavily armed occupying army. At that time he wrote a poem, "Those Passing between Passing Words,"[25] in which he asks the occupiers to withdraw from the occupied land and to let its people lead their normal lives, of which they have been deprived. In a highly emotive metaphorical language, he clearly outlines the sharp differences between the Palestinians and their occupiers with regard to the values of justice and peace and conflicting historical claims. He invites the occupiers to take their share of Palestinian blood and leave, because the time for them to leave has come. They should live and die wherever they wish, but not among Palestinians who, he says, have a lot of work to do in their land and want to live as they themselves wish.[26]

From this survey of Maḥmūd Darwīsh's poetry we can see how his concept of identity has been strongly related to the land of Palestine, its past and its present. His identity is also strongly oriented to the future, to what the Palestinians wish to do in their land, in freedom and in accord with their own values. He envisions a future in which Palestinians will attempt without malice to preserve themselves and their culture for upcoming generations and to live in peace on the only land they know to be their own.

Notes

1. On Maḥmūd Darwīsh's life and poetry, see Rajāʾ al-Naqqāsh, *Maḥmūd Darwīsh: Shāʿir al-Arḍ al-Muḥtalla,* 2nd ed. (Cairo: Dār al-Hilāl, 1971). See also Muhammad Siddiq, "Maḥmūd Darwīsh," in *Encyclopedia of World Literature in the 20th Century,* vol. 5 (New York: Continuum Publishing Company, 1993), 161–63.
2. Maḥmūd Darwīsh, *Dīwān Maḥmūd Darwīsh,* 13th ed. (Beirut: Dār al-ʿAwda, 1989), 73–76.
3. *Ibid.*, 76. All English translations of poems in this chapter are mine.
4. *Ibid.*, 77–163.
5. *Ibid.*, 311–62.
6. *Ibid.*, 363–457.
7. *Ibid.*, 365.
8. *Ibid.*, 618–32.
9. *Ibid.*, 619.
10. *Ibid.*, 630.
11. For a larger portion of this poem translated by Lena Jayyusi and Christopher Middleton, see Salma Khadra Jayyusi, ed., *An Anthology of Modern Palestinian Literature* (New York: Columbia University Press, 1992), 145–51.
12. Darwīsh, *Dīwān,* 41.
13. *Ibid.*, 618–31.
14. *Ibid.*, 595–608.
15. *Ibid.*, 192–94.
16. *Ibid.*, 181–82.
17. *Ibid.*, 359–62.
18. *Ibid.*, 632–35.

19. *Al-Yawm al-Sābiʿ*, December 1, 1986, cited in Shākir al-Nābulusī, *Majnūn al-Turāb: Dirāsa fī Shiʿr wa Fikr Maḥmūd Darwīsh* (Beirut: al-Muʾassasa al-ʿArabiyya li al-Dirāsāt wa al-Nashr, 1987), 241–42.
20. *Ma aṭyaba l-ʿaysha law anna l-fatā ḥajarun*
Tanbū l-ḥawādithu ʿanhu wa-hwa malmūmu.
(How good life would be if man were a stone
From whom events bounce while he remains collected.)
See *Dīwān al-Shiʿr al-ʿArabī,* 3 vols., ed. ʿAlī Aḥmad Saʿīd (Beirut: Dār al-Fikr, 1986), vol. 1, 202.
21. *Ḥiṣār li-Madāʾiḥ al-Baḥr,* 2nd ed (Beirut: Dār al-ʿAwda, 1985), 7–8. Originally published in Tunis in 1984, this was the first collection of poetry published by Darwīsh following his move from Lebanon to Tunisia as a result of the Israeli invasion of Lebanon in 1982.
22. "Taḍīq binā al-Arḍ," in *Ḥiṣār li-Madāʾiḥ al-Baḥr,* 143.
23. *Ibid.*
24. Maḥmūd Darwīsh, *Maʾsāt al-Narjis wa Malhāt al-Fiḍḍa* (London: Riad El-Rayyes Books, 1989), reprinted in Darwīsh's collection *Arā Mā Urīd* (Casablanca: Dār Tubqāl li al-Nashr, 1990), 49–78.
25. Maḥmūd Darwīsh, *ʿĀbirūn fī Kalām ʿĀbir* (Casablanca: Dār Tubqāl li al-Nashr, 1991), 41–43.
26. For a detailed study of this poem, see Issa J. Boullata, "An Arabic Poem in an Israeli Controversy: Maḥmūd Darwīsh's 'Passing Words,'" in *Humanism, Culture, and Language in the Near East: Studies in Honor of Georg Krotkoff,* eds. Asma Afsaruddin and A.H. Mathias Zahniser (Winona Lake, IN: Eisenbrauns, 1997), 119–28.

10

Palestinian Identity in Literature

Salma Khadra Jayyusi

We, the Palestinians

Palestinian identity is rooted in collective identity, the individual belonging to the wider compass of the group, the nation, the village, the party, or the brotherhood. This is an integral part of the inherited outlook of the individual, which pulls him away from his individual self to merge with the community. This heritage was dominant in pre-Islamic times with the Arab's close sense of tribal allegiance and tribal unity, and it was carried on into Islam, which is first and foremost a communal religion that draws all believers together into one flock standing before God. In Islam the individuality of men is diminished within the religion, absorbed into something greater than itself, but also released to exhibit its individual temper within the all-protective vigilance of the group.

The Palestinians' collective attitude is enhanced by their collective struggle to liberate their land and preserve their own identity. The closeness of members in the same political group and their passion for the struggle are poignantly depicted in both the personal and fictional accounts that are written to proclaim the Palestinian story to the world. The group spirit pulls them together, and it is often this group spirit that dictates the tone and theme of Palestinian literature.

To give a single example from personal-account literature, the narrative written by Muʿīn Basīsū (pronounced Bseiso) on his experience as a man wanted by the Egyptian authorities who ruled his hometown of Gaza reflects communal experience and communal goals. A good example from fiction is Saḥar Khalīfa's novel *Al-Ṣubbār* (Wild Thorns), which brilliantly portrays the clash between individual concerns and communal solidarity, with the communal winning in the end. The absolute egocentricity of the father, an extreme example of the older generation of the formerly petit-bourgeois Palestinians who are spent, capitulating, and decrepit, stands in shocking contrast to the self-sacrifice and determination of the younger generation of Palestinian men and women who have persevered in the enduring struggle for Palestinian rights. One of the characters in the novel, Ṣābir, at first chooses survival for himself and his family by keeping his peace and joining the work force of Arab laborers going daily to work in Israel, but in the end he experiences a sudden reversal, joins the fight, and is killed in his first encounter with the enemy.

Among Palestinians an individual may suffer and die alone, but his general plight is always linked to the plight of the community and the nation. When Palestinians think of themselves they always think of "us," the Palestinians: the afflicted; the impoverished; those robbed of home, identity, and possessions; those thrown into destitution, terrorized, tortured, abandoned by the world, and buried alive; but they also think of themselves as dedicated, courageous, self-sacrificing, intelligent, successful, pioneering, enterprising, and—despite their tragedies—robustly alive. This collective nature of Palestinian identity has been an integral part of the national narrative, and it has also played a great role in the process of resistance, in which a collective identity is a cementing factor, pointing to a resemblance in kind and a shared experience that warms the heart.

Memory

Memory has played a great role in the staying power of the Palestinians' struggle to preserve their identity. Memory has been particularly preserved in fiction, personal accounts, and poetry. Because of its capacity to linger in the mind, both folk and formal poetry have most powerfully preserved the memory of the harrowing Palestinian experience that has persisted during a good part of the twentieth century. In so doing modern Palestinian poetry can be seen as the progeny of the poetry that has immortalized Arab triumphs and losses over centuries of experience, keeping memory alive and informed with passion. Throughout its history Arabic poetry has served as a permanent agent of confirmation and unification. It has played a unifying and vitalizing role, as it has helped to propagate the Arab spirit, to mold many of the worldviews and ethical concepts that Arabs still hold as part of their psychological make-up, and to preserve the chronicles of the past. The enlivening memory of Saladdin's triumphs as he reconquered the holy citadel of Jerusalem has never died from the hearts of Arabs. It has gloriously reverberated throughout the centuries, recorded in history texts, which few people read, but carried over vibrantly in poetry, which most people remember. The loss of al-Andalus, on the other hand, has never ceased to bring pain and tears to the eyes, even five hundred years after the event. To give a single example, the famous and highly evocative verses that Shawqī wrote in Spain during his exile in the second decade of the twentieth century cannot fail, even to this day, to move the heart of any Arab who hears them.

In this light, it would be erroneous to evaluate the identity question without taking into account poetry, this unifying, constantly dynamic agent with its rich repertoire of wisdom and memories, its rhetorical sway, its vivid emotional bounce, its recurrent motifs of places and events, and its heart-rending reminders. Even in an era of new poetry that is more muted and has different orientations, the major Palestinian poet Maḥmūd Darwīsh still evokes, no less than Shawqī, Jawāhirī, and Abū Rīsha in their day, the surge of passion in crowds, holding memory alive in the hearts and consciousness of the millions, keeping vigil over the vicissitudes of Palestinian life and searching for an outlet in the dark labyrinth that hems his people in.

A Well-Defined Palestinian Perspective

Despite their thriving cultural achievements in modern times, the Arabs are suffering a cultural malaise with roots in their painful relationship with the West. Since early in the twentieth century there has been a widespread assumption among Arabs of the superiority of Western cultural and artistic output. Up to the 1970s, quite a few prominent, Western-educated Arabs have asserted this notion of Western "superiority," and often they have engaged in an equally concentrated attack on the Arab Islamic heritage, or at least in a snobbish neglect of or biased indifference toward it. During that long period, the defense of the classical cultural repertoire, one of the richest in the history of world cultures, was taken up mainly by traditionalists lacking the critical tools that could impose a decisive argument offered in modern terms. Thus, the unrivaled cultural achievements of the Arabs in medieval times were ignored and remained cast off in the recesses of old libraries or burdensome academic assignments. There was a general capitulation not simply to the idea of Western cultural superiority, but also to the belief in the rigidity and utter uselessness of the inherited literature and its irrelevance to modern times.

This attitude changed with the rise, in the 1970s, of a new, more rigorous, and more sophisticated scholarship in both the Arab and Western worlds. Contemporary Arabs, however, have not yet fully resolved the challenging problems imposed on them during this century. They are now more confident in their own culture and more aware of the connections among culture, politics, and colonialism. They have begun to believe that the West is culturally antagonistic to them, and they feel that its major interest in Arab and Islamic culture is to look for flaws in either the theoretical basis on which this culture is built or in the applications of fundamentals. Its interest in how Islam deals with the rights of women, for example, or with fundamentalism (two issues that are not yet resolved in the West itself) far outstrips any interest in other areas of culture that could reflect a more luminous image, including travel accounts, philosophical works, chronicles, and folk epics, as well as Islam in its original state.

In addition, Arabs today are torn between their admiration for the liberal, humanistic aspects of Western culture; their suspicions about the Western approach to their own culture; the still-unresolved feelings of tension toward their heritage; and the horrid political situation they have been driven into—both internally (by the coercive Arab establishments, lack of freedom and democracy, and constant encroachment on human rights) and externally (by Israel, mainly, but also by the Gulf War of 1991, which destroyed the economy and the mental and physical health of a whole nation and left American military installations camped on Arab land). Due to all this, contemporary Arabs suffer from a deep perplexity about what they were, what they are, and what they will become in the future. Belonging neither to the fundamentalist front nor to the now much less formidable Marxist front, most Arab intellectuals entertain nascent uncertainties toward and mistrust of ideologies. This situation has resulted in a fragile hold on goals and a disjunction of outlook. The major positive trend they display is perhaps their aspiration for democracy and the implementation of human rights, but these are two hazardous quests that are often approached only on a theoretical basis.

Palestinian cultural and literary identity is perhaps more defined and more distinctly concrete than that of other Arabs, due to their greater concern to preserve their identity and history and to struggle to attain the well-defined goals of freedom, justice, security, and national liberation. To the Palestinian writer the Palestine issue, which is central in his or her work, is clear, its history well known, its dangers anticipated, and its future gloomy, threatening a long period of struggle and sacrifice. As Murīd al-Barghūthī ominously predicts:

> O Lifetime of ours, go on! Parents!
> Give our children plenty of milk
> Prepare what light for them you can
> save for them every matchstick
> keep the lanterns, and the oil
> For the night means to inhabit us for a long time.[1]

And in the words of Muḥammad al-Asʿad:

> What will come next
> Will be even darker.[2]

The Palestinian creative writer identifies the Palestinians as singled out to suffer monumental tragedies and wage a sustained and dedicated struggle over a long time. This writer's vision is well defined: he predicts the Palestinian destiny and accepts its predictable frontiers. Only if the newly formed Palestinian National Authority, reflecting the style of Arab governments elsewhere, begins to clamp down on writers and their quest for democracy and the implementation of human rights will doubts and uncertainties begin to assail the firm concepts of the writer and his view of his national responsibility.[3] Most Palestinian authors have no time or inclination to entangle themselves in the intricacies of contradictory, self-consuming notions. The central vision in their work is the Palestinian cause, with its clear, well-defined demarcations, dealing with the stuff of human tragedy and with the notions of resistance, self-sacrifice, and faith.

The Touchstone of a Unifying Ritual

The semantics of such concepts as resistance, courage, honor, duty, patriotism, and responsibility have been a driving force in the Palestinians' spiritual survival. It must be emphasized here that in *good* Palestinian literature the verbal utterance of these abstracts has faithfully been avoided; the contemporary sophisticated aesthetics and the modernizing agents that have become a religion to contemporary writers would not tolerate such a verbal utterance of abstract concepts. Instead, they are conveyed in the tone, the subject matter, and the descriptive account of what has happened and still happens to Palestinians. At least in literature, and particularly in poetry, Palestinian identity is well preserved in its pride and convictions, its aspiration to heroism, its resilience, and its rejection of the role of the complete victim; but also in its contemplation of its own counterviolence, its assumed self-righteousness, even sometimes its arrogant defiance. This has been the moral landscape dictated by harsh political reality as well as the living pan-Arab heritage of a glorified, twentieth-century, anticolonialist struggle that recalls its martyrs forever. Ernest Hemingway once said that "abstract words such as glory, honor, courage, or hallow were obscene beside the concrete names of villages, the numbers of roads, the names of rivers." This can be well applied to Palestinian literature. It has been the names of villages, mountains, and rivers that have been the touchstone that has never failed to arouse deep reaction in the listener or reader. While the abstract words have been kept at low gear, there is no writer who has not stood at the side of the freedom fighter, the Intifada child, the demonstrating schoolgirl, and the fallen martyr. One can see in this literature that there is no doubt in the minds of the writers or the nation as a whole regarding the righteousness of the struggle and the complete aggression of the enemy.

The conviction of the Palestinians that their cause is just and that a great injustice has been dealt to them and to their land allows the writers to maintain a singularly powerful moral position in the world. There is almost nothing in Palestinian literature like the doubts so many American writers[4] had regarding the American government as a consequence of the Vietnam War. As one American writer has noted, "While the war was being fought with Americans actively participating, there was hardly a poet who did not contribute to the flood of war protest poetry in one way or another. [The returning American fighters oscillated between] victim and executioner."[5] Honorable mention is due here to the high-minded Israeli and Jewish writers and activists who have opposed by many methods the dangers of the Israelis' flawed policy in Palestine. The Palestinian scene, however, is different. Palestinian literature harbors no such protest and does not engage in the reexamination of national myths: Palestinian heroes remain heroes, and Palestinian villains remain villains.

Palestinians, however, have been critical of other Arabs. No worthy Palestinian writer, to my knowledge, has condoned the cruelty imposed on the Palestinians in the Diaspora by other Arabs in whose countries most Palestinian refugees settled. Murīd Barghūthī writes of this issue with irony and sarcasm. Addressing the Palestinian, he says:

> To every citizen there is one ruler.
> You alone are favored with twenty
> in twenty capitals.
> If you made one of them angry,
> the law would claim your head
> and if you honored one of the them
> the rest would want you dead.[6]

In both prose and poetry there is a demarcation line between an Arab state and its people. The state in the Arab world is, on the whole, the object of attack by its own writers and poets, either directly or indirectly. And it is the works of literature which malign the corruption of some Arab governments, or at least their weaknesses and lack of determination, that are most popular on a regional and a pan-Arab level. Many poets acquire their reputation because of their involvement in the fight against the political malaise in the Arab world. The vast halls of Arab cities in which poetry is read to huge audiences have often experienced bursts of frenzied excitement at the declamation of the political poet attacking Arab establishments. This is why when Palestinian literature complains of unjust treatment by other Arabs it is seen as a welcome contribution to the Arab world.

A Terrible Clash of Identities

The confirmation of Palestinian identity has been strengthened by the necessity to confront a strong Israeli identity, which has been belligerent, overreaching, and self-imposing, as well as capable of addressing through various methods the world at large. The Israelis have excelled in inventing the argument that rationalized their acts of aggression against the Palestinians. They have had to go into elaborate, make-believe accounts, often self-deluding in nature to the extreme, in which the Israeli aggressor is transformed into a victim and the Palestinian victim is transformed into a bloodthirsty terrorist who had no right to be in the country.

When the State of Israel established itself in 1948, the Palestinians who remained in Palestine found themselves second-class residents in their own birthplace. It was mainly the defiant or ironic rejoinders to this biased and racist situation in Palestinian literature that captured the hearts of all Arabs. Maḥmūd Darwīsh's simple, poignant early poem, "Write Down 'I am an Arab' " became the rage in the 1970s when it reached the Arab world, as did Tawfīq Zayyād's defiant verses "Here We Remain," which were sung all over the Arab world. Imīl Ḥabībī's brilliant novel, *The Secret Life of Said the Pessoptimist,* portrays a small-time Palestinian collaborator with the Israeli authorities who acts the perfect fool to save his neck in a place, once his own country, that had suddenly become threatening and menacing. This novel has been highly successful and has received numerous rave reviews in the Arab world. Readers were particularly drawn to the fact that the protagonist undergoes two experiences: he does not escape Israeli suspicion and is therefore imprisoned and tortured, and he meets in prison a real Palestinian hero under whose influence he experiences a reversal and rebels against both himself and his Israeli masters.

While the Israelis have related to the country as if the Palestinians did not exist, the Palestinian literary identity has never been invisible to the Israelis, and could never be. I think that the Israelis know its importance, know that it is the conscience of its people, the profound expression of their inner promptings, and most importantly the register of their recent history. Furthermore, it is, on the whole, an accomplished literature, potent, flowing more profusely every year, rich, vibrant, humane, and to a great extent honest in its convictions and in its proclamations of its own experiences of loss and suffering, of a terrible injustice endured, but also of self-betrayal, agonizing shortcomings, and tragic failures. Its literary strength stems from the deeply entrenched roots of the Arabic language and literary tradition. It also draws on the joyful contemplation of its modern burgeoning, the discovery of its potency, the recent explosion of its genius, and above all its initial innocence, the burning memory of its having been wrenched away, unawares, from normal life and plunged into an inferno of suffering while still at the borderline of awakening into twentieth-century life in the twilight zone between pre-modern stupor and modern consciousness.

The Palestinian Cultural Identity

Has there been any change in the cultural identity of Palestinians or in the way they contemplate their own cultural output since 1948? It may come as a surprise to hear me answer that yes, a fantastic change in the cultural identity of the Palestinian poet and writer of fiction has indeed taken place since 1948. This, however, was due not to cultural encounter with Israelis, but to the fact that the Palestinians in the Diaspora, living at large in the Arab homeland and elsewhere, where they came into direct contact with the vibrant literary currents blowing over the Arab world, have come finally into their own, discovered their creative potency, and acquired new ambitions that the pre-1948 generations did not experience.

In several of my writings on modern Arabic literature, I have shown that Palestinians living in the land of Palestine were little exposed to the literary currents that, since the Arab literary renaissance in the nineteenth century, have been blowing over the rest of the Arab heartland, producing a continuous effervescence of literary creativity and thereby creating a chain of development that culminated in the late 1940s in the greatest revolution ever known to Arabic poetry, making it ready to embrace modernism. In Palestine at this time, however, there was, comparatively speaking, a paucity of real creative endeavor. So many talents remained dormant, and genius often stayed undiscovered or was waylaid on traditional roads. Unless the poetic utterance was political, it was submerged in obscure labyrinths.

The fact that modern Palestine was not the home of great literary activity before the 1950s and its poets and writers were rarely counted among the major literary figures of the pre-1948 Arab world was not simply the result of the unsavory political situation at the end of World War I into which the Palestinian people had been unknowingly plunged. This momentous reality only helped to complicate a cultural situation that had historically suffered from a kind of semi-isolation keeping Palestinians away from the cultural currents that joined the Shīʿa centers of Iraq (Kufa and Najaf) with those of Lebanon (Sidon and Tyre); the Sunni centers of Baghdad with those of Damascus, Aleppo, Istanbul, and Cairo; and Christian Aleppo with Lebanon and Rome. Palestine was not influenced by any of these currents, nor was it the home of great and powerful patrons of literature.

After scrutinizing the cultural situation during the pre-1950s period, the observer would easily discover that Palestinian talent would emerge, and even sometimes explode, when the writer would go to live outside the borders of his country and thereby come into actual contact with other creative talents actively at work. To give two examples: when he was a consul in Bordeaux at the turn of the century, Rawḥī al-Khālidī wrote an authoritative treatise on comparative literature; and Ibrāhīm Ṭūqān's talent burgeoned and surged when, as a student in Beirut, he came into contact with poets from several regions of the Arab world.

In recent decades, however, exile has sharpened the talent of Palestinians everywhere. Palestinian literature has made a decisive leap to the highest level of the modern literary experiment. Particularly in the Palestinian Diaspora, where the young generation of evacuee poets and writers of fiction has grown up in the active and blossoming literary atmosphere of the Arab world at large, it boasts some of the best modernist poets and writers of fiction of the whole Arab world and has produced one of the most famous and original poets now writing in Arabic, Maḥmūd Darwīsh. This, which I would describe as the "great divide" in the modern history of Palestinian literature, has changed the way Palestinians view their cultural identity. No longer in relative isolation, Palestinian writers are now major originators and sometimes leaders of new trends.[7] The death of the Palestinian novelist Jabrā Ibrāhīm Jabrā in 1995, for example, was a major Arab literary event, mourned by countless critics and writers. Last but not least is the outstanding figure of Edward Said, whose writings have made a great difference in the way the Orientalist scholars look at the Arabs, and indeed have changed the view of Arab identity throughout the world.

Notes

1. Salma Khadra Jayyusi, ed., *Anthology of Modern Palestinian Literature* (New York: Columbia University Press, 1992), 131. The translation is by Lena Jayyusi and W. S. Merwin.
2. *Ibid.,* 121. The translation is by May Jayyusi and Jack Collom.
3. The clarity of the struggle, the straightforward action, and the literature on it have always been clear cut and well defined in Arabic literature when fighting colonial aggression. Ambiguity and the resort to camouflage and oblique and convoluted expression are seen when the coercive enemy is the ruler of one's country.
4. Such as P. Caputo, Harold Rosenberg, and Robert Bly, who in his long poem, "The Teeth Mother Naked at Last" (1980), compares the American actions in Vietnam with the Pharaohs' treatment of the Jews.

5. Robert Lifton, *Home From the War: Vietnam Veterans: Neither Victims Nor Executioners* (New York: Simon and Schuster, 1973).
6. Murīd Barghūthi, *Ṭāla al-Shatāt* (Long Is This Exile) (Beirut: Dār al-Kalima, 1987), 113. The translation is mine.
7. In addition to the outstanding and highly original poetic experiments of Maḥmūd Darwīsh, there has also been the rise of a handful of poets who have absorbed genuine modernity, despite the involvement of Palestinian literature with the political cause, including Ṭāhir Riyāḍ, Walīd Khāzindār, Ghassān Zaqṭān, Zakariyyā Muḥammad, Muḥammad al-Asʿad, Zuhayr Abu Shayeb, and others. In fiction, the accomplishments of Palestinian writers are not less than those in poetry. In fact, some of the most original and fascinating experiments in Arabic fiction since the 1960s were created by Palestinian authors: Imīl Ḥabībī's *The Pessoptimist,* Ghassān Kanafānī's *All That's Left to You,* and the amazing postmodern novel of Ibrāhīm Naṣrallāh, *Prairies of Fear.* All three novels have been translated by the Project of Translation from Arabic (PROTA) and offered to the English-speaking reader with full introductions.

Living on Borderlines:* War and Exile in Selected Works by Ghassān Kanafānī, Fawaz Turki, and Maḥmūd Darwīsh

Kamal Abdel-Malek

> For the last half-century or so, to be Palestinian was, in part by upbringing, in part by sensibility, to be a wanderer, an exile, a touch moon-mad, always a little different from others. Our name, which we acquired after 1948, was not so much a national title—we had had no nation—as an existential term. Palestinians enjoyed the freedom to go beyond the confining thresholds of national torpor. We had the freedom to remember, to dream of a different reality, to deliver ourselves into history's keeping.[1]

The literary depiction of the deep scars war and exile have inflicted on Palestinians can be understood in light of recent Western literary scholarship on marginality and anthropological studies of liminality. Arnold van Gennep sees the "liminal" as the middle point in the three stages typically found in rites of passage: separation, liminality, and reaggregation. Victor Turner adds a spatial dimension to van Gennep's definition of the liminal. For Turner liminality can be a state in its own right and not a transient one.[2] Gustavo Perez Firmat points out the subversive nature of the liminal when he states that "the liminal entity, whatever its nature (an individual, a group, an event, a text) is one that at a given situation takes up a position of eccentricity, one that occupies the periphery in relation to a contextually determined center."[3] This chapter shows that major works by Palestinian writers as different as Ghassān Kanafānī, Fawaz Turki, and Maḥmūd Darwīsh include characters, techniques, and literary tropes that can be characterized as liminal entities that, in turn, represent the central Palestinian experience of living a marginal existence on literal and figurative borders.

Ghassān Kanafānī's *Men in the Sun:* The Aborted Rite of Passage:

Men in the Sun (1966) depicts the fate of three Palestinian refugees who are smuggled through the borders into Kuwait inside an empty tanker truck. The three are left in the truck for too long as the border inspection is being negotiated. Under the sun, the three men die of suffocation, unable to alert anyone to their presence. The oldest of the refugees, Abu Qais, is an elderly man who lives in abject poverty with his wife and children. He hopes to slip through the border of Kuwait in order to work there and send money to his family. The novel opens with this passage about him:

> Abu Qais rested his chest on the damp ground, and the earth began to throb under him, with tired heartbeats, which trembled through the grains of sand and penetrated the cells of his body. Every time he threw himself down with his chest to the ground he sensed that throbbing, as though the heart of the earth had been pushing its difficult way towards the light from the utmost depths of hell, ever since the time he had lain there. Once when he said that to his neighbour, with whom he shared the field in the land he left ten years ago, the man answered mockingly:
>
> "It's the sound of your own heart. You can hear it when you lay your chest close to the ground."
>
> What wicked nonsense! And the smell, then? The smell which, when he sniffed it surged into his head and then poured down into his veins. Every time he breathed the scent of the earth, as he lay on it, he imagined that he was sniffing his wife's hair when she had just walked out of the bathroom, after washing with cold water. The very same smell, the smell of a woman who had washed her hair with cold water and covered her face with her hair while it was still damp. The same throbbing, like carrying a small bird tenderly in your hands.[4]

Abu Qais slowly becomes aware that he is somewhere near where the Tigris and the Euphrates rivers meet and form one river. (Notice here the confluence of the two rivers as a liminal entity reminiscent of the

Qur'anic reference to the confluence of the two seas *majmaʿ al-baḥrayn.*)[5] He is there waiting to be smuggled into Kuwait. As the passage illustrates, the present is sensed through recollecting the past: his conversations with his neighbor, the voice of his geography teacher in a Palestinian school before 1948, going over a lesson about the Tigris and the Euphrates forming one river. Abu Qais's own present, therefore, "is an amalgam of disjointed memory with the gathering force of his difficult situation now; he is a refugee with a family, forced to seek employment in a country whose blinding sun signifies the universal indifference to his fate."[6]

Abu Qais's fellow refugee Assad is wanted for unknown political activities. Like Abu Qais, Assad hopes to flee his precarious existence to a life of security. He is helped to flee by his uncle, who hopes to marry him off to his daughter Nada. But Assad does not want to marry his cousin Nada. As Assad poignantly puts it, his uncle wants "to buy him for his daughter as you buy a sack of manure for a field."[7]

Marwan, at age sixteen, is the youngest of the three refugees. Zakariyya, his older brother, had left for Kuwait many years ago. Although for a time Zakariyya would send the family money from Kuwait, he no longer does. Marwan, therefore, is now faced with the responsibility of fending for his mother and young siblings in the refugee camp where they live. He is determined to seek a new life in Kuwait and send every penny he earns to his family.

Abul Khaizuran is the truck driver who smuggles people into Kuwait for a sum of money. He is described as a skilled driver who worked for the British army during the Palestine mandate. In a battle with Zionist forces, he was hit between his thighs and became impotent. He is destined to live with the physical scars of the war in whose aftermath he lost both home and manhood.[8] It is ironic that his Arabic name literally means "father of the bamboo stick," an obvious phallic symbol. Kanafānī appears to suggest that much like Abul Khaizuran, Arab or Palestinian leadership became impotent in 1948 and after, and yet kept pretending to be aroused by the desire to do battle with Israel.[9]

The novel describes the journey of the four Palestinians. Theirs is a passage, both in the sense of a journey and of a rite of passage. But unlike the conventional rites of passage that end with postliminal incorporation by means of a reunion with the community, theirs ends with death, the ultimate separation. The journey proceeds through several stages, which the author identifies as "the Deal," "the Road," "Sun and Shade," and "the Grave." In "the Deal" there is the bargaining over the price of smuggling the main characters into another country, literally crossing borders. "The Road" describes the ordeal of going through the scorching heat of the desert, where "the sun was pouring its inferno down on them without any respite."[10] The road, a liminal entity, is described by Abul Khaizuran as the *ṣirāṭ,* "the path which God in the Qur'ān promised his creatures they must cross before being directed either to Paradise or to Hell. If anyone falls he goes to Hell, and if anyone crosses safely he reaches Paradise. Here the angels are the frontier guards."[11] Both "Sun and Shade" and "the Grave" provide powerful descriptions of the fateful journey, which ends in the gratuitous death of the smuggled men.

The novel blends past and present. Characters articulate their predicament by means of present voices intercepted by past echoes. For example, as Assad is negotiating another attempt at getting himself smuggled into Kuwait, he recalls his first attempt, when "the earth turned into shining sheets of yellow paper. . . ."[12] At this point in the narrative, the figurative yellow sheets remind him of the real yellow writing sheets on the desk:

> Suddenly the yellow sheets began to fly about, and he stooped to gather them up.
>
> "Thanks. Thanks. This damned fan makes the papers fly about in front of me, but I can't breathe without it. Ha! What have you decided?"[13]

Elsewhere we come across the word "rats" in different but juxtaposed scenes. In one scene we read:

> "Oh. This desert is full of rats. What on earth do they eat?"
>
> He answered quietly:
>
> "Rats smaller than them."
>
> "Really?" said the girl. "It's frightening. Rats themselves are horrible, frightening animals."

Then in another scene that immediately follows this one we read:

> The fat man who owned the office said:
>
> "Rats are horrible animals. How can you sleep in that hotel?"
>
> "It's cheap."[14]

Key words here appear as liminal entities. They are made to act like a bridge, or isthmus, between blocks of past events and present ones, as in the case of the word "rats"[15] in the passages quoted above—uttered by two different characters in two different episodes, otherwise unrelated. Note also the word "light" in another passage, which connects two episodes in Abul Khaizuran's distant and recent past[16]—the piercing light of the operating room in a 1948 scene when he "lost his manhood" and the blazing light of the sun in a different scene several years later. Humans are depicted not as pure types, not as bipolar entities of good versus evil or friend versus foe. For example, Marwan's father is described as "someone who did something horrible [by divorcing Marwan's mother and marrying another woman], but which of us doesn't from time to time?"[17] Thoughts of the four characters leak into one another: "the thoughts seemed to run from one head to another, laden with the same suspicions. . . ."[18]

At the end of the novel, Abul Khaizuran takes the corpses out of the tank and throws them onto a municipal waste dump. After he leaves the place, he returns to take away the possessions of the dead men. He climbs into his truck then shouts, "Why didn't you knock on the sides of the tank? Why didn't you say anything? Why?"[19] The desert, we read, echoes back his questions. Here Kanafānī seems to suggest that Palestinians be called upon to embark on their national struggle in word (shouting) and in deed (knocking). Otherwise, they are destined to be both physically and existentially banished outside the borders of their homeland and world attention.

Kanafānī's *Men in the Sun* merges present with past; key words in it serve as connective tissues between writing segments, between units of time and geography. His Palestinian characters are on-the-move, restless, marginalized individuals—misguided, it seems. Theirs is a journey that can be seen as a reenactment of the rites of passage, even though the characters are stuck midway at the liminal stage. Borders spell death for these characters—borders are *ḥudūd,* not only in the sense of limits, boundaries, but also, as in the Islamic legal terminology, penalties.

Fawaz Turki: Exile as a Permanent Habitat

In his book *The Disinherited,* Fawaz Turki[20] describes his family's flight from Haifa to Beirut during the Arab-Israeli war in 1948 and how they all ended up living in a refugee camp. "With our memories," says Turki, "of places and times we had known before, rational and good, floating in the space around us and within us, we existed not in the present tense, the tense of reality, but the future imperfect, when next year, next time, next speech, the wrongs will have been righted, the grievances removed, and our cause justified... Godot, for whom we waited, never arrived."[21]

Growing up as a refugee in Beirut, with no regular education or work, Turki became a street kid and a petty thief. After some years of aimless life, he fortunately was offered an opportunity to go to school and to study in England for three and a half years. When he returned to the Middle East, he says, he was "more embittered, more disillusioned, more unhappy than when I left."[22] In one incident, he runs into Um Ismael, a neighbor in his Beirut refugee camp. He now finds Um Ismael a frail broken woman, no longer able to defy the world, to utter vociferous threats and obscenities. "How was it?" asks Turki, "When was it that the Palestinian mind wrinkled with gloom and saw the whole world as the land of no man?"[23] In his heart, he urges Um Ismael to be defiant again:

> Swear, Um Ismael, swear woman. Say ben sharmoota [literally, son of a whore] on the camp, on the world, on the Zionists, on the two-bit Lebanese; say ben sharmoota on God; throw rocks and garbage at passing army trucks as you used to do, woman. Don't give up. We are becoming a defeated people, fading, descending. A piece of fluff blowing hither and thither in the air, disintegrating.[24]

Turki left Lebanon for Saudi Arabia. He found work with Aramco. But soon his unruly behavior got him into trouble with his superiors and he lost his job. The immediate reason for the clash with his superiors had to do with the preferential treatment offered the American employees at the company. He then returned to Beirut to realize more than before that for him and his fellow Palestinians living in this kind of limbo, divested of any hope for a solution to the national predicament and unable to alter the cruel circumstance of life in exile "defeated some of us. It reduced and distorted and alienated others."[25] Turki considers himself as part of the "defeated" who had to leave the Arab world altogether and go to places like India or Australia or the United States, to wrestle, as he says, with his own and his people's plight and to understand. But soon he came to the bitter realization that "[A]fter twenty-five years of living in the ghourba, of growing up permanently reminded of my status as an exile, the diaspora for me, for a whole generation of Palestinians, becomes *the* homeland. Palestine is no longer a mere geographical entity but a state of mind. The reason, however, that Palestinians are obsessed with the notion of Returning, though indeed there is no Palestine to return to . . . is because the Return means the reconstitution of a Palestinian's integrity and the regaining of his place in history."[26]

In his *Exile's Return: The Making of a Palestinian American* (1994),[27] Turki describes his return to the homeland for a visit, after more than forty years of living in exile. "My book is the story of one Palestinian exile who tries to come to grips and, finally, to terms with his condition. . . . [T]he book is both a backward glance at my life as a Palestinian writer, activist, and an unhoused wanderer, and an account of my visit to Palestine on the eve of the Persian Gulf War, in which I reflect on the tensions that exist between Palestinians who have always lived in their homeland and those, who, like myself, have lived in exile."[28] He says that whereas the English-speaking readers may find his book informative, his fellow Palestinians in the Palestine Liberation Organization (PLO) will find it scandalous, and others of his people will be "shocked by its harsh critiques of Palestinian popular culture and its antiquated mores."[29]

Turki attacks several aspects of social life in the Palestinian "homeground" and the Arab world at large, most notably formal literary Arabic. For Turki, Arabs have three different varieties of the same language that are as different as Chaucer's, Churchill's, and African-American English are from one another. These varieties are Classical Arabic; Formal Arabic (what is commonly referred to as Modern Standard Arabic), which he describes as the one invented by the "age of neobackwardness," his ironic label for the Arab *nahḍa* (renaissance) that started in the second half of the nineteenth century; and Oral Arabic, dubbed by him as the language of the masses "whose vocabulary, chaotic grammar, structure, and tonality reflect the mutilated world Arabs inhabit."[30]

During his stay in the homeland Turki visits Haifa, his birthplace, as well as Jerusalem, Ramallah, and other places both inside Israel and in the Occupied Territories. He is always on the move, in search for what he calls the magic country behind the mountain. As he does in *The Disinherited,* he also describes here how he grew up in a refugee camp in Lebanon and how all his life there and elsewhere he suffered from the humiliation of material deprivation and the severe brutality of exile.

Turki tells us of encounters with high-ranking Palestinian politicians and activists. One politician he meets is a perfect example of a liminal entity, living astride two worlds but not belonging to either one:

> Shaath was addressing me in English. He spoke faultless textbook English, but his archaic imagery was quintessentially Arabic. Like other Westernized Palestinian intellectuals, especially those who now embrace Islam and reject the West as the Great Satan, Shaath is tormented by the dilemma of a man

> who has gone far—but not deep—into an alien culture to which he suddenly realizes he can never belong, and is now drawn back to an Arab culture to which he can never return.[31]

As readers, we may find ourselves asking whether Turki is not in some ways like Shaath, torn between two worlds and really belonging to neither.

In this book, Turki's return is anticlimactic. In his birthplace, Haifa, Turki says that he "felt nothing." He gives up on the idea of returning to his homeland. "I need not live in Nablus or Jericho or Gaza. . . . And I need not die in Haifa, Safad, or Jaffa. Washington will do."[32] The only return for him is a symbolic one. At the end of the book, Turki enacts this return to Haifa by summoning the spirit of his father. It is through the son that the father has symbolically returned to Haifa. Echoing his conclusion in his earlier book, *The Disinherited,* Turki states, "[F]orty-five years of exile are homeland enough."[33] The exile is destined to live in a perpetual state of liminality; the threshold has become his permanent habitat.

Unlike Kanafānī's men, Turki did return to the homeland, but only to discover that after years of living in exile, the bond between him, the native son, and the land had expired, as it were. The death of his hope for reunion with his fellow Palestinians in the land that was called Palestine was slow and drawn out, whereas theirs was a sudden and gratuitous death. Having been banished from the centrality of the homeland, Turki, the exile, the liminal entity, can be seen as a menace to the established order, threatening to subvert both customary laws and literary conventions. In this sense, he is unlike Kanafānī's men, who have in the end died as helpless victims of their exile.

Maḥmūd Darwīsh's *Memory for Forgetfulness:* The Text That Falls Betwixt and Between

Genres in Memory for Forgetfulness

Maḥmūd Darwīsh's *Memory for Forgetfulness* [34] recounts the poet's harrowing experiences in Beirut during the summer of 1982 when it was besieged and relentlessly bombarded by the Israeli army. The first thing that strikes us in this book is its seemingly contradictory title, *Memory for Forgetfulness.* Memory in the title refers many times to Darwīsh's life in the homeland, while the Israeli invasion of Lebanon and the siege of Beirut are the things he would hope to forget. Here the poles of memory and forgetfulness are intertwined in such a manner as to form a new intermediary combination that owes its existence to both but does not totally belong to either. The liminality of the text, as reflective of the position of its author and his fellow Palestinians in war-torn Lebanon, is therefore established early on.

Intertextuality in Memory for Forgetfulness

The text opens with a dream and ends with the author going to sleep at the end of the day. Between his waking and sleep, events take place and memories of the past are invoked; both are interwoven in the act of writing. Writing serves as a witness (*shāhid*) to the events the author describes. Writing is also the metaphor of all existence in the Arab and Islamic view. According to this view, expressed by the medieval historian Ibn al-Athīr, "God . . . created the Pen and commanded it, so that it wrote into being everything that will exist till the Day of Judgment."[35] The text of the Qur'ān is believed by Muslims to be recorded on the "Preserved Tablet" (*al-lawḥ al-maḥfūẓ).* According to this view, words in the Qur'ān are God's own (*kalām allāh)* and it is with words that God creates, for He says to the thing: "Be!" and it becomes (*kun fa-yakūn).* The author has only words with which to create the memory. He writes into being the memory of times past. He erects writing as a witness *(shāhid),* a testimony to what is already gone. But a text may carry its own contradiction so that by calling writing a witness (*shāhid*), the text may also be its own gravestone or epitaph (both are *shāhid* in Arabic).[36]

Darwīsh quotes another passage from the medieval book, *al-Kāmil fī l-Tārīkh* (A Complete History) by Ibn al-Athīr:

> He [God] created the earth on a whale, and the whale is the letter Nune [sic] . . . . The whale was in the water, and the water was on a wide, smooth stone, and the stone was on the back of an angel, and the angel on a rock, and the rock was in the wind. This was the rock mentioned by Luqman, which is neither in the sky nor on earth. The whale moved, and the earth was disturbed and shook, whereupon God set the mountains on it and it stayed in place.[37]

This medieval passage is immediately followed by another in which Darwīsh brings the reader to besieged Beirut in 1982: "I walk down the street, exactly in the middle, not caring to know where I'm going. As if I were sleepwalking. I don't come out of anything, and I don't go into anything. But the rage in my conflicting emotions rises higher than the roar of jets, which I ignore."[38] The juxtaposition links the mythic with the real, the cosmic with the momentary, pointing out the precariousness of human existence in both the image of the earth's unstable foundation and the vulnerable civilian about to be blown up any moment by the enemy's shells.

Quotes from the medieval work *al-Bidāya wa l-Nihāya* (The Beginning and the End) by Ibn Kathīr are followed by quotes from another medieval work, by Usāma ibn Munqidh, concerning the Franks. Israelis are alluded to as the modern counterparts of the Franks; both laid siege to Muslim lands and engaged in war atrocities. Between the two medieval sources, the cruelties as well as the venalities of the enemies are illustrated. "That year," Darwīsh quotes Ibn Kathīr, "the Franks took Jerusalem and killed more than sixty thousand Muslims. They broke into homes, wreaking havoc wherever they went. . . ."[39] Then he follows the long quote with one from Ibn Munqidh that illustrates the "lack of zeal and jealousy" among the Franks. One day, we are told, a Frank soldier went home and found a man lying in bed with the Frank's wife.

> He asked him, "What could have made thee enter into my wife's room?" The man replied, "I was tired, so I went in to rest." "But how," asked he, "didst thou get into my bed?" The other replied, "Well, the bed is hers. How could I therefore have prevented her from using her own bed?" "By the truth of my religion," said the husband, "if thou shouldst do it again, thou and I will have a quarrel." Such was for the Frank the entire expression of his disapproval and the limit of his jealousy.[40]

Anecdote after anecdote of this type are cited in order to ridicule the Frankish enemies, and in each one of these anecdotes, medieval Muslims are shown resisting the foreign occupation against all odds, now by the sword, now by the pen. It is as though Darwīsh were saying: "There was a time when we fought off the enemy, when we devastated the enemy by the sharp sword and the pointed pen, in the battlefield and in the written text in which we subjected the enemy to our own interpretation."

Another example of Darwīsh's intertextual technique is his meditation on the meaning and significance of water at a time when the Israeli army during the summer months of 1982 cut off the water supply to Beirut. "What is water?"[41] asks Darwīsh. It is, he declares, more than its chemical composition; it is "the joy of the senses and the air that surrounds them."[42] He then quotes the Qur'ān, "We made from water every living thing," (Qur'ān: 21:20),[43] and the tenth-century epistle of Ibn

Faḍlān, which records his journey into Russia and his disgust at the sight of Russian soldiers using one vessel of water to wash.[44] He then describes the treachery of the Israelis, referred to as "leftover Crusaders,"[45] who cut off the water supply to thirsty Beirutis, and he contrasts it with the magnanimity of the Muslim commander Saladin who used to send ice and fruit to the Crusader enemies in the hope that "their hearts would melt."[46] When we Arabs were in a position of power in the distant past, Darwīsh appears to suggest, we enjoyed not only military superiority over Westerners but also superior knowledge about them; centuries ago we understood that knowledge was power.

For Darwīsh, such was the powerful position of medieval Arabs. At present the tables are turned and the contemporary Arabs find themselves robbed of their civilizational roles; robbed in fact, Darwīsh suggests, of all their roles, even the one of being victims of Israeli aggression. "I didn't rejoice over the demonstrations in Tel Aviv, which continues to rob us of all our roles. From them the killer, and the victim, from them the pain, and the cry; the sword, and the rose; the victory, and the defeat." He goes on to explain that he did not rejoice "because their intent was to banish the heroes from the stage. They had grown accustomed to easy wars and easy victories. . . . The victor was defeated from within. The victor was afraid to lose his identity as victim."[47] "From them," Darwīsh continues, "the sin, and from them the forgiveness. From them the killing, and the tears. From them the massacres, and the justice of the courts."[48] The Palestinians, Darwīsh suggests, are not only banished from their birthplace but also from world attention; both their land and their historical role as victims have been usurped. "Is there," asks Darwīsh, "anything more cruel than this absence: that you should not be the one to celebrate your victory or the one to lament your defeat? That you should stay offstage and not make an entrance except as a subject for others to take up and interpret."[49]

Another example of intertextuality is Darwīsh's allusion to the Bible. He bitterly describes an imagined conversation that takes place when a Maronite woman welcomes an Israeli soldier, a reference to the welcome given to the Israeli army in the early days of the invasion by members of the Maronite community. Some parts of this imagined dialogue ironically evoke the biblical Song of Songs:

> Yesterday's newspapers showed the carnation ladies throwing themselves at the invaders' tanks, their bosoms and thighs bare in the summer nakedness and pleasure, ready to receive the saviors.

> *"Kiss me on the lips, Shlomo! O kiss me on the lips! What's your name, my love so I can call you by your name, my darling? Shlomo, come into my house, slowly, slowly, or all at once so that I can feel your strength. How I love your strength, my love!"*[50]

Metaleptic Reversals in Memory for Forgetfulness

Metalepsis is a literary trope that "places the present before the past, effect before cause, epigone before precursor."[51] As a reversal of the normal order of things, it appears that metalepsis "takes up a position of eccentricity, one that occupie[s] the periphery in relation to a contextually determined center"[52] of established order. Darwīsh employs metalepsis to drive home the paradoxes of life in Beirut under Israeli siege. It is not the metal of weapons that engages human flesh but the other way around: "The day human flesh clenched the muscles of its spirit and cried: 'They shall not pass, and we will not leave!' Flesh engaged metal: it won the difficult arithmetic, and the conquerors were halted by the walls."[53] Meaning seems to predate its word, meaning looks for its word: "Meanings will find their words again."[54] The soul is not inside the body but rather it is the body that is inside the soul. Addressing the Israelis, Darwīsh says: "They shall not pass as long as there's life in our bodies. Let them pass then, if they can pass at all, over what corpses the spirit may spit out."[55] Under war conditions imminent death arouses lust. Darwīsh asks, "Is it part of the nature of war to create this lust?"[56] and he later exclaims, "How beautiful to overcome the war within us with this fear that unites two bodies!"[57]

Throughout his book, Darwīsh uses a discourse that is journal, history, memoir, fiction, myth, and allegory all together. He quotes from Arabic classical chronicles; from the Bible, both the Old and New Testaments; from the reports about the Prophet Muḥammad; from Qur'ān exegesis; and from ordinary conversations. All of these elements do not exist as discrete units but rather as a lively blend. In Darwīsh's text discrete units lose their borderlines and leak into one another. It is, as Darwīsh himself says, a war that is declared on borders.[58] Although intertextuality "reflects breakdown, it also embodies a synthesis. Suspended between wholeness and fraction, the text, like Palestine, is a crossroads of competing meanings."[59]

Conclusion

Kanafānī's misguided characters and their aborted journey, Turki's disillusionment with the cause of returning to the "homeground," and Darwīsh's unclassifiable text all seem to be molded by the crushing conditions of war and exile. The works of these three writers in turn appear to reflect the betwixt-and-between, contingent, social, political, and existential state of the stateless Palestinians.

Notes

* This part of the title is borrowed from Jacques Derrida's article, "Living on Border Lines," in *Deconstruction and Criticism,* ed. Geoffrey Hartman (New York: The Seabury Press, 1979).

1. Fawaz Turki, *Exile's Return: The Making of a Palestinian American* (New York: The Free Press, 1994), 272.
2. Victor Turner, *The Ritual Process: Structure and Anti-Structure* (Chicago: Aldine Publishing Company, 1969), 95.
3. Notably Gustavo Perez Firmat, *Literature and Liminality: Festive Readings in the Hispanic Tradition* (Durham: Duke University Press, 1986); Victor Turner, *The Ritual Process* and *Process, Performance and Pilgrimage* (New Delhi: Concept Publishing Company, 1979); Arnold Van Gennep, *The Rites of Passage,* trans. Monika B. Vizedom and Gabrielle L. Caffee (Chicago: The University of Chicago Press, 1960); Jacques Derrida, "Living on Border Lines," *Deconstruction and Criticism,* 75–176; and Jonathan Culler, *On Deconstruction* (Ithaca: Cornell University Press, 1982).
4. Ghassān Kanafani, *Men in the Sun,* trans. Hilary Kilpatrick (Washington, DC: Three Continents Press, 1993), 9.
5. For this and other terms in the Qur'ān see Kamal Abdel-Malek, *Muḥammad in the Modern Egyptian Popular Ballad* (Leiden: E.J. Brill, 1995), 2.
6. Edward Said, *The Question of Palestine* (New York: Vantage Books, 1980), 151.
7. Kanafani, *Men in the Sun,* 19–20.
8. *Ibid.,* 38.
9. Muhammad Siddiq, *Man is a Cause: Political Consciousness and the Fiction of Ghassan Kanafani* (Seattle: University of Washington Press, 1984), 12.
10. Kanafani, *Men in the Sun,* 36.
11. *Ibid.*
12. *Ibid.,* 18.
13. *Ibid.*
14. *Ibid.,* 21.
15. *Ibid.* Note the association between "rat" and the "fat owner of the office:" big rats victimize smaller ones just as the "fat owner of the office," Abul Khaizuran, and the smugglers are seen to victimize the helpless Palestinian characters in the novel.
16. *Ibid.,* 38.
17. *Ibid.,* 25.

18. *Ibid.*, 48.
19. *Ibid.*, 56.
20. Fawaz Turki was born in Haifa in 1940. He is a poet and the author of several prose works in English, all accounts of his life as a Palestinian in exile: *The Disinherited: Journey of a Palestinian Exile* (1972), *Soul in Exile* (1988), and *Exile's Return: The Making of a Palestinian American* (1994). His book of prose poems, *Tel Zaater Was the Hill of Thyme,* was published in 1978. For more on Turki, see Salma Khadra Jayyusi, ed., *Anthology of Modern Palestinian Literature* (New York: Columbia University Press, 1992).
21. Turki, *The Disinherited,* 16.
22. *Ibid.*, 75.
23. *Ibid.*, 76–77.
24. *Ibid.*, 77.
25. *Ibid.*, 9.
26. *Ibid.*, 175–76.
27. Fawaz Turki, *Exile's Return: The Making of a Palestinian American* (New York: The Free Press, 1994).
28. *Ibid.*, vi.
29. *Ibid.*
30. *Ibid.*, 120.
31. *Ibid.*, 216–17.
32. *Ibid.*, 273.
33. *Ibid.* Cf. "After twenty-five years of living in the ghourba, of growing up permanently reminded of my status as an exile, the diaspora for me, for a whole generation of Palestinians, becomes *the homeland.*" Turki, *The Disinherited,* 176.
34. Maḥmūd Darwīsh was born in 1942 in the Palestinian village of Birweh, which the Israelis destroyed in 1948. He worked as an editor and translator for the Rakah (Communist) Party newspaper and was imprisoned several times. By 1971 he left Israel for Lebanon where his reputation as a gifted poet was quickly established. He became affiliated with the PLO and soon was regarded as Palestine's national poet. Darwīsh stayed in Beirut through the Israeli invasion of Lebanon in 1982, and it was about his experiences in besieged Beirut that he wrote his book, *Memory for Forgetfulness* (Dhākira li l-Nisyān, 1986). After 1982, Darwīsh became a wandering exile, living in such Arab and European capitals as Cairo, Tunis, and Paris. At present he moves between Amman, the capital of Jordan, and Ramallah on the West Bank.
35. Darwīsh, *Memory for Forgetfulness: August, Beirut, 1982* trans. with an introduction by Ibrahim Muhawi (Berkeley: University of California Press, 1995), 42.

36. *Memory for Forgetfulness,* translator's introduction, xx. Such monumental nature of writing has been noted by such Western poets as T. S. Eliot, whom the translator quotes in his introduction (xx):

    Every phrase and every sentence is an end and a beginning
    Every poem an epitaph
    ("Little Giddings" in *Four Quartets*).

37. *Ibid.*, 44.
38. *Ibid.*, 45.
39. *Ibid.*, 111.
40. *Ibid.*, 116.
41. *Ibid.*, 33.
42. *Ibid.*
43. *Ibid.*
44. *Ibid.*
45. *Ibid.*
46. *Ibid.*, 33–34.
47. *Ibid.*, 109–10.
48. *Ibid.*, 110.
49. *Ibid.*
50. *Ibid.*, 18.
51. Firmat, *Literature and Liminality,* 21. For more on metalepsis, see Abdel-Malek, *Muḥammad in the Modern Egyptian Popular Ballad,* 114–18.
52. Firmat, *Literature and Liminality,* xiv.
53. Darwish, *Memory for Forgetfulness,* 11.
54. *Ibid.*
55. *Ibid.*
56. *Ibid.*, 129.
57. *Ibid.*, 130.
58. *Ibid.*, 49.
59. *Ibid.*, translator's introduction, xvii.

Part III

Roundtable Discussion on Israeli and Palestinian Identities

Roundtable Discussion on Israeli and Palestinian Identities

YOAV PELED: I actually have been thinking since this morning, not about identity, but about post-identity. Maybe we have exhausted the issue of identity. When we say "identity," especially in this conference, but I think also in general, we immediately assume some kind of ascripted type of identity. In other words, we think in terms of nationalism, religion, ethnicity, and so on. And these identities, certainly in the cases we are talking about, are integrally involved with conflict. Now the question is what happens to identity if and when the conflict is resolved? (I think that at least some of us believe that it is being resolved right now.) I think the answer, which is actually discouraging, is evident already in at least certain segments of Israeli society, and that is the replacement of this belligerent, conflictual identity with a totally self-centered and, I would say, mindless and empty individualism, which rejects any kind of collective association. I think this is very unfortunate and very dangerous and very bad. I don't know how to do it, but I think it is time to begin to think about what kind of collective and social identities can be developed that will not be belligerent and hostile, that would replace those national, religious, and other identities. This is especially true in the case of Israelis and Palestinians and, I think, in other cases as well. We can go forward on the basis of some kind of collective association that is not hostile and belligerent towards others, and that can be the basis for some kind of social cooperation.

AMI ELAD-BOUSKILA: This question of a search for identity is typical not only in modern Palestinian literature, or in modern Hebrew literature, but as I mentioned before also in modern Arabic literature throughout the world and especially in literature of the Maghrib. In connection with this crucial topic I would like to quote, not a Palestinian writer, and quite surprisingly not an Israeli or a Hebrew writer, but a Moroccan writer. Al-Muʿṭī Qabbāl, one of the significant Moroccan writers of the younger generation, who writes in Arabic and French and translates from and into both languages, addresses this question in the following way:

> The issue of bilingualism in the Maghrib opens up an entire debate: on the one hand, the nationalists argue that with decolonization, there is no reason for French to continue its cultural dominance, that decolonization should also take effect in the writing, the literature. On the other hand, Maghrib authors who write in French treat the language not as an end, but as a means, and believe that writing in French gives them distance from themselves, a chance to come out of themselves. The novels of al-Ṭāhir b. Jallūn, Muḥammad Dīb, Kātib Yāsīn, and others—who write in French—are all drawn from the cultural and ritualistic milieu of the Maghrib and portray it that way, i.e., through their writing. The question of bilingualism is not just cultural, but also political. Bilingualism as a philosophical question touches upon identity, the question of the other, and the role of the other in the cultural space of these countries reflecting the hardship. Although the question is an open one, those who write in Arabic are the majority; they give voice to a political and cultural attitude replete with resentment for the language of the conqueror. But their desire to banish this language is an illusion; bilingualism is a window to modernity. (Ami Elad-Bouskila and Erez Biton, eds., "Le Maghreb: Littérature et Culture," *Apirion* 28 [1993]: 11–12.)

NEIL CAPLAN: I just have one observation that I think I will pose as a question to some of my fellow participants in the conference, and that is the question of symmetry. When I started to compose my presentation on victims versus victims, I knew that there was another half of an equally valid master story of the Palestinians' victimization and victimhood. Having heard Salma Jayyusi's discussion of poetry and Fawaz Turki's personal remarks, I could see that if they would choose to dignify the topic with their energy, they could come up with a paper outlining this notion and probe the question whether or not there is at least, on an intellectual level, a symmetry between the perceptions that the parties have of themselves as victims.

I know, of course, that symmetry is too simplistic a concept and breaks down in realpolitik. Certainly, both in negotiation theory and in dialogue attempts, one has to take into account the actual power relationships between the partners in the dialogue. Thus, when you are exploring parallels, no situation is exactly the same from the point of view of power. Finally, victimization is not just an abstract concept: it is a real-life tragedy for many people. So, I would like some of the panelists to explore, if they consider it appropriate, whether or not they see among the Palestinians a symmetrical mirror image of what I have said on this topic regarding the Israelis.

SALMA KHADRA JAYYUSI: I think that a conference like this must look to the future. It is no use talking about what has happened, if you don't have an eye to the future. Now, how can the writer change the future? This is a big responsibility that the writer has, but we can also expect and hope that the writer will write responsibly. There are social and psychological dimensions to the problem that will prohibit certain advances from certain people, like the Arabs, for instance. You can't expect, and I would never expect, an Arab writer to compromise, an Arab poet to write positively about what is happening. It is impossible, because what is happening is that there is aggression against Palestinian rights. When the Egyptian dramatist Ali Salim came back to Cairo from his visit to Israel, he suffered so much rejection in response to his trip that he had to go to a psychiatrist, and the psychiatrist told him that the best thing for him was to leave the country, because he was so ostracized by everybody. Many of my friends and I get many invitations to participate in cultural activities with Israelis, but I can't accept them; I cannot go because there is still aggression against our rights. I can't compromise, it's impossible. I would never compromise. There is aggression according to some Israeli writers. I think that Israeli writers should continue to voice more criticism of the aggression. If writing and art can do anything about the situation, it must first be done by the Israeli writers. The Arabs are a very good-hearted people. We don't feel a racist hatred. We will accept the defense of their own rights by the Israelis, and we will be very happy about this. I think that the responsibility of the Israeli writers is to make the first big step. The Palestinians cannot do this. I really want you to understand this. There is a movement in Israel to have cultural normalization. It is not happening, because you can expect only what is possible. As long as there is aggression, as long as there are impediments to peace, to a real peace, it's impossible. Any Palestinian writer who compromises will have happen to him what happened to Ali Salim. So, I think it is up to the Israeli writer to begin the process.

FAWAZ TURKI: Can the writer compromise? The answer, of course, is a categorical, emphatic no. The writer's role in society is both response and responsibility. In other words, he or she is not just responsible for reflecting in his or her writing the ebb and flow of the dynamic of the society he or she inhabits, but indeed he or she has the responsibility of trying to define what that society should be doing. This is where I depart dramatically from the posture adopted by my fellow Arabs here: I have a very adversarial relationship with Arab culture. I believe that Arab culture is degraded and dehumanized, and I believe that the individual in Arab society is socialized on the ethic of fear. We are socialized to fear authority figures. We are socialized to look upon orthodoxy as the norm in our lives. We are socialized to fear the notion of originality and as such, we are brought up in a milieu where we fear the notion of confronting the new. It is true; it is very, very true. I grew up in a society that in fact socializes the individual to fear any form of originality. We are socialized to look upon the authority figure as someone to fear. This notion of socialization is reflected in the way we speak our language. Arabic is a language that is not suitable for logical thinking. Arabic is probably the most degraded and dehumanized language in the entire world. It blocks us from being able to be part of the global dialogue of culture. Why is that? Because language is culture. We come from a culture that is repressive; the language we speak is equally repressive. So we have a problem here on two levels: the problem is to liberate ourselves from occupation and on the other level to liberate ourselves, to have an Intifada, directed against our own home.

SAMMY SMOOHA: If identity is as fluid and as changing as has been suggested at this conference, then I can tell you it is worthless as a scientific concept. If identity changes from day to day or from year to year, and if it changes from one situation to another that easily, then what do you need this concept for? So, we have to be more reasonable about our approach to identity. It's more tenacious; it's more permanent than we usually think. I think that identity takes a long time to change. I think this is the power of the concept of identity, only because it has permanence; otherwise it is not a powerful concept.

My next comments are about something that is much more baffling to me. This is an interdisciplinary conference, which includes historians, comparative literature scholars, political scientists, sociologists, and others. I can tell you it is very hard for me to speak to other sociologists. Now when I have to speak to people from other disciplines, it is extremely hard. Listening today to the literature session as a sociologist, I was really thinking: What are these people talking about? What kind of identity are they talking about? From a novel that is the creation of one person, the writer, how can you really generalize about the changing identity of Israelis?

Let me put what I am saying in a far more generalized way. Most historians are still, unfortunately, doing diplomatic history. They analyze the statements of diplomats, the statements of, generally speaking, the elite. They take texts of the elite and they try to reconstruct reality from these texts. The same is true in the case of writers. Today we have heard that the writers do not even project reality; they criticize reality. As a social scientist, I would like to know how from analyzing various texts or novels or poetry and so forth I can understand the identity of people as it is, not only how it is criticized. I am really more interested in popular views, which is why I take public opinion polls, which give me the sense how the people really feel, how they perceive the world, and what their identity is and not just the projections of the elite and leaders and critics.

I would like to offer a generalization about Israeli identity and its presumed crisis. Contrary to the impressions gleaned from literary works, there are no sociological studies attesting to an identity crisis among Israeli Jews. Israeli Jewish identity has been rather continuous over a long period. It has not become post-Zionist. Post-Zionists are a tiny minority in Israeli society today, found mostly among the intellectual elite and within academia. Perhaps post-Zionism is the wave of the distant future. Yet it is hard to see it appealing to the Jewish masses, because they have a vested interest in keeping Israel Jewish and Zionist.

The Israeli-Arab conflict is coming to an end not because of a change in Israeli and Palestinian identities. The phasing out of the conflict is occurring without a change of heart or soul searching on either side. It is happening while both sides keep their belligerent identities and mirror-image narratives in which each side sees itself as the victim. The end of the conflict is the offshoot of a configuration of forces, including the end of the Cold War, attrition, fatigue, and the realization that this fateful conflict is a destructive game that no one will win. While identity transformation has not contributed to the termination of the Israeli-Arab dispute, it may be its outcome in the long run.

ISSA J. BOULLATA: I will agree with Professor Smooha that change in identity takes place over a period of time, but it does happen. In the case of Maḥmūd Darwīsh, about whom I spoke earlier, there has been change in his own self-identification. It has not been a basic change, but there has been change. You may remember that I quoted Darwīsh as saying, "I have often said that the Israeli repression transformed me into an Arab, and that disappointment with the Arabs transformed me into a Palestinian." Here is an occasion where the same person feels he is being transformed by what is happening around him. Change happens. When it does, it is gradual and it takes a long time. An important thing that I have noticed is that whatever changes in identity occur and whatever are the causes, it is *I* who defines who *I* am in the last resort. You cannot tell another person, "Your identity is such and such; you must be that and nothing else." Identity cannot be imposed on you by the other, however strong the other or the outside forces are. It is a person himself or herself who will in the long run define his or her identity as such, and then inasmuch as there is individual identity there is also a totality of a collective identity. And in the case of the Palestinians there is such an identity, and Maḥmūd Darwīsh speaks out for this.

I had an interesting conversation with one member of the audience here during the intermission before this panel. She objected to Maḥmūd Darwīsh's idea that one's land is inherited as one's language is. She came from an Eastern European country and is living now in the United States, and she told me that her parents were not permitted to have land in Europe, and they lost all that they had and came as refugees here. Therefore, land does not define them, but it is the language that defines your identity. And you can carry your language wherever you go; you cannot carry your land with you. Why this insistence on land, therefore? And she said something even about the Zionist project, that it is regressive that there is so much insistence on land. She referred to the movement of people around the world in these days of refugees, of the globalization of human beings with demography changing so much that we cannot adhere to the idea of land being so much a part of one's identity. On one hand, my response was that in the case of the Palestinians, land continues to be a very strong component of Palestinian identity as much as it is for many or all Zionists. And that is at the basis of the conflict that we have today. On the other hand, as one thinks of reality and what reality gives us, one must not lose sight of the ideal state that one must keep thinking of. In my conversation with this lady I referred to the prophets. The prophets have always told us ideal things, and we unfortunately sometimes don't do the ideal thing and we have to adhere to practical things like holding onto one's land. God's gift to the world for everybody is that everybody, ideally speaking, should be at home wherever he or she would like to be. Unfortunately, the world is not that ideal and human beings are not that idealistic; therefore we must come to terms with reality, at the same time keeping ideals in mind.

I would like to take this occasion to say to my friend Fawaz Turki that he is not alone in criticizing Arab culture, especially in the way it relates to authority. There are many other Arab intellectuals, most of whom are still living, who do exactly this. I published a book in 1990, *Trends and Issues in Contemporary Arab Thought,* and many of the thinkers I studied in that book do actually speak about this concept of authority and how Arabs are socialized into being dominated by authority, whether it begins with the father at home, the teacher at school, the policeman in the street, the prime minister or whoever is the head of the country. Authority has a powerful influence that permeates all Arab society, and you have intellectuals in the Arab world who have been dealing with this issue. There are some who have dealt with this on the level of religion (Muḥammad al-Nuwayhī is one of those), or culture in general (such as Adonis and a few others), and there are women who are also writing on this (Fatima Mernissi of Morocco is one of them, and she is totally against the present system of authority, particularly in the way it deals with women).

NURITH GERTZ: It is true that not all Israeli writers have written against the oppression of the Arabs. Nevertheless, many of them have done so, and I am amazed that the Arab participants in this conference are not aware of the great waves of Israeli protest poetry written against the Israeli government and army during the Lebanese War and the Intifida. Some Israeli poetry of the Intifida period even goes so far as to identify with Arab children throwing stones at Israelis. I think, however, that the more important role of Israeli literature and cinema has been that it has changed the image of the Arab, showing that the Arab has a fully human identity. One example is the Israeli film *Avanti Popolo,* about two Egyptian soldiers fleeing the victorious Israeli army in the Sinai desert after the Six-Day War. One of the soldiers is an Arab actor, who is best known in Egypt for playing the role of Shylock in Shakespeare's *Merchant of Venice.* Since as the Egyptian soldiers travel through the desert they cannot find any water, they quench their thirst on vodka and eventually become intoxicated. At one point in the film they encounter Israeli soldiers, and in a desperate effort to save their lives, the Egyptian actor kneels before the Israeli soldiers and begins to recite the famous speech of Shylock: "I am a Jew. Hath not a Jew eyes? Hath not a Jew hands, organs, dimensions, senses, affections, passions?" In this scene the film suggests to Israelis the possibility that there are other ways of viewing the Arab, that the Arab other is not just an image, not just a monster, but that he actually is an individual who should be seen as a fellow human being. This film is one of many examples of works of Israeli literature and cinema that preceded and contributed to the emergence of the political peace process by humanizing for Israelis the image of their Arab enemies.

ARNOLD J. BAND: There is one aspect of identity that I don't think we have discussed, though it is implicit, in our deliberations, and that is the identity of the speakers at this conference. All the speakers here have their own identities. They have their specific backgrounds, and they have their points of view. There are Israelis and there are Palestinians. The Israelis are not all the same, nor are the Palestinians. There are participants who are neither Israelis nor Palestinians. Some of us are Americans. And I think this is an issue we have to put on the table. You are not hearing the voices of nonpersons; you are hearing the voices of people who have very definite points of view often shaped by their origins and academic training.

Allow me to make a few remarks, therefore, based on this perception. Sammy Smooha, a social scientist, dismissed as nonsense the use of both literature and literary criticism in the context of our deliberations. With the fall of the Berlin Wall, I found two reasons to celebrate. First, of course, was the fact that this marked the end of the repressive Communist regimes; second, it brought a temporary stop to the pontifications of my colleagues in political science who clearly had no idea over the years regarding what was really happening in Eastern Europe. So much for the wisdom of the social scientists.

After calling attention to the question of the identities of the speakers, let me raise the importance of the very situation of this conference at Brown University. Let us not forget that this conference is being held in an American university that has a distinctive history and very specific ways of looking at reality and conducting a discourse. The language in which the conference is held also implies many things. It is being held in English, the international language of communication, and not in one of the languages of the Middle East. The American identity, with its Jeffersonian tradition of individualism, surely is a factor in the ambiance of our discussions. I think, furthermore, that we would all grant that Americanization is one of the dominant cultural features in the world today. We have talked about Israelization; we have talked about Palestinization; but we have not talked about Americanization and the globalization of American values. That is another issue we should put on the table today.

Finally, since I too am a product of a specific background and training, I have my own identity and my own take on historical events. We have heard many rash statements about the evil decisions of statesmen. For me, with my classical background, the great text on politics and history is not Machiavelli, or the book of Joshua, or the book of Esther, but Thucydides' *Peloponnesian Wars.* In that great work the author, writing "for eternity," comes to the conclusion that there are aggressors on both sides of a conflict and that human beings can be both magnanimous or bestial. They can also be very foolish. At times, the best intentions lead to disasters. Not all decisions of leaders that turn out bad were designed to be that way. We would be wise to heed this voice of experience.

Contributors

KAMAL ABDEL-MALEK is an assistant professor of Arabic and Islamic Studies in the Department of Comparative Literature, Religion, Film and Media Studies at the University of Alberta, Canada. He also taught at Brown University and Princeton University. He is a specialist in modern Arabic language and literature and author of *Muḥammad in the Modern Egyptian Popular Ballad, Celebrating Muḥammad* (with Ali Asani and Annemarie Schimmel), and *A Study of the Vernacular Poetry of Aḥmad Fu'ād Nigm;* and co-editor (with Wael Hallaq) of *Tradition, Modernity, and Postmodernity in Arabic Literature* (forthcoming). He is the editor of the forthcoming *America in an Arab Mirror*. In 1998, he was the winner of the prestigious Henry Merritt Wriston Fellowship competition, awarded by Brown University to "outstanding members of the faculty in support of innovative research." His current research focuses on studying Arab-Jewish encounters in Palestinian literature and the portrayal of the American in Arabic travel literature.

ARNOLD J. BAND is a professor of Hebrew and Comparative Literature at the University of California at Los Angeles, where he has served as chair of the Department of Comparative Literature and director of the Center for Jewish Studies. He has also served as president of the Association for Jewish Studies. He has been a research fellow at the University of Pennsylvania Center for Judaic Studies. He is the author of *Nostalgia and Nightmare: A Study in the Fiction of S.Y. Agnon; Nahman of Bratslav: The Tales;* and numerous articles on Israeli and modern Jewish literature.

ISSA J. BOULLATA was born in Jerusalem, Palestine. He is a professor of Arabic literature and language at McGill University. His publications include *Outlines of Romanticism in Modern Arabic Poetry* and *Badr Shākir al-Sayyāb: His Life and Poetry,* both in Arabic, and *Modern Arabic*

Poets, an anthology in English translation. He is also the editor of *Critical Perspectives on Modern Arabic Literature* and (with Terri DeYoung) *Tradition and Modernity in Arabic Literature.* His *Trends and Issues in Contemporary Arab Thought* is an analysis of contemporary Arab thought since 1967. He has served as co-editor of *The Muslim World* and editor of *Al-ʿArabiyya.* He has also published several translations of Arabic literature into English. In 1998, he published an Arabic novel in Beirut entitled *ʿĀʾid ilā al-Quds* (Return to Jerusalem), and his latest work as editor is *Literary Structures of Religious Meaning in the Qurʾān.*

NEIL CAPLAN is a professor in the Humanities Department at Vanier College in Quebec, Canada. He has also taught in the Departments of Political Science at Concordia and McGill Universities. His research includes the history of the Arab and Jewish communities of British Mandatory Palestine. More recently, he has done research into international efforts to resolve the Arab-Israeli conflict between 1948 and 1956. His publications include *Palestine Jewry and the Arab Question, 1917–1925; The Lausanne Conference, 1949: A Case Study in Middle East Peacemaking;* and *Futile Diplomacy,* a multivolume documentary history of the Arab-Israeli conflict. His latest work (with Laura Z. Eisenberg), *Negotiating Arab-Israeli Peace: Patterns, Problems, Possibilities,* analyzes the Arab-Israeli peace process from 1977 to 1997.

AMI ELAD-BOUSKILA is a scholar, critic, and anthologist. He chairs the Arabic Department at Beit Berl College in Israel. In addition to his teaching and research activities, he has extensively translated Arabic literature into Hebrew, especially in his former position as general editor of *Bidayat* (Beginnings), a series of Arabic literary works translated into Hebrew. Among his current projects are anthologies of Arab women's writing, Palestinian novellas, and Maghribian short stories. His publications include *Arabic Literature in Hebrew Dress* [Hebrew] and *The Village Novel in Modern Egyptian Literature.* He is also the editor of *Writer, Culture, Text: Studies in Modern Arabic Literature* and *Near Lights: An Anthology of Modern Arabic Short Stories* [Arabic]. His book on Palestinian literature is soon to be published. He was the Israeli Visiting Fellow at St. Antony's College of Oxford University in 1997–98. In addition to his current research on Palestinian literature, he is also engaged in research on the Sudanese writer al-Ṭayyib Ṣāliḥ.

NURITH GERTZ is an associate professor. She teaches Hebrew literature, culture, and cinema at the Open University and at Tel Aviv University. She has also been a research fellow at the University of Pennsylvania Center for Judaic Studies and has taught at Yale University and the University of California at Berkeley. Her publications include *Amos Oz: A Monograph* [Hebrew], *Literature and Ideology in Eretz Yisrael in the Thirties* [Hebrew], *Motion Fiction: Literature and Cinema* [Hebrew], and *Captive of a Dream: National Myths in Israeli Culture* [Hebrew].

DAVID C. JACOBSON is an associate professor of Judaic Studies at Brown University. He has previously taught at University of Michigan, Ben-Gurion University, University of Pennsylvania, and Wesleyan University. He is the author of *Modern Midrash: The Retelling of Traditional Jewish Narratives by Twentieth-Century Hebrew Writers* and *Does David Still Play Before You? Israeli Poetry and the Bible,* as well as other studies in modern Hebrew literature. His current research is on issues of religious doubt and faith in twentieth-century Hebrew literature.

SALMA KHADRA JAYYUSI is a poet, scholar, critic, and anthologist. She spent her childhood and early youth in Acre and in Jerusalem. She has taught at several Arab and American universities. In 1980, she founded the Project of Translation from Arabic Literature (PROTA), and in 1992 she founded East-West Nexus. Her publications include a collection of her poetry, *Return from the Dreamy Fountain,* and a two-volume critical literary history, *Trends and Movements in Modern Arabic Poetry.* She is the editor of *Modern Arabic Poetry, The Literature of Modern Arabia, Anthology of Modern Palestinian Literature, Modern Arabic Drama* (with Roger Allen), *Modern Arabic Fiction,* and *The Legacy of Muslim Spain.*

YOAV PELED is a senior lecturer in political science at Tel Aviv University. He previously taught at the Hebrew University and Ben-Gurion University and has held visiting positions at the University of California, Los Angeles; the University of California, San Diego; the University of Miami; and the University of Pennsylvania. He is the author of *Class and Ethnicity in the Pale: The Political Economy of Jewish Workers' Nationalism in Late Imperial Russia* and co-editor of a number of collections of scholarly essays. In recent years he has been working in the field of the political sociology of Israeli society. He has recently completed (with Gershon Shafir) a study entitled *The Dynamics of Israeli Citizenship: Between Colonialism and Democracy.*

GERSHON SHAFIR is a professor of sociology at the University of California, San Diego. He received a B.A. in economics and a B.A. in political science and sociology from Tel Aviv University and a Ph.D. from the University of California, Berkeley. He is the author of *Land, Labor, and the Origins of the Israeli-Palestinian Conflict, 1882–1914* and *Immigrants and Nationalists,* as well as the editor of *The Citizenship Debates.* His articles have appeared in the *American Journal of Sociology,* the *British Journal of Sociology, International Journal of Middle East Studies,* and other journals. He has recently completed (with Yoav Peled) a study entitled *The Dynamics of Israeli Citizenship: Between Colonialism and Democracy.* His current research projects include "Decolonization and Peacemaking in South Africa and Israel/Palestine" and "Was the Yom Kippur War Unavoidable?"

SAMMY SMOOHA is a professor of sociology at the University of Haifa. He has taught at the University of Washington at Seattle, SUNY at Binghamton, and Brown University. He has also served as a research fellow at the Annenberg Research Institute in Philadelphia, the Oxford Centre for Hebrew and Jewish Studies, Arnold Bergstraesser Institut in Freiburg, and the Wissenschaftszentrum Berlin für Sozialforschung. He has published widely on the internal divisions in Israeli society. His books include *Israel: Pluralism and Conflict* and a two-volume study, *Arabs and Jews in Israel.*

SALIM TAMARI is an associate professor of sociology at Birzeit University and director of the Institute of Jerusalem Studies in Jerusalem. He has also been a visiting professor at Cornell University and at New York University. He serves as coordinator and delegate to the Working Group on Refugees in the Multilateral Peace Negotiations. He is associate editor of the journal of the Middle East Research and Information Project (MERIP). His research interests include Eastern Mediterranean urban issues and Palestinian culture and political economy. His most recent publications are *Palestinian Refugee Negotiations; From Madrid to Oslo II;* and *Jerusalem 1948: The Arab Neighborhoods and Their Fate in the War.*

FAWAZ TURKI was born in Haifa, Palestine. He is a poet and the author of prose accounts of his life and those of other Palestinians in exile. He has published several books in English, including his autobiographical accounts *The Disinherited: Journal of a Palestinian Exil*e and *Soul in Exile,* as well as a volume of prose poetry, *Tel Zaatar Was the Hill of Thyme.*

He has been a writer-in-residence at the Virginia Center for the Creative Arts, a professor at the State University of New York in Buffalo, and a frequent speaker at conferences and panels dealing with the Middle East and the Third World. He lives in the United States.

Index